New Casebooks

GEORGE ORWELL

New Casebooks

PUBLISHED

Antony and Cleopatra	*Mansfield Park* and *Persuasion*
Hamlet	*Middlemarch*
King Lear	*Toni Morrison*
Macbeth	*Mrs Dalloway* and
A Midsummer Night's	To the Lighthouse
Dream	*George Orwell*
Shakespeare on Film	*Sense and Sensibility* and
Shakespeare's History Plays:	*Pride and Prejudice*
Richard II to Henry V	*Sons and Lovers*
Shakespeare's Tragedies	*Tess of the d'Urbervilles*
Twelfth Night	*Tristram Shandy*
	The Turn of the Screw and
	What Maisie Knew
Feminist Theatre and Theory	*Villette*
Waiting for Godot and	*Wuthering Heights*
Endgame	

Bleak House	*William Blake*
Wilkie Collins	*Chaucer*
Joseph Conrad	*Coleridge, Keats and Shelley*
David Copperfield and	*Seamus Heaney*
Hard Times	*Philip Larkin*
Emma	*Victorian Women Poets*
E. M. Forster	*Wordsworth*
Frankenstein	
Great Expectations	*Postcolonial Literatures*
Jane Eyre	

Further titles are in preparation

New Casebooks Series
Series Standing Order
ISBN 0–333–71702–3 hardcover
ISBN 0–333–69345–0 paperback
(outside North America only)

You can receive future titles in this series as they are published by placing a standing order. Please contact your bookseller or, in case of difficulty, write to us at the address below with your name and address, the title of the series and the ISBN quoted above.

Customer Services Department, Macmillan Distribution Ltd
Houndmills, Basingstoke, Hampshire RG21 6XS, England

New Casebooks

GEORGE ORWELL

EDITED BY GRAHAM HOLDERNESS,
BRYAN LOUGHREY AND NAHEM YOUSAF

First published 1998 by
MACMILLAN PRESS LTD
Houndmills, Basingstoke, Hampshire RG21 6XS
and London
Companies and representatives throughout the world

ISBN 0–333–67978–4 hardcover
ISBN 0–333–67979–2 paperback

A catalogue record for this book is available from the British Library.

This book is printed on paper suitable for recycling and made from
fully managed and sustained forest sources.

10   9   8   7   6   5   4   3   2   1
07 06 05 04 03 02 01 00 99 98

Typeset by EXPO Holdings, Malaysia

Printed in Hong Kong

Published in the United States of America 1998 by
ST. MARTIN'S PRESS, INC.,
Scholarly and Reference Division,
175 Fifth Avenue, New York, N.Y. 10010

ISBN 0–312–21465–0

Contents

Acknowledgements

The editors and publishers wish to thank the following for permission to use copyright material:

Beatrix Campbell, for 'Orwell – Paterfamilias or Big Brother?' in *Inside the Myth – Orwell: Views from the Left*, ed. Christopher Norris (1984), pp. 126–38, by permission of Lawrence & Wishart; Simon Dentith, for '"The journalists do the shouting": Orwell and Propaganda' in *A Rhetoric of the Real* (1990), pp. 148–73, Harvester Wheatsheaf, by permission of Prentice-Hall, Europe; Richard Filloy, for 'Orwell's Political Persuasion: A Rhetoric of Personality' in *Literary Nonfiction: Theory, Criticism, Pedagogy*, ed. Chris Anderson (1989), pp. 51–69. Copyright © 1989 by the Board of Trustees, Southern Illinois University, by permission of the Southern Illinois University Press; Lynette Hunter, for '*Animal Farm*: Satire into Allegory' in *George Orwell: The Search for a Voice* (1984), pp. 178–90, Open University Press, by permission of the author; Stephen Ingle, for 'The Anti-Imperialism of George Orwell' in *Literature and the Political Imagination*, ed. John Horton and Andrea Baumeister (1996), pp. 218–37, by permission of Routledge; Alan Kennedy, 'The Inversion of Form: Deconstructing *1984*' in *Reading, Resistance, Value* (1990), pp. 129–48. Copyright © Alan Kennedy, by permission of Macmillan Ltd and St. Martin's Press, Inc; V. C. Letemendia, for 'Revolution on *Animal Farm*: Orwell's Neglected Commentary', *Journal of Modern Literature*, 18:I (1992), 127–37, by permission of the Foundation for Modern Literature; James Phelan, for 'Character, Progression, and Thematism in *1984*' in *Reading People, Reading Plots* (1989), pp. 28–43, by permission of the University of Chicago Press; Patrick Reilly, for '*Nineteen Eighty-Four*: The Insufficient Self' in *The Literature of Guilt* (1988), pp. 92–113, by permission of Macmillan Ltd; John Rodden, for 'On the Political Sociology of Intellectuals: George Orwell and the London Left Intelligentsia' in *The Revised Orwell*, ed. Jonathan Rose, Michigan State University Press (1991), pp. 207–9, 214–33, by permission of the author; Richard Rorty, for 'The Last Intellectual in Europe: Orwell on Cruelty' in *Contingency, Irony, and Solidarity* (1989), pp. 169–88, by permission of Cambridge University Press; Michael Walzer, for 'George Orwell's England' in *The Company of Critics: Social Criticism and Political Commitment in the Twentieth Century* (1988), pp. 117–35. Copyright © 1988 by Michael Walzer, by permission of Peter Halban Publishers and Basic Books, a division of HarperCollins Publishers, Inc.

Every effort has been made to trace the copyright holders but if any have been inadvertently overlooked the publishers will be pleased to make the necessary arrangement at the first opportunity.

General Editors' Preface

The purpose of this series of New Casebooks is to reveal some of the ways in which contemporary criticism has changed our understanding of commonly studied texts and writers and, indeed, of the nature of criticism itself. Central to the series is a concern with modern critical theory and its effect on current approaches to the study of literature. Each New Casebook editor has been asked to select a sequence of essays which will introduce the reader to the new critical approaches to the text or texts being discussed in the volume and also illuminate the rich interchange between critical theory and critical practice that characterises so much current writing about literature.

In this focus on modern critical thinking and practice New Casebooks aim not only to inform but also to stimulate, with volumes seeking to reflect both the controversy and the excitement of current criticism. Because much of this criticism is difficult and often employs an unfamiliar critical language, editors have been asked to give the reader as much help as they feel is appropriate, but without simplifying the essays or the issues they raise. Again, editors have been asked to supply a list of further reading which will enable readers to follow up issues raised by the essays in the volume.

The project of New Casebooks, then, is to bring together in an illuminating way those critics who best illustrate the ways in which contemporary criticism has established new methods of analysing texts and who have reinvigorated the important debate about how we 'read' literature. The hope is, of course, that New Casebooks will not only open up this debate to a wider audience, but will also encourage students to extend their own ideas, and think afresh about their responses to the texts they are studying.

John Peck and Martin Coyle
University of Wales, Cardiff

Introduction

GRAHAM HOLDERNESS, BRYAN LOUGHREY and
NAHEM YOUSAF

George Orwell (1903–50) was a controversial writer who produced a wealth of fictional and non-fictional writing which has provoked numerous and diverse critical responses. He has been championed by the left as well as, paradoxically, by the right, whilst his most well known works, *Animal Farm* and *Nineteen Eighty-Four*, have found a place on school syllabuses. That said, there has not been as much theoretical criticism of his work as one might suppose, and what there is has tended to focus on the well known texts, either completely overlooking such novels as *Down and Out in Paris and London* (1933), *Burmese Days* (1935), *A Clergyman's Daughter* (1935), *Keep the Aspidistra Flying* (1936), and *Coming Up For Air* (1939), or affording them a cursory mention. The essays in this collection are by no means intended as inclusive but they attempt to engage with key issues in Orwell's work that have proved problematic or controversial. In putting this collection together we became increasingly aware of a dearth of theoretically informed published material, which takes its point of departure from within debates in the areas of poststructuralism, feminism, psychoanalysis or cultural materialism. There has been a tendency to move away from biographical detail when considering writers but this is not the case with Orwell whose life and beliefs still influence most readings of his writing. The essays that comprise this collection have been selected for their particular engagements with critical and theoretical paradigms and positions and all were written after 1984. They may also be read for the ways in which they explore his writing as cutting across the boundaries between fiction and politics, auto-biography and criticism, genres and disciplines. We include one essay that focuses on *Burmese Days* and Orwell's imperial experi-ence, a selection of views on the more consistently read and studied novels *Animal Farm* and *Nineteen Eighty-Four*, and a further four which focus on Orwell as a political writer and on his position *vis-à-vis* the state and socialism.

I

In order to appreciate fully the political nature of George Orwell's writing one must return to those moments that shaped him and had a profound influence on both his fiction and his politics. Eric Arthur Blair was born in India in 1903 but spent much of his early life in England. His childhood and adolescence were characterised by little family contact and a public school education at Eton. After Eton, Orwell joined the ranks of the Imperial Police in Burma, thus con-tinuing his family's connection with the British imperial project – his father, Richard Walmesley Blair, was an administrator in the Opium Department of the Indian Civil Service, whilst his maternal grandfather had been a teak merchant in Burma and his paternal grandfather a member of the Indian Army.

After spending some five years in what he felt was 'an un-suitable profession' Orwell resigned from the Imperial Police in 1927 for reasons he made clear in 'Shooting an Elephant', via his narrator:

> I had already made up my mind that imperialism was an evil thing and the sooner I chucked up my job and got out of it the better. Theoretically – and secretly, of course, I was always for the Burmese and all against their oppressors, the British. As for the job I was doing, I hated it more bitterly than I can perhaps make clear. In a job like that you see the dirty work of Empire at close quarters.[1]

The second sentence sums up Orwell's move toward self-definition against Empire and against the ruling classes. He expressed his feel-ings for, and loyalties to, the oppressed and marginalised groups when he asserted that

> I felt I had got to escape not merely from imperialism but from every form of man's dominion over man. I wanted to submerge myself, to

get right down among the oppressed, to be one of them and on their side against their tyrants ... It was in this way that my thoughts turned towards the English working class. It was the first time that I had ever been really aware of the working class, and to begin with it was only because they supplied an analogy. They were the symbolic victims of injustice, playing the same part in England as the Burmese played in Burma.[2]

Orwell's Burmese experience was formative in radically reshaping his views of the working class, an idea that is explored in Stephen Ingle's essay (12) in this volume. In *The Road to Wigan Pier* Orwell writes that as an Eton schoolboy he had 'no notion that the working class were human beings' and he 'hated and despised them', considering them 'brutal and repulsive'.[3] His choice of adjectives is interesting in that it fits a pattern of imperial discourse traditionally used in descriptions of the colonised 'Other'. Indeed, Orwell was to state in later life that

My starting point is always a feeling of partisanship, a sense of injustice. When I sit down to write a book, I do not say to myself, 'I am going to produce a work of art.' I write it because there is some lie that I want to expose, some fact to which I want to draw attention, and my initial concern is to get a hearing.[4]

Raymond Williams calls this '*negative identification*' which involves a rejection of one's 'initial and formative social experience'.[5] Orwell did indeed reject his middle-class upbringing and his training for a life as a loyal employee of Empire but it was his Burmese experience which opened his eyes to the disparity between the lives and living conditions of the rulers and the ruled.

In an effort to understand the conditions of those who inhabited the 'lower depths', Orwell embarked upon a mission to tell their stories which was inspired by the need to 'expiate' an 'immense weight of guilt'.[6] He spent some time living as a 'down and out' in London's East End before moving to Paris to experience life on the streets there. His foray into the world of tramps and tramping resulted in *Down and Out in Paris and London* published in 1933. The novel conveys the experiences of a disparate group of individuals trapped by a system which ensured that while the rich remained in power the poor were treated as little more than drudges living a hand-to-mouth existence: 'the mass of the rich and the poor are differentiated by their incomes and nothing else ... Everyone who has mixed on equal terms with the poor knows this quite well.'[7] In this, his first book, we find 'the white-hot reaction of a sensitive, observant, compassionate young man to poverty, injustice and the callousness of the rich'.[8] *Down and Out* established Orwell as a writer of conscience, a committed and interrogative writer, whose style has been called 'clear, direct and precise'.[9]

II

In his second novel, *Burmese Days*, Orwell explores the power relations between the coloniser and the colonised, but it is not a classic text of Empire so much as an example of anti-imperialist writing. As Elleke Boehmer has suggested, it is 'distinguished from earlier colonial writings by its knowingness – its anti-adventure cynicism, its penetrating insights into the less than honourable mechanisms of empire ... Orwell with *Burmese Days* signals the closing down of an entire genre of imperial heroics, as well as, by implication, the system that sustained it.'[10] Despite the 'anti-adventure cynicism' and the attempt to produce a counter-narrative, Orwell nevertheless borrows from Kipling and Conrad which prompts Boehmer to conclude that he 'does not diverge significantly from a colonialist semiotic'.[11] Indeed, intertextual references to the above named writers abound. Furthermore, Orwell is inevitably trapped in the position of representer, attempting on the one hand an anti-imperial invective while remaining on the other within the boundaries of his colonial master position. In attempting to display his unease with Britain's imperial project, Orwell produced an ambivalent text which, in turn, has produced ambivalent readings. But, as Homi Bhabha reminds us, the category of 'literature' is itself a form of representation whose 'reality is not given but produced: its meanings transformative, historical and relational rather than revelatory' and its 'continuity and coherence underscored by division and difference'.[12]

The critical study of Orwell's work is further complicated by the recognition that the term 'representation' is semantically unstable and the cultural codes which underlie representations prompt a kind of intellectual archaeology on the part of the critic. Edward Said in his essay 'Representing the Colonized: Anthropology's Interlocutors' thinks through the kind of history of imperialism that underpins a text like *Burmese Days*:

> Once again *representation* becomes significant, not just as an academic or theoretical quandary but as a political choice. How the anthropologist represents his or her disciplinary situation is, on one level, of course, a matter of local, personal, or professional moment. But it is in fact part of a totality, one's society, whose shape and tendency depend on the cumulatively affirmative or deterrent and oppositional weight made up by a whole series of such choices ... The point is that anthropological representations bear as much on the representer's world as on who or what is represented.[13]

Orwell's position as a writer of fiction, extrapolated from his experience of serving in the Imperial Police, can be read in light of Said's argument here. The literary representation that is *Burmese Days* rests on the 'personal or professional moment' but is inextricable from the ideological totality of his society's values and beliefs. Anti-imperialism was not synonymous with anti-racism at the time Orwell was writing, but he recognised that it was ideologically necessary for exponents of imperial power to undermine the races who were subjected to that power. Orwell retains this power relationship in *Burmese Days* and while he is clearly critical of imperialism we do not find in this text a critique of the racist assumptions that facilitate imperial expansion. JanMohamed observes that:

> The European writer commodifies the native by negating his individuality, his subjectivity, so that he is now perceived as a generic being that can be exchanged for any other native (they all look alike, act alike and so on).[14]

Is Orwell guilty of such 'commodification'? Certainly textual examples from *Burmese Days* and 'Shooting an Elephant' suggest his complicity in this. The representation of Dr Veraswami, for example, as the white man's mouthpiece who espouses the view that without the British India would remain in the dark ages, can be read as colonial brainwashing:

> They are the salt of the earth. Consider the great things they have done – consider the great administrators who have made British India what it is. Consider Clive, Warren Hastings, Dalhousie, Curzon. They were such men – I quote your immortal Shakespeare – as, take them for all in all, we shall not look upon their like again![15]

Veraswami is the only example of an Indian character that Orwell provides in the book and he is clearly unable to transcend the racially constructed boundaries that contain and demean him and others like him. He has adopted the Orientalist mindset that has the 'natives' riddled with 'apathy and superstition'[16] whilst seeing the colonial businessmen develop the resources of the country: '... your officials', he comments, 'are civilising us, elevating us to their level.'[17]

The bastion of Britishness in the bush remains the European Club which is the last outpost against the 'natives' and when this sacred institution is threatened with the election of a 'native member' Ellis's response is characteristic and even expected:

> He's asking us to break all our rules and take a dear little nigger-boy into this Club. *Dear* Dr Veraswami, for instance. Dr Very-slimy, I call him. That *would* be a treat, wouldn't it? Little pot-bellied niggers breathing garlic in your face over the bridge-table.[18]

Ellis is obnoxious and barely tolerated by the Club members but he can be secure in his reliance on their support since they will stay loyal to the Empire and to the idea of Englishness in the face of outsiders. For example, Maxwell sees the Burmese as little more than game with his desire to hunt and shoot them, and even the drunkard Lackersteen can muster the courage and sobriety to state unequivocally:

> 'Keep the black swabs out of it. *Esprit de corps* and all that.' Mr Lackersteen could always be relied upon for sound sentiments in a case like this. In his heart he did not care and never had cared a damn for the British Raj, and he was as happy drinking with an Oriental as with a white man; but he was always ready with a loud 'Hear, hear!' when anyone suggested the bamboo for disrespectful servants or boiling oil for Nationalists. He prided himself that though he might booze a bit and all that, dammit, he *was* loyal. It was his form of respectability.[19]

Faced with such vehement opposition to the idea of electing a 'native' member to the Club, Flory is strong willed enough to hold his position in nominating Veraswami. However, Flory is acting as a single man who realises the imperial project's prime concerns:

> I don't want the Burmans to drive us out of this country. God forbid! I'm here to make money, like everyone else. All I object to is the slimy white man's burden humbug ... Even those bloody fools at the Club might be better company if we weren't all of us living a lie the whole time ... the lie that we're here to uplift our poor black brothers instead of to rob them.[20]

Flory cannot do other than participate in a master/slave relationship with the non-Europeans around him and, ultimately, he remains an impotent victim of his own circumstances and position as a *white man*. Flory's ambivalent situation leads to his suicide.

III

Orwell continued to pursue his explorations of the relationship between the oppressors and the oppressed in other contexts. *Burmese Days* was followed by *A Clergyman's Daughter* and *Keep the Aspidistra Flying* and throughout this period of prolific production Orwell managed to create a niche for himself as a writer of informed fiction. As Raymond Williams suggests, 'Orwell's reputation at this time, as a writer and journalist, was based mainly on his accounts of poverty and depression. His expeditions and then his convincing reports had given him a particular though limited identity in the literary world.'[21] At first sight this seems a fairly accurate description of Orwell's writing career at this juncture, but what Williams fails to note is that the so-called 'limited identity' paved the way for Orwell to make further forays into the world of the dispossessed and marginalised. His reputation meant that he secured a contract to write about the condition of the working class in the north of England for the Left Book Club, to explore their feelings about and attitudes to the British class structure and the north/south divide. Furthermore, this project gave him the opportunity to state explicitly his attitudes towards members of his own class and to discuss his formative experiences. In Part Two of *The Road to Wigan Pier* he informs us that, as a boy, he was 'taught the lower classes smell' and that he had imagined them being 'brown all over'.[22] Whilst in itself this might seem a trivial point, it is important in illustrating the ways in which Orwell was exposed to a bourgeois ideological indoctrination of ideas that he highlights in his representation of Ellis, and his attitude towards the Orientals in *Burmese Days* who are so offensive to him precisely because they 'smell'. The equation of the English working class with the Burmese natives establishes a connection between two prejudices and highlights the limited and stereotypical perspective held by the middle class whose knowledge of both the working class and 'natives' was largely based on the dominant representations they encountered, either via magazines like *Punch* or through literature, but never, for the most part, from direct experience.

The Road to Wigan Pier clearly reveals Orwell's growing interest in politics and, particularly, socialism. In Part Two of the book Orwell states that

> ... at the age of seventeen or eighteen ... I loosely described myself as a Socialist. But I had not much grasp of what Socialism meant, and no notion that the working class were human beings. At a distance ... I could agonise over their sufferings, but I still hated them and despised them when I came anywhere near them.[23]

This autobiographical interlude shows Orwell's honest attitude towards the working class and confirms that he little understood the principles of socialism. It is also an attack on those middle-class socialists whose attitude towards the working class did not differ significantly from his when he was at Eton. The essential point here is that it is very difficult to ignore one's formative experiences, as Orwell realised only too well, writing

> All my notions – notions of good and evil, of pleasant and unpleasant, of funny and serious, of ugly and beautiful – are essentially *middle-class* notions; my tastes in books and food and clothes, my sense of honour, my table manners, my turns of speech, my accent, even the characteristic movements of my body, are the products of a special kind of upbringing and my special niche about half-way up the social hierarchy.

And that only

> When I grasp this I grasp that it is no use clapping a proletarian on the back and telling him that he is as good a man as I am; if I want real contact with him, I have to make an effort for which very likely I am unprepared. For to get outside the class-racket I have got to suppress not merely my private snobbishness, but most of my other tastes and prejudices as well. I have got to alter myself so completely that at the end I should hardly be recognisable as the same person.[24]

For Orwell organised socialism could only succeed if and when its key proponents acknowledged cultural and class differences to be important but also recognised that the focus could shift to what he saw as the main similarity between the classes, namely income.[25] In Orwell's analysis the 'sinking middle classes' would have nothing to lose but 'our aitches' and focusing upon income would have the desired effect of uniting the middle and working classes. Socialism as practice could only work when it presented a united front against fascism, but as long as socialism was associated with a 'picture of vegetarians with wilting beards, of Bolshevik commissars (half gangster, half gramophone), of earnest ladies in sandals, shock-headed Marxists chewing polysyllables, escaped Quakers, birth-control fanatics, and Labour Party backstairs-crawlers'[26] it would fail. For Orwell the appeal of socialism was in its simple call for justice and equality and not in the jargonistic speech and literature of its doctrinaire adherents which he believed had the effect of alienating and frightening prospective followers into considering fascism as an alternative.

Orwell's conception of socialism, with its initial and mobilising influence being not the 'pea-and-thimble trick with those three mys-terious entities, thesis, antithesis, and synthesis'[27] but the notions of justice and liberty, is not without its inherent problems. *The Road to Wigan Pier* demonstrates that Orwell saw little that he consid-ered positive or admirable in working-class intellectuals and this is a point that Beatrix Campbell takes up when she asserts that 'Orwell insists on a separation between the working class and its activist intelligentsia' and points to his inability to 'conceive of the working class itself as a *thinking* class with its own history, with a history of making itself. The result is the representation of a class which is thoughtless and leaderless, and class in its natural state.'[28] Of course, this suits Orwell's purpose by giving him the scope to develop his own ideas about the working class and its relation to socialism. Furthermore, the first part of the book is not without its own weaknesses: focusing on the mine workers Orwell produces an image of 'noble savages by his panegyric on their physique' and his limited perspective on this 'most masculinised profession' masks the role that women have played in the mining industry. And it is indeed true to say that 'women do not appear as protagonists in Orwell's working class'.[29] Orwell's understanding of the working-class family is an idealised image that is itself replete with stereo-typical undertones:

> I have often been struck by the peculiar easy completeness, the perfect symmetry as it were, of a working-class interior at its best. Especially on winter evenings after tea, when the fire glows in the open range and dances mirrored in the steel fender, when Father, in shirt-sleeves, sits in the rocking chair at one side of the fire reading the racing finals, and Mother sits on the other with her sewing, and the children are happy with a pennorth of mint humbugs, and the dog lolls roasting himself on the rag mat.[30]

The atmosphere evoked by this description is one of internal harmony, away from the middle-class family where the family members would be 'nagging and badgering him night and day for failing to "get on"' and his wife would be encouraging him to 'blackleg and get the other fellow's job'.[31] In the working-class home the woman knows her place as it is the man who is the 'master and not ... the woman or the baby'.[32] Beatrix Campbell's essay (4) in this volume addresses directly representations of working-class women and families, taking Raymond Williams's reading of this feature of Orwell's work as her starting point.

Contrary to Williams's claim that there is not much sense of family in *The Road to Wigan Pier*, we would argue that the image of a united family is a recurring one in Orwell's writing, particularly with reference to the condition of England and ideas of nationhood. In the essay 'England Your England' Orwell posits his understanding of the English character and his belief that

> England is the most class-ridden country under the sun. It is a land of snobbery and privilege, ruled largely by the old and the silly. But in any calculation about it one has got to take into account its emotional unity, the tendency of nearly all its inhabitants to feel alike and act together in moments of supreme crisis.[33]

For Orwell, England is a 'nation ... bound together by an invisible chain'[34] which finally he describes as

> ... a family, a rather stuffy Victorian family, with not many black sheep in it but with all its cupboards bursting with skeletons. It has rich relations who have to be kow-towed to and poor relations who are horribly sat upon, and there is a deep conspiracy of silence about the source of the family income. It is a family in which the young are generally thwarted and most of the power is in the hands of irresponsible uncles and bedridden aunts. Still, it is a family ... A family with the wrong members in control.[35]

The image of a family that is, despite some internal differences, nevertheless united is a problematic one. Orwell's analysis may be blighted by his inability to see capitalism as 'an economic and political system'[36] but his deployment of the image of the family as a microcosm of community is an important feature in his elucidation of the belief that the sinking middle class should unite with the working class in a revolutionary effort to overthrow the 'wrong members', namely the 'upper classes', who remain in control.

Orwell's deployment of the family as a political trope, as an item in his rhetorical lexicon, needs to be seen in relation to his preoccupation with the rise of fascism which, in many ways, precluded a more detailed analysis of middle-class socialism. His writing is really more public and polemical in its concerns than philosophical and speculative.

Totalitarianism was in some senses Orwell's lifelong study and from his warnings against fascist dictatorships to his practical involvement in the Spanish Civil War, his commitment to freedom remained paramount. His most famous and, paradoxically, controversial fictions *Animal Farm* and *Nineteen Eighty-Four* both satirise and warn against a left-leaning complacency that could be replaced by the power-hungry totalitarian regimes that he spent his life fighting against. However, Orwell's commitment has been called into question from perspectives such as Stephen Sedley's. Sedley writes:

> Orwell's argument [in *Animal Farm*] ... is that socialism in whatever form offers the common people no more hope than capitalism; that it will be first betrayed and then held to ransom by those forces which human beings have in common with beasts; and that the inefficient and occasionally benign rule of capitalism, which at least keeps the beasts in check, is a lesser evil.[37]

Sedley does not elucidate what he means by 'whatever form' but one can assume that he ignores the notion of revolution. This point is important; Orwell's Spanish experience taught him that for socialism to really work, a workers' revolution would be inevitable. In *Homage to Catalonia* Orwell stresses the part played by the USSR's supply of arms to the Spanish Government and its indirect involvement in the suppression of the POUM and mass revolution

> ... the Communists stood not upon the extreme Left, but upon the extreme Right. In reality this should cause no surprise, because the tactics of the Communist Party elsewhere ... have made it clear that Official Communism must be regarded, at any rate for the time being, as an anti-revolutionary force.[38]

IV

The final legacy of George Orwell is steeped in controversy. The plain-speaking man's creative and critical output has allowed him to be positioned as both the champion of the political left as well as its enemy. George Woodcock's comments are telling:

> From the day he published *The Road to Wigan Pier* in 1936, until his death in 1950, not only the Communists, who frankly hated him, but also many doctrinaire Socialists within the Labour Party felt that their movement would have been better off without an advocate so given to prickly criticism and so liable to lapse into embarrassing bouts of conservatism.[39]

Orwell's political position did not consist of a fixed set of assumptions and opinions; rather, his was a shifting and developing – if occasionally contradictory – subject position, from which he attempted to address a range of problematic issues. Raymond Williams perhaps summarises the most eminently sensible approach to Orwell and his body of work when he writes that

> ... the contradictions, the paradox of Orwell, must be seen as paramount. Instead of flattening out the contradictions by choosing this or that tendency as the 'real' Orwell, or fragmenting them by separating this or that period or this or that genre, we ought to say that it is the paradoxes which are finally significant. No simple explanation of them will do justice to so complex a man ...[40]

The essays that follow exemplify the difficulties of getting hold of 'the man' and the contradictions that arise when one attempts to draw conclusions about his work. Along with the sense of form or narrative, the reader/critic is forced to engage with the political philosophy that underlies the texts, with their rhetoric, an element that a number of the essays here endeavour to get to grips with, and their satirical energy. Orwell remains a challenging writer and the debates about his work continue.

NOTES

1. George Orwell, 'Shooting an Elephant', in George Bott (ed.), *George Orwell: Selected Writings* (Oxford, 1958), p. 25.

2. George Orwell, *The Road to Wigan Pier* (Harmondsworth, 1983), p. 130.

3. Ibid., p. 122.

4. *George Orwell: Selected Writings*, p. 103.

5. Raymond Williams, *George Orwell* (London, 1971), p. 20.

6. Orwell, *The Road to Wigan Pier*, p. 130.

7. George Orwell, *Down and Out in Paris and London* (Harmondsworth, 1989), p. 121.

8. Dervla Murphy's Introduction to George Orwell, *Down and Out in Paris and London*, p. xii.

9. Lynette Hunter, *George Orwell: The Search for a Voice* (Milton Keynes, 1984), p. 1.

10. Elleke Boehmer, *Colonial and Postcolonial Literature* (Oxford, 1995), p. 163.

11. Ibid., p. 162.

12. Homi Bhabha, 'Representation and the Colonial Text: A Critical Exploration of Some Forms of Mimeticism', in Frank Gloversmith (ed.), *The Theory of Reading* (Hemel Hempstead, 1984), p. 96.

13. Edward Said, 'Representing the Colonized: Anthropology's Interlocutors', *Critical Inquiry*, 15 (1989), 224.

14. Abdul JanMohamed, 'The Economy of Manichean Allegory: The Function of Racial Difference in Colonialist Literature', *Critical Inquiry*, 12 (1985), 64.

15. George Orwell, *Burmese Days* (Harmondsworth, 1967), p. 36.

16. Ibid., p. 41.

17. Ibid., p. 40.

18. Ibid., pp. 22–3.

19. Ibid., p. 234.

20. Ibid., p. 39.

21. Williams, *George Orwell*, p. 11.

22. Orwell, *The Road to Wigan Pier*, p. 112.

23. Ibid., p. 122.

24. Ibid., p. 141.

25. Ibid., pp. 107–9.

26. Ibid., p. 190.

27. Ibid., p. 155.

28. Beatrix Campbell, pp. 65–6 below.

29. Ibid.,

30. Orwell, *The Road to Wigan Pier*, p. 104.

31. Ibid., p. 103.

32. Ibid., p. 72–3.

33. George Orwell, *The Lion and the Unicorn* (Harmondsworth, 1982), p. 52.

34. Ibid., p. 53.

35. Ibid., pp. 53–4.

36. Williams, *George Orwell*, p. 26.

37. Stephen Sedley, 'An Immodest Proposal: Animal Farm', in Christopher Norris (ed.), *Inside the Myth* (London, 1984), p. 158.

38. George Orwell, *Homage to Catalonia* (London, 1959), p. 58.

39. George Woodcock, *The Crystal Spirit* (Harmondsworth, 1966), p. 218.

40. Williams, *George Orwell*, p. 87.

1

Revolution on *Animal Farm*: Orwell's Neglected Commentary

V. C. LETEMENDIA

In the last scene of George Orwell's 'fairy tale', *Animal Farm*, the humbler animals peer through a window of the farmhouse to observe a horrible sight: the pigs who rule over them have grown indistinguishable from their temporary allies, the human farmers, whom they originally fought to overthrow.[1] The animals' fate seems to mirror rather closely that of the common people as Orwell envisaged it some six years before commencing *Animal Farm*: 'what you get over and over again is a movement of the proletariat which is promptly canalised and betrayed by astute people at the top, and then the growth of a new governing class. The one thing that never arrives is equality. The mass of the people never get the chance to bring their innate decency into the control of affairs, so that one is almost driven to the cynical thought that men are only decent when they are powerless.'[2] Obviously *Animal Farm* was designed to parody the betrayal of Socialist ideals by the Soviet regime. Yet it has also been interpreted by various readers as expressing Orwell's own disillusion with any form of revolutionary political change and, by others, as unfolding such a meaning even without its author's conscious intention. It is time now to challenge both of these views.

Orwell himself commented of *Animal Farm* that 'if it does not speak for itself, it is a failure'.[3] The text does indeed stand alone to reveal Orwell's consistent belief not only in democratic Socialism, but in the possibility of a democratic Socialist revolution, but there is also a considerable body of evidence outside *Animal Farm* that can be shown to corroborate this interpretation. The series of events surrounding its publication, and Orwell's own consistent attitude towards his book provide evidence of its political meaning.[4] Meanwhile, of the two extant prefaces written by Orwell, the one designed for the Ukrainian edition, composed in 1947, is of particular political interest.[5] Orwell's correspondence with his friends and acquaintances on the subject of *Animal Farm* provides a further source of information. Some of these letters are well known to Orwell scholars, but his correspondence with Dwight Macdonald, with whom he became friends when he was writing for the American journal, *Partisan Review*, does not appear to have been fully investigated. Macdonald himself raised a direct question about the political intent of *Animal Farm* and was given a specific answer by Orwell, yet this fascinating evidence has apparently been neglected, in spite of the generous access now available to his correspondence in the Orwell Archive.[6]

Commentators on Orwell find it easy to conclude from *Animal Farm* the utter despair and pessimism either of its author, or of the tale itself.[7] It must be remembered, however, that through his allegory Orwell plays a two-sided game with his reader. In some ways, he clearly emphasises the similarities between the beasts on Animal Farm and the humans whom they are designed to represent; at other times, he demonstrates with both humour and pathos the profound differences separating animal from man – differences which in the end serve to limit the former. In doing so, he forces his reader to draw a distinction between the personalities and conduct of the beasts and those of the human world. Of course, the animals are designed to represent working people in their initial social, economic, and political position in the society not just of Animal Farm but of England in general. The basic antagonism between working class and capitalist is also strongly emphasised by the metaphor: pig and man quarrel fiercely at the end of the story. The diversity of the animal class, like the working class, is equally stressed by the differing personalities of the creatures. Just because all have been subjected to human rule, this does not mean that they will act as a united body once they take over the farm. The qualities which, for Orwell, clearly unite the majority of the animals with their human counterparts, the common working people, are a concern for freedom and equality in society and a form of 'innate decency' which prevents them from desiring power for any personal gain. While this decency hinders the worker animals from discovering the true nature of the pigs until the final scene, it also provides them with an instinctive feeling for what a fair society might actually look like. Yet Orwell was obviously aware, in using this metaphor, that the animals differ fundamentally from their human counterparts. Unlike men, the majority of the beasts are limited naturally by their brief lifespan and the consequent shortness of their memory. Moreover, their differentiated physical types deny them the versatility of humans. Their class structure is fixed by their immutable functions on the farm: a horse can never fill the role of a hen. The class structure of human society, in contrast, is free from such biological demarcations. These two profoundly limiting aspects of the animal condition, in which men share no part, finally contribute to the creatures' passivity in the face of the pig dictatorship. The metaphor, then, cannot be reduced to a simple equivalence, in the way that the pigs reduce the seven Commandments of Animal Farm to one.[8]

Evidently the animals lack education and self-confidence in spite of the active role which most of them played in the first rebellion and, in the case of some, are naturally stupid. Orwell is not implying by this the hopelessness of a proletarian revolution: he rather points to the need for education and self-confidence in any working-class movement if it is to remain democratic in character. Both of these attributes, he appears further to suggest, must come from within the movement itself. The crude proletarian spirit of the common animals necessarily provides the essential ingredient for a revolution towards a free and equal society, but it needs careful honing and polishing if it is not to fall victim to its own inherent decency and modesty. If this simple, instinctive decency is to be preserved in the transition from revolution – which is all too easy – to the construction of a new society – which is not – other kinds of virtue are also necessary and must at all costs be developed by the working class if it is not to be betrayed again. The text itself, however, hints at disaster for the rule of the pigs. Their single tenet asserting that some animals are more equal than others is in the end a meaningless absurdity. In spite of their great intellectual gifts, the pigs are ultimately the most absurd of all the farm animals, for they are attempting to assume a human identity which cannot belong to them. It is left to the reader to ponder the potential for political change, given the evident weakness and vanity at the core of the pig dictatorship. The final scene of the book, moreover, reveals the disillusionment of the working beasts with their porcine leaders, an essential step in the process of creating a new revolution.[9]

Evidence external to the text of *Animal Farm* is not required to establish the political meaning within its pages. Yet an examination of Orwell's attitude towards the book during the difficult period in which he tried to have it published only strengthens the conclusions drawn here. Even before *Animal Farm* was finished, Orwell was quite aware that it would cause controversy because of its untimely anti-Stalinist message, and he predicted difficulties in publishing it.[10] He was, of course, correct: the manuscript was refused by Gollancz, André Deutsch, and Jonathan Cape – in the latter case on the advice of the Ministry of Information. Meanwhile, Orwell declined an offer to publish the book in serial form in Lady Rhondda's *Time and Tide*, explaining that the politics of the journal were too right-wing for his tale, only to be turned down by T. S. Eliot at Faber and Faber, his next choice of publisher. The end of the story is well known to Orwell scholars: Orwell went finally to Frederick Warburg, who accepted the manuscript, and upon its publication in August 1945, it was well received and soon selected by the Book-of-the-Month Club.[11] Orwell's interest in the major publishing houses, as well as his reluctance to approach Frederick Warburg as a first choice and his willingness at one desperate point to pay himself to have the work reproduced in pamphlet form show that he wanted it to reach the public at all costs and to address as wide an audience as possible from as unprejudiced a political context as he could find. Naturally, Lady Rhondda's journal would not have been suitable: his purpose was not to congratulate conservatives or even liberals on the failure of the Russian Revolution, however scathing his criticism of the Stalinist regime within the allegory. Furthermore, Orwell stood firmly against any suggested alterations to the text, particularly in the instance of his representation of the Bolsheviks as pigs. He made no excuses for *Animal Farm* – as he would in the case of *Nineteen Eighty-Four* – and must have considered its message to be fairly clear, for he offered no press releases to correct misinterpretations of the book from either right- or left-wing political camps.[12] On the contrary, it rather seems that he was proud of the quality, as much as the political timeliness, of the book and expected it to require no external defence or explanation; this opinion did not appear to change.[13]

Some further indication of Orwell's own view of *Animal Farm* may be found in the two prefaces he wrote for it. Of the two, only the Ukrainian preface was actually published. Its original English version, written early in 1947, has never been found, and only a translation from the Ukrainian is available to Orwell scholars. This presents the possibility that various errors or subtle alterations of meaning might have remained uncorrected by the author when it was first translated from English to Ukrainian.[14] Written two years after the English preface, the Ukrainian piece obviously betrays a purpose very different from that of its predecessor, as a result supplying the reader with far more direct commentary on the text. Orwell makes it clear here that he 'became pro-Socialist more out of disgust with the way the poorer section of the industrial workers were oppressed and neglected than out of any theoretical admiration for a planned society'. His experiences in Spain, he states, gave him first-hand evidence of the ease with which 'totalitarian propaganda can control the opinion of enlightened people in democratic countries'. Not only were the accusations against Trotskyists in Spain the same as those made at the Moscow trials in the USSR; Orwell considers that he 'had every reason to believe that [they] were false', as far as Spain was concerned. Upon his return to England, he discovered 'the numerous sensible and well-informed observers believing the most fantastic accounts of conspiracy, treachery and sabotage which the press reported from the Moscow trials'. What upset him most was not the 'barbaric and undemocratic methods' of Stalin and his associates, since, he argues, 'It is quite possible that even with the best intentions, they could not have acted otherwise under the conditions prevailing there.' The real problem, in his view, was that Western Europeans could not see the truth about the Soviet regime, still considering it a Socialist country when, in fact, it was being transformed 'into a hierarchical society, in which the rulers have no more reason to give up their power than any other ruling class'. Both workers and the intelligentsia had to be disabused of this illusion which they held partly out of wilful misunderstanding and partly because of an inability to comprehend totalitarianism, 'being accustomed to comparative freedom and moderation in public life'. To make possible, then, a 'revival of the Socialist movement' by exposing the Soviet myth, Orwell writes that he tried to think of 'a story that could be easily understood by almost everyone and which could be easily translated into other languages'.[15]

He claims that although the idea came to him upon his return from Spain in 1937, the details of the story were not worked out until the day he 'saw a little boy, perhaps ten years old, driving a huge cart-horse along a narrow path, whipping it whenever it tried to turn'. If the horse could only become aware of its own strength, the boy would obviously have no control over it. Orwell found in this a parallel with the way in which 'the rich exploit the proletariat', and he proceeded from this recognition 'to analyse Marx's argument from the animals' point of view'. For them, he argues, the idea of class struggle between humans was illusory; the real tension was between animals and men, 'since whenever it was necessary to exploit animals, all humans united against them'. The story was not hard to elaborate from this, Orwell continues, although he did not actually write it all out until 1943, some six years after the main ideas had been conceived of. Orwell declines to comment on the work in his preface, for 'if it does not speak for itself, it is a failure'. Yet he ends with two points about details in the story: first, that it required some chronological rearrangement of the events of the Russian Revolution, and, second, that he did not mean pigs and men to appear reconciled completely at the end of the book. On the contrary, 'I meant it to end on a loud note of discord, for I wrote it immediately after the Teheran Conference [parodied by the final scene in *Animal Farm*] which everybody thought had established the best possible relations between the USSR and the West. I personally did not believe that such good relations would last long. ...'[16]

It seems, then, that as much as Orwell wanted to explain how he had arrived at Socialism and at his understanding of totalitarianism, he sought to indicate in this preface to Ukrainian readers how workers and intelligentsia in Western Europe, but especially in England, misperceived the difference between the Soviet Union of 1917 and that of twenty and thirty years later. *Animal Farm* was, according to its author, an attempt to strip away the mythical veil shrouding the Stalinist regime; simultaneously, however, he was trying to renew what had been lost through this deception and to revive the original spirit of the Socialist movement. It seems possible to conclude that Orwell is suggesting the presence of just such a double intention within the allegory. One point in the preface, however, requires clarification. Orwell's reference to the animals' view that the real class struggle lay between animals and humans suggests, in the context of the allegory, the absence of any significant class struggle between members of the ruling class – or humans – since they will readily forget their differences and unite to oppress animals. This appears confusing when applied to Marx's theory, which Orwell claims as the theoretical basis of this insight, and furthermore it does not capture the thrust of the story itself, in which the divisions between animals are exposed in detail, rather than those between humans, or even between humans and animals.[17] But Orwell makes it quite clear here that he refers to an animal perspective in defining the class struggle as one between humans and beasts. Certainly the point of departure was, in both the Russian situation and in this particular allegory, the identification and removal of the most evident class of oppressors. In this initial movement, the oppressed class was not mistaken politically; what came afterwards in both instances, though, demonstrated that the first movement of revolutionary consciousness had not been sustained in its purity, since the goals of the revolution gradually began to be violated. Orwell's remark in the preface that '[f]rom this point of departure [the animals' view of the class struggle], it was not difficult to elaborate the rest of the story' cannot be taken as an admission that the animals' perspective was perfectly correct.[18] Of course, the book debunks such a simplistic interpretation of the class struggle, in spite of its initial accuracy.

By revealing the divisions within the animal ranks, Orwell is cautioning his reader to question the animal view of the class struggle, for the crucial problem that even the wise Old Major does not predict in his identification of the real enemy is the power-hunger of the pigs. By allegorical implication, this points rather interestingly to Orwell's identification of a flaw in the Marxian theory of revolution itself. Although its starting point is clearly the animals' partially accurate but insufficient analysis of the class struggle, the allegory in its course reveals more and more drastically the inadequacy of such a view as a basis for post-revolutionary society. Part of Old Major's vision is indeed debunked, while the truth of the initial insight about class struggle is never denied, and the story, as has been seen, ends on a note of hope. Orwell's final point in the preface constitutes the only correction and very mild apology that he would make about the text, even though he had had roughly two years to assess the critical response – and hence the variety of misinterpretations – circulating about *Animal Farm*. Here he is warning his reader about the subtlety of his allegory: pigs and humans may come to look the same at the end, but they are still essentially enemies and share only a greed for power. For it is indeed the dispute between farmers and pigs which completes the transformation of pig to man and of man to pig.

If the Ukrainian preface was written for an unknown audience, the English preface was designed for readers with whom Orwell was much more familiar. Written in 1945, when he was still bitterly upset over the difficulties of printing unpopular political commentary in wartime Britain, the English preface is concerned not with the content of the story but with the question of whether he would be free to publish it at all because of current political alliances, intellectual prejudices, and general apathy over the need to defend basic democratic liberties.[19] Attacking as he does here the political toadying of the Left intelligentsia in Britain to the Stalinist regime, Orwell presents *Animal Farm* as a lesson for the well-educated as much as the uneducated.[20] Meanwhile, the fact that he makes no reference in this preface to the details of the book indicates his strong confidence in its political clarity for English readers, although his bitter tone shows, as Crick suggests, Orwell's acute sense that he was being 'persecuted for plain speaking' before *Animal Farm* was published.[21] Since the English preface does not actually offer an interpretation of *Animal Farm* explaining Orwell's political intention, it is necessary to look for this information in his more private communications on the subject.

Orwell commented explicitly on his book to his friends Geoffrey Gorer and Dwight Macdonald. Crick states that Orwell gave a copy of *Animal Farm* to Gorer having marked in it the passage in which Squealer defends the pigs' theft of the milk and apples. He told Gorer that this 'was the key passage'.[22] This emphasis of Orwell's is reiterated and explained more fully in a letter to Dwight Macdonald written shortly after *Animal Farm* first appeared in the United States, in 1946. Macdonald was one of a group of American intellectuals who had broken with Soviet Communism as early as 1936 and had gone to work with Philip Rahv and William Phillips on *Partisan Review*.[23] From January 1941 to the summer of 1946, Orwell had sent regular 'letters' to the review and had had cause to correspond with Macdonald fairly frequently. Macdonald was later to move to the editorship of *Politics*, described by Orwell in a letter to T. S. Eliot as 'a sort of dissident offshoot' of *Partisan Review*, and had already championed a review written by Orwell that had been rejected for political reasons by the *Manchester Evening News*.[24] This shared political understanding soon developed into a literary friendship which lasted until Orwell's death in 1950.[25]

In September 1944, Orwell had already written to Macdonald expressing his views about the Soviet Union. Given that only a few months separated the completion of *Animal Farm* from this letter, it seems safe to assume that the views expressed in both might be similar. To Macdonald, Orwell stated, 'I think the USSR is the dynamo of world Socialism, so long as people believe in it. I think that if the USSR were to be conquered by some foreign country the working class everywhere would lose heart, for the time being at least, and the ordinary stupid capitalists who never lost their suspicion of Russia would be encouraged.' Furthermore, 'the fact that the Germans have failed to conquer Russia has given prestige to the idea of Socialism. For that reason I wouldn't want to see the USSR destroyed and think it ought to be defended if necessary.' There is a caution, however: '[b]ut I want people to become disillusioned about it and to realise that they must build their own Socialist movement without Russian interference, and I want the existence of democratic Socialism in the West to exert a regenerative influence upon Russia.' He concludes that 'if the working class everywhere had been taught to be as anti-Russian as the Germans have been made, the USSR would simply have collapsed in 1941 or 1942, and God knows what things would then have come out from under their stones. After that Spanish business I hate the Stalin regime perhaps worse than you do, but I think one must defend it against people like Franco, Laval etc.'[26]

In spite of its repressive features and its betrayal of basic human freedoms, then, Orwell still considered the Soviet regime to be vital as an example to the working class everywhere. The real danger lay in the idea that it defined Socialism. What was most needed was a new form of democratic Socialism created and maintained by the people. He offers meanwhile the possibility that such democratic forms of Socialism elsewhere might actually have a benign effect on the Russian regime.[27] In the allegorical context of Animal Farm, Napoleon's dictatorship would still seem to be a step forward from that of the human farmers – according to Orwell's letter, the rule of 'the ordinary stupid capitalists'. For animals outside the farm, it would provide a beacon of hope – so long as the truth about the betrayal taking place within was made plain to them. For it would now become their task to build their own movement in a democratic spirit which might, in Orwell's words, 'exert a regenerative influence' on the corruption of the pigs' realm.

When *Animal Farm* finally appeared in the United States in 1946, Macdonald wrote again to Orwell, this time to discuss the book:

'most of the anti-Stalinist intellectuals I know ... don't seem to share my enthusiasm for *Animal Farm*. They claim that your parable means that revolution always ends badly for the underdog, hence to hell with it and hail the status quo. My own reading of the book is that it is meant to apply to Russia without making any larger statement about the philosophy of revolution. None of the objectors have so far satisfied me when I raised this point; they admit explicitly that is all you profess to do, but still insist that implicit is the broader point. ... Which view would you say comes closer to your intentions?'[28]

Orwell's reply deserves quoting in full: 'Of course I intended it primarily as a satire on the Russian revolution. But I did mean it to have a wider application in so much that I meant that that kind of revolution (violent conspiratorial revolution, led by unconsciously power-hungry people) can only lead to a change of masters. I meant the moral to be that revolutions only effect a radical improvement when the masses are alert and know how to chuck out their leaders as soon as the latter have done their job. The turning point of the story was supposed to be when the pigs kept the milk and apples for themselves (Kronstadt). If the other animals had had the sense to put their foot down then, it would have been all right. If people think I am defending the status quo, that is, I think, because they have grown pessimistic and assume there is no alternative except dictatorship or laissez-faire capitalism. In the case of the Trotskyists, there is the added complication that they feel responsible for events in the USSR up to about 1926 and have to assume that a sudden degeneration took place about that date, whereas I think the whole process was foreseeable – and was foreseen by a few people, e.g. Bertrand Russell – from the very nature of the Bolshevik party. What I was trying to say was, "You can't have a revolution unless you make it for yourself; there is no such thing as a benevolent dictatorship".'[29]

Yes, *Animal Farm* was intended to have a wider application than a satire upon the Russian regime alone. Yes, it did indeed imply that the rule of the pigs was only 'a change of masters'. Yet it did not condemn to the same fate all revolutions, nor for a moment suggest that Farmer Jones should be reinstated as a more benevolent dictator than Napoleon. According to Orwell's letter, the problem examined by *Animal Farm* concerns the nature of revolution itself. Unless everyone makes the revolution for him or herself without surrendering power to an elite, there will be little hope for freedom or equality.

A revolution in which violence and conspiracy become the tools most resorted to, one which is led by a consciously or unconsciously power-hungry group, will inevitably betray its own principles.[30] Failing to protest when the pigs kept the milk and apples for themselves, the other animals surrendered what power they might have had to pig leadership. Had they been 'alert and [known] how to chuck out their leaders'[31] once the latter had fulfilled their task, the original spirit of Animal Farm might have been salvaged. The book itself, Orwell makes clear in his letter, was calling not for the end of revolutionary hopes, but for the beginning of a new kind of personal responsibility on the part of revolutionaries. The most important barrier in the way of such a democratic Socialist revolution was the Soviet myth: if people outside still thought that that particular form of revolution could succeed without betraying its goals, nothing new could be accomplished. The final note of Orwell's letter is optimistic: if people mistook his message for a conservative one, it was precisely their problem. They had no confidence in the possibility of an alternative to either capitalism or dictatorship. In a sense, they would be like those animals who, when forced into making a choice between a false set of alternatives by Squealer – either the return of Farmer Jones or unquestioning obedience to the rule of the pigs – failed to consider the possibility of a third choice, a democratic Socialist society. For although Orwell was prepared to provide a fairly detailed explanation of his animal story for his friend Macdonald, his letter makes it quite evident that the burden of understanding *Animal Farm* still lay with its reader.

Given the striking congruity between the text and Orwell's political commentary about it, it would be rash to argue that he had lost control of his allegory in *Animal Farm*. If it takes time and effort to expose the political intricacies behind the stark prose of his animal fable, this must have been partly his intention: the lesson of democracy was not an easy one to learn, and the next revolutionary move towards democratic Socialism could surely not be allowed to repeat the mistakes of Old Major. Still, we may wonder if the grain of hope provided by the final scene of the book is not, in this light, too insubstantial to feed a new generation of revolutionaries. Yet if Orwell had presented an easy political resolution to the horrors of totalitarianism, his warning would lose its force. His reader could remain complacent, detached from the urgent need for personal involvement in political change so emphasised by the animal allegory. If he had designed a political solution for the other beasts, furthermore, he could be accused of hypocrisy: his whole argument both inside and outside the text rested on the proposition that the people had to make and retain control of the revolution themselves if they wanted it to remain true to its goals. The deceit of the pigs was not the only failure on Animal Farm, for the foolish simplicity of the other animals and, indeed, of Old Major's naïve idea of revolutionary change were as much to blame for the dictatorship which ensued. Orwell had to warn his readers that their apathy and thoughtlessness were as dangerous as blind admiration for the Stalinist regime. Only when all members of society saw the essential need for individual responsibility and honesty at the heart of any struggle for freedom and equality could the basic goals of Socialism, as Orwell saw them, be approached more closely. Meanwhile, no single revolutionary act could create a perfect world, either for the animals or for the humans whom they represent in the story. Acceptance of the notion of class struggle could not lead to an instant transformation of society unless those who would transform it accepted also the difficult burden of political power, both at the time of and after the revolution. While the most corrupting force on Animal Farm was the deception practised upon the other animals by the pigs, the greatest danger came from the reluctance of the oppressed creatures to believe in an alternative between porcine and human rule. Yet it was in the affirmation of dignity, freedom, and equality tacitly provided by the nobler qualities of the presumed lower animals that Orwell saw the beginnings of such an alternative. So it is that, in the last moment of the book, he leaves open the task of rebuilding the revolution on a wiser and more cautiously optimistic foundation.

From *Journal of Modern Literature*, 18:1 (1992), 127–37.

NOTES

[V. C. Letemendia asserts that *Animal Farm* is not finally a pessimistic overview of the Soviet myth nor an anti-Socialist tract, but is rather Orwell's attempt to explicate the need for new revolutionary tactics and strategies. She, interestingly, refers to Orwell's correspondence with the American anti-Stalinist intellectual Dwight Macdonald, material which has received little previous critical inquiry and which offers insights into Orwell's feelings about *Animal Farm* and Russian Socialism. This essay, in its emphasis on the historical and political background to *Animal Farm*, effectively complements Lynette Hunter's essay (2) in the collection which is a study of the rhetoric of the text. Eds]

1. George Orwell, *Animal Farm* (New York, 1946), p. 118. Further references to the text are to this edition and are given parenthetically.

2. Sonia Orwell and Ian Angus (eds), *The Collected Essays, Journalism and Letters of George Orwell* (Harmondsworth, 1971), vol. I, p. 372. (This four-volume collection will be referred to henceforth as *CEJL*.) Even when Orwell wrote this, in deep distress after his experience of the Spanish Civil War, he was not completely pessimistic, as he remarked with some surprise: see *Homage to Catalonia* (Harmondsworth, 1984), p. 220.

3. *CEJL*, III, p. 459.

4. Much of Orwell's other writing, particularly that which is contemporary to the creation of *Animal Farm*, also supports the interpretation offered here. See, for example, *CEJL*, II, pp. 83 and 280–2; 'Tapping the Wheels', *Observer*, 16 January 1944, p. 3. This is not to mention Orwell's radical writing of the earlier war years, exemplified by his revolutionary enthusiasm in *The Lion and the Unicorn* (see *CEJL*, II, pp. 74–134) and his two essays for Gollancz, *'The Betrayal of the Left* (1941), 'Fascism and Democracy' and 'Patriots and Revolutionaries' (pp. 206–14 and 234–45). After *Animal Farm*, Orwell's position remained unchanged; see, for example, 'The British General Election', *Commentary*, November 1946, pp. 65–70, and 'What is Socialism?' *Manchester Evening News*, 31 January 1946, p. 2.

5. For the Ukrainian preface, see *CEJL*, III, pp. 455–9; see also 'The Freedom of the Press', *The Times Literary Supplement*, 15 September 1972, pp. 1036–8.

6. The author would like to thank the staff of the Orwell Archive, University College, University of London, for their very kind assistance in searching out the relevant materials for this discussion, as well as for their help in finding resources for the larger work on Orwell's politics of which it is but a small part. She would like to thank the estate of the late Sonia Orwell and Martin Secker & Warburg for permission to publish extracts from their collection of Orwell's correspondence. She would also like to thank the Yale University Library for permission to publish extracts from the Dwight Macdonald Papers and its generosity in making available to her copies of other letters in their Manuscripts and Archives collection.

7. See, for example, Patrick Reilly, *George Orwell: The Age's Adversary* (London, 1986), pp. 266–7; Alan Sandison, *George Orwell: After 1984* (London, 1986), p. 156; Alok Rai, *Orwell and the Politics of Despair* (Cambridge, 1988), pp. 115–16; Stephen Sedley, 'An Immodest Proposal: *Animal Farm*', in Christopher Norris (ed.), *Inside the Myth* (London, 1984), p. 158; and Alex Zwerdling, *Orwell and the Left* (New Haven, CT, 1984), pp. 90–4.

8. A full discussion of the animal–human metaphor and its political purpose is not within the scope of this brief study, but is elaborated upon fully in the author's doctoral dissertation, 'Free from Hunger and the Whip: Exploring the Political Development of George Orwell' (University of Toronto, 1992).

9. Raymond Williams, in his *George Orwell* (New York and Ontario, 1971), shares this view: see pp. 74–5.

10. Bernard Crick, *George Orwell: A Life* (Harmondsworth, 1980), p. 450; for an indication of Orwell's own fears about the unpopularity of his book, see *CEJL*, III, pp. 71–2, 118–19 and 168–70.

11. For a full account of the publication problems and the reception of *Animal Farm*, see Crick, *George Orwell: A Life*, pp. 452–8 and pp. 487–90.

12. For an account of Orwell's own criticism of *Nineteen Eighty-Four*, the conditions under which it was written, and the statement which he issued in order to correct political misinterpretations of it, see Crick, *George Orwell: A Life*, pp. 546–51 and 565–70.

13. For evidence of his apparent satisfaction with the book, see *CEJL*, I, p. 29. His friend William Empson recalls him complaining when the book first appeared that 'not one of [the reviews] said it's a beautiful book'. See Audrey Coppard and Bernard Crick (eds), *Orwell Remembered* (London, 1984), p. 183.

14. Peter Stansky and William Abrahams, in their *Orwell: the Transformation* (London, 1981), also consider this worth mentioning: see p. 185. Peter Davison, at present in the process of editing *The Complete Works of George Orwell*, has already discovered a surprising number of mistakes or changes made during the past publication of Orwell's work in English: it seems logical that the potential inaccuracies of a re-translated translation uncorrected by its original author should be contemplated seriously. For a brief account of Davison's discoveries, see *The Sunday Times*, 2 March 1986, p. 5.

15. *CEJL*, III, pp. 455–8.

16. *CEJL*, III, pp. 458–9.

17. Stephen Sedley concludes from this that '[t]he muddle is remarkable' and that 'the book begins and ends by debunking' the idea of a class struggle between animals and humans, whether it be attributed to the animals or to Orwell himself (Sedley, 'An Immodest Proposal', p. 161). Rai, meanwhile, argues from the Ukrainian preface that '*Animal Farm* had been intended as an allegory of the common people, awaking to a realisation of their strength and overthrowing their oppressors', but that '[i]n working out the fable, however, in the winter of 1943–4, the euphoria collapsed' (Rai, *Orwell and the Politics of Despair*, p. 115). Rai seems to forget

Orwell's own comment at the beginning of the preface that the idea for *Animal Farm* was linked to his experience in Spain and explicitly designed to debunk the Soviet myth. This already suggests a story with a far from idyllic ending. It was only after the idea had been conceived of, according to Orwell, that he decided on the details of the story. It would thus appear likely that Orwell had thought through the political message of his story long before the winter of 1943.

18. *CEJL*, III, p. 459.

19. Orwell, 'Freedom of the Press', pp. 1036–8.

20. Orwell considered that many such intellectuals had substituted for love of their own country a far more slavish regard for the Soviet Union. For his ideas on this issue, see 'Notes on Nationalism', *CEJL*, III, pp. 410–31. In other writing of the time, his language was even stronger than that of the English preface: see, for example, p. 263.

21. Crick, *George Orwell: A Life*, p. 463. Orwell was not, however, the only writer to feel this: as his friend Arthur Koestler explains, 'George and I were the only anti-Stalinists who could get printed. We felt we were persecuted by the *New Statesman* etc., and what appalled us was not just the refusal to print what we had written, but the systematic suppression of fact so that people simply did not know what was going on. Sources of truthful information were the privately circulated news sheets ... But people like Beaverbrook suppressed a great deal. I remember the "Beaver" saying how we all liked "Uncle Joe" and therefore mustn't say too much against him' (in Audrey Coppard and Bernard Crick [eds], *Orwell Remembered* [1984] pp. 167–8).

22. Crick, *George Orwell: A Life*, p. 490. It is a pity that Crick does not provide here the source of this important information.

23. David Caute, *The Fellow Travellers* (London, 1973), pp. 88–9; see note. See also Crick, *George Orwell, A Life*, p. 392.

24. See letter from Orwell to T. S. Eliot, 5 September 1944 in the Orwell Archive, reproduced by kind permission of the estate of the late Sonia Orwell and Martin Secker & Warburg. For details of the rejected book review, see *CEJL*, III, pp. 169–70.

25. An indication of its depth is that Sonia Orwell, when first considering the possibility of contravening her husband's dying wish and authorising a biography of him, wrote to Macdonald to see if he would undertake it. He accepted with enthusiasm, but she later withdrew her offer, having decided that it was too early for a biography to appear. See correspondence between Sonia Orwell and Dwight Macdonald in the Orwell Archive.

26. Letter from Orwell to Macdonald, 5 September 1944, Dwight Macdonald Papers, Manuscripts and Archives, Yale University Library;

copy in the Orwell Archive, reproduced by kind permission of the estate of the late Sonia Orwell and Martin Secker & Warburg. Orwell made a similar point in a later letter to Frank Barber, in which he states: 'My attention was first drawn to this deliberate falsification of history by my experiences in the Spanish civil war. One can't make too much noise about it while the man in the street identifies the cause of Socialism with the USSR, but I believe one can make a perceptible difference by seeing that the true facts get into print, even if it is only in some obscure place' (15 December 1944, Orwell Archive), reproduced by kind permission of the estate of the late Sonia Orwell and Martin Secker & Warburg. At this date, of course, Orwell was still waiting for *Animal Farm* to 'get into print'; it might be that his comment about 'some obscure place' could refer to the book itself.

27. In another letter to Macdonald written at the time that Orwell was in-volved with his final novel, he argues with an optimism which might surprise some of his critics: 'Communism will presently shed certain unfortunate characteristics such as bumping off its opponents, and if Socialists join up with the CP they can persuade it into better ways' (2 May 1948, Dwight Macdonald Papers).

28. Letter from Macdonald to Orwell, 2 December 1946. The argument to which Macdonald objects is still a favourite with Orwell's critics on the Left: Stephen Sedley offers it in his critique of *Animal Farm*.

29. Letter from Orwell to Macdonald, 5 December. It is interesting to compare this statement with one made by Orwell in a commentary on Randall Swingler's *Violence* published in *Polemic*, 5 (September–October, 1946), pp. 45–53: 'I do not believe in the possibility of benevolent dictatorship, nor, in the last analysis, in the honesty of those who defend dictatorship. Of course, one develops and modifies one's views, but I have never fundamentally altered my attitude towards the Soviet regime since I first began to pay attention to it some time in the nineteen-twenties. But so far from disappointing me, it has actually turned out somewhat better than I would have predicted fifteen years ago' (p. 53).

30. This is not to argue that Orwell defended pacifism; his fighting in Spain and his urgent and frequent attempts to join the army during the Second World War demonstrate his acceptance of the need for violent combat in order to defend basic human liberties. Yet he was evidently aware of the ease with which violence and conspiracy could be turned against the initial purpose which seemed to justify them. In the text of *Animal Farm*, Boxer's sorrow at the necessity of violence even in the struggle to overthrow human rule suggests a deeper wisdom than he is often given credit for (see pp. 36–7).

31. Letter from Orwell to Macdonald, 5 December 1946.

2

Animal Farm: Satire into Allegory

LYNETTE HUNTER

The complex satire of *Animal Farm* is built upon an awareness of the power that language wields. The interaction between politics and language does not just establish one-to-one relationships between animal characters and historical figures but creates an understanding of a particular set of rhetorical techniques that have a broad political application. Further, it does not simply criticise certain forms of government but suggests reasons for why they occur and what contributes to their success. However, what limits the tale to satire, no matter how constructive it is in its suggestions, is the sense of inevitability, of describing an insoluble problem, ending on a note of negativity and cynicism. At the same time though the reader cannot ignore the coincident tongue-in-cheek humour of the narrating voice. The melodramatised character of the elderly Clover, the formal dance of speeches with their all-too-neat structure, the final exaggerated irony, all belie the negative pattern of the satire.

What turns the writing into positive allegory is the establishing of genre conventions that are shifted and reversed. In these changes the narrator takes a positive stance that contrasts sharply with the satirical voice; and the primary and most obvious reversal is that to which we are alerted in the subtitle of the book, 'A Fairy Story'. The function of allegory depends on differences. Yet to repeat part of the earlier discussion, what is commonly termed 'allegory' is one-to-one use of representational emblems, similarities: hardly a subtle genre. The dissatisfaction with it comes from the limited and reduced nature of stance. If acted well the movements can afford a similar pleasure to that of chess, but as with chess the more significant aspects of the game lie in the battle between the players not that between the pieces on the board. Restricting themselves to those pieces and what they are capable of, the players limit the scope of their interaction and the involvement of their audience. The supposed author of this kind of reduced generic 'allegory' is limited by the overtly representational nature of his structure. It takes great skill to maintain the grounds of his alternative world and to avoid the sense of inevitability that arises from the associative links and habitual connotations that are established. At the same time simple destruction of those links can be just as reductive; something positive needs to be suggested to open out the dialogue and make interaction possible. The complex satire of *Animal Farm* is generated by the process of allegory out of a reductive satire about events in Russian history. Its positive nature is found in its broad applicability to politics and language. But it is still limited to the criticism and exposure of weaknesses, to saying what not to do rather than what to do.

However, there is also the broader, interactive allegorical stance of *Animal Farm* which removes itself one step further from the representational, by turning to literary conventions which establish the bases for difference. The writer spends much of the first chapter getting the narrator to set up the genre conventions that surround fairy stories. Yet from the beginning there is a counter-element which indicates why this particular genre has been chosen. Elements to note are the simple phrasing and the repetition of grammatical structures which create a formal rhythm in the prose. There is also use of specific constructions such as 'there was a stirring and a fluttering' or the literal use of common expressions like 'chewing the cud' that are traditionally allied to the genre. Especially distinctive is the formal and detached quality of the narrator generated by these elements. It is as if he has a specific recognised role as tale-teller, because individual style is played down. Even before the more personalised descriptions of the animals begin, these details alert and orientate the reader to a genre.

For several reasons, the convention is immediately effective. The form is instantly recognised as non-novelistic. The reader does not expect the naturalism of psychological exploration or 'round characters'. What he does look for is a formal structure for teaching and knowing, by way of a conventional and non-representational mode. From the beginning, we are involved in an expected manner, alerted to certain rules. The narrator has the freedom to state, and present 'types', without appearing to dictate or over-control. He also has a convention that encourages detachment because its formality states his stance for him. However, at the same time he is part of the narration in a manner that a tale-teller would not be. He throws forward the convention he is using with the addition of extraneous comment, such as the Major's alternative name being 'Willingdon Beauty'. The use of brackets at this particular point in itself indicates a grammatical 'aside' different from his formal role. The use of fairy story is further highlighted by the humour which emerges in applying human description to animals, which is unusual for the genre. The mare Clover 'had never quite got her figure back after her fourth foal',[1] and Benjamin's cynicism is undercut by a devotion to Boxer. Neither character will regain the formal distance of a fairy story figure after such description.

These effects are generated by the unusual use of animals as the main elements in the fairy story. The effect for the reader is that he can identify with the animals because they fit recognisable types, but the humour in their human description allows one to remain detached. We see the humanity in them because of their lack of it. The two views are the key to the allegory. The fairy story genre conditions one to certain expectations, an inevitability, a certain and set ethical development of specific issues in which the 'good' get rewarded and the 'bad' punished, according to the terms of the society they are written for. Excitement, adventure and apparent change occur only to reaffirm the basis of the society. Working against this all the way through is the fact that the characters are animals not humans. As a result many incongruous and ludicrous comparisons surface which detract from the formality of the fairy story and call into question its ethical inevitability.

Over and above the interconnection of these two is the interplay of the narrative allegory with the satire. After all the Major's speech dominates the first chapter. It is an example of a rhetoric containing within it the seeds of negative persuasion. The premises of that speech establish a power-wielding, knowledgeable, acceptable identity; they evidence total control over the development of the logic; and they encourage acceptance and group participation in agreed custom. The fairy story elements of the first chapter also do this. If we are aware of the manipulation involved in the Major's speech we should be doubly aware of the negative rhetorical elements in the fairy story. In this interplay and in the interaction of fairy story and humour, the allegory of the writing may be discerned. However, on first reading the dominant note is that of the fairy story not its disruption. Similarly, it is difficult to be immediately aware of the implications of the Major's speech. Yet I would suggest that this is a positive aspect of the writer's stance. The reader's gradual learning about the negative use of language parallels his gradual recognition of the subversion of the fairy story convention. The process of learning involves the active participation of the reader, draws him into a personal assessment necessary to the positive rhetoric of the writing.

The second chapter begins with the narrator retreating to an unobtrusive position to let the reader get on with the activity of recognition, disagreement and questioning. Only following the Rebellion does the overtly humorous voice re-enter again to balance out the conventions of fairy story. The humour is an unspoken irony based on the animals seeing human things from their point of view and the reader seeing them from his. The difference in the standards being applied need not be defined by the narrator because they are so clear. For example, the pathetic comedy of the statement that 'hams hanging in the kitchen were taken out for burial' (p. 21) is obvious. But because the humour is a result of the animals' different perspective rather than their ignorance, it is not simply a reason to laugh at them but to understand them and further, to reflect on the justification for our own standards. The humour of the irony sets up possibilities of choice for the reader. During this section of the satire it is made clear that the characters are being defined through their use of language and this is also true of the narrator. But while the pigs move only to imposing a control, the narrator in contrast has the ability to focus in and out, controlling but also asking his reader to control.

During the third chapter, the narrator retreats even further, pulling back his humorous comments closer to himself. His detachment is underlined when he clearly fails to make the usual narratorial comments. As a result he is not just formally but personally detached. The techniques of juxtaposition, resonance and the downplaying of incidents that take over, require the reader to partipate; they alert him to discrepancies, to meanings other than the habitual. Whereas the narrator himself did this at first, now the reader has to do it. Yet in setting the farmers off against the animals in the fourth chapter the narrator places himself firmly on the side of the animals by involving the reader in the decisions between the two. The tone of presentation defines part of his attitude. When describing the humans he uses longer sentences, idiomatic language and limited characteristics. They are 'types' not people. By contrast the animals are presented by way of a more direct, simple and straightforward language, the logic is easy to follow and there are few clichés and generalisations.

Although the narrator is able to maintain a distance from the story, the shift in his expression when presenting animals and humans indicates that he cannot be impartial. The alignment against the humans and with the animals is not a serious compromise of stance. In the first place it is defused by the humour of the contrasts. It is further controlled by the insistence on the overt fictionality which makes the humans 'types' and undercuts the achievements of the animals by limiting them to fairy story. However, his alignment with the other animals against the pigs by making the pigs more like humans in their speech, is a more subtle and questionable stance, and the reader must assess how it is to be justified. The reader's trust in the narrator's alignment is partly derived from his involvement in the techniques which gives a certain share in the assessment. But what really leaves the question open and allows for impartiality is not what is said or implied against the pigs, but what the other animals have or lack in comparison with them. These elements are supplied purely by the reader and the possibility of involving ourselves to this extent creates trust in the narratorial stance.

Chapter 5 is a highly ambiguous chapter in which the fairy story elements become so accepted that one is right inside the convention. The narrative reports, observes and states with little intervention, and even the implicit comments of the involving techniques are excised. Here a pattern of narratorial stance is developing, in which as the narrator aligns himself with a group he adopts their linguistic expression. The more the narrator aligns himself with the animals, the less he says because they are linguistically limited. The result is an expression of the ambiguity and confusion that they feel.

It is in this chapter that we are told that the animals would have argued 'if they could have found the right arguments' (p. 40) and for the reader the stance here requires even more involvement with the animals, assessing from their actions and partial verbalisations if we are to understand anything at all. For example, it is important that the narrator refrains from commenting on the kind of logic that the animals use to work out the apparent treachery of Snowball. Boxer restricts himself to the maxim that 'Napoleon is always right' and Clover turns to the written evidence of the Commandments. If the narrator were to spell out the processes and their implications, the limitations would appear too obvious. As it is, the reader has to make the evaluations himself and realises that it is not easy. Indeed on a first reading the importance of doing so may not even be apparent. But the narrator's alignment is carefully balanced. Only toward the end of the chapter do the pigs increasingly show in a bad light.

What is interesting about chapter 6 is the inclusion of more reported rather than direct speech from the pigs. It becomes even less easy for the reader to identify with them and to understand the significance of their words. When Squealer's explanations are reported they appear more plausible because they are at one remove, gaining a false objectivity, and they come from the narrator whom we trust. It is exactly the effect achieved by Napoleon's orders going through Squealer, or when Boxer and Clover explain the pigs' decisions to the other animals. Again the intercommentary on the rhetoric of politics demonstrates the problems involved in the narration itself and how we should not take it for granted. During the description of the second Battle, activity is restrained by the exaggerated ironic tone of the narrator. The animals are 'shocked beyond measure', and quite coincidentally the treacherous Snowball's footprints are found 'Almost immediately'. The artificiality of the response underlines the growing need to fit into the acceptable forms of expression wanted by the pigs. Not only are the other animals more personally restrained, but when they do speak they adopt conventional, easily identified modes for expression. As a whole the chapter separates more clearly between the pigs and the other animals, but also introduces more complexity, ambiguity and confusion so that it is difficult for the reader to know what to do about the separation.

The increasing identification of the narrator with the cause of the animals against the pigs carries on into chapter 7. Initially he narrates for them, and the reader, because of this, is led to identify with them. At the same time there is a growing inability on the reader's part to note the discrepancies between human and animal figures. While this used to be a source of humour and detachment, it becomes a worrying ignorance. No matter which reading is involved, a first or a subsequent, the reader will never be able to fully assess the situation. The process of confusion is stopped by the incident of the chickens during which the narratorial voice changes and quickens pace. This event may be read quite straightforwardly, and the reader can distinguish that the chickens are being killed, not dying naturally. It is reasonable to assume since the narrator is narrating for the animals, that the animals can also make the distinction. The suspicious reserve of 'It was given out ...' backs this up. But such distinction is double-edged because one is then left wondering what to do about it, and the animals do nothing. Our identification with them is put under considerable stress, for we observe a self-deception on their part that we know they are aware of.

Meanwhile the whole fairy story genre is called radically into question: rewards are not being meted out as they should be, something is going wrong with our expectations. Indeed so much so that when the animal 'confessions' and swift retributions come, it is necessary to re-read to see if one has missed some salient point. The event fits no convention whatever. At this point the narrator moves from the discursive and patient to the immediate with short quick phrases following rapidly on one another, a quickly moving rhythm that repeats itself and resonates. To begin with we hear of a formal 'arrangement' and the confessions spill out 'without further prompting' as if organised. The confessions are mechanical, expected, using an 'and/and/and' construction. But then there is the sudden shock of 'the dogs promptly tore their throats out', the internal resonance of 'prompt' linking the two actions in a horrific manner. The next animals 'were slaughtered'; the following deaths become even less specific being 'all slain upon the spot', and finally just 'a pile of corpses'. The control of pace and formal repetition turns the efficient narration into an almost ritual account.

The chapter concludes with the transition into a 'pastoral' scene from the unreal and completely upset convention of fairy story. The transition into these rather different generic elements can be read at least three ways. In the first it can be seen as a true pastoral of reassessment in which case it could legitimately conclude a fairy story. On the other hand it can be interpreted ironically as an escape into nostalgia by self-deceiving animals in which case the reader assumes a different position but with the same knowledge; or it can be read allegorically as a failed pastoral which succeeds in analysing its failure because our knowledge is not simply greater but different in kind from that of the animals. The scene has all the elements of pastoral. It portrays a removal from society which leads to looking back at it from a detached point of view so that one can see its faults. The pastoral motifs of a country scene with the 'gilded' quality common to the genre, and the 'desirable' nature of what is being viewed, all place it firmly in a pastoral tradition. In common with classic pastoral Clover realises that something is wrong; the situation is 'not what they had looked forward to'; and she decides to go back and correct rather than change it. 'There was no thought of rebellion or disobedience in her mind' (p. 60), times are still better than life under Jones.

It is the quality of acceptance that makes the scene potentially nostalgic. Clover's decision may be read not pastorally but ironically as self-deception, an escape into a dignified role which has been encouraged by the pigs to provide simple answers in terms of absolutes. Just as with the evasive 'act' that the animals do to cope with Snowball's treachery or the implications of the chickens' deaths, they turn to the melodramatic concepts of absolute good and evil offered by the pigs. Something, such as Snowball, is simply designated 'bad'. There is no actuality beyond the word; it just is so. The pigs use a rational logic perverted to 'prove' their case, in which personal reasoning and assessment is denied, and an ironic reading of this scene accepts that the animals go along with it.

The two stages of simple pastoral and ironic perspective are those which the reader has been taken through already in terms of this chapter itself and the narrative as a whole. To accept the pastoral reading we are asked simply to identify with the animal point of view. But this may be read as a delusion, in which case we detach ourselves, recognise the self-deception by the animals, step back from identification and criticise. Yet either way we neglect narratorial stance. The stance throughout Clover's scene is different. It neither identifies with the animals nor criticises them but sets up a new convention to express what is actually in Clover's mind. The convention treats her as if she were human. The reader is explicitly led, held by the hand and shown, that it is neither ignorance nor self-deception at work, but an inability to speak and to argue out. We identify but differently. It is not a matter, as it has been, of being for or against; the perception of failure on the animals' part is here presented as a matter of lack not of omission. As Clover is accorded full human status, in other words, the ability to express herself through the temporary device of narratorial voice, so also is her inhumanity demonstrated.

The inhumanity lies in significant contrast to the inhumanity of the pigs, and sets up a discrepancy essential to a positive reading of *Animal Farm*. On the one hand Clover is inhuman because she lacks certain human qualities of speaking and verbal reasoning; she cannot express the values she believes in. On the other hand the pigs are inhuman not because they lack these qualities but because they lack the standards that would use them responsibly. The reader can separate himself from Clover not ironically but allegorically, recognising that there is a piece missing and that in that piece lies the ability and responsibility to understand, protest and fight back. The animal is not unwilling but is incapable of doing so. A corollary to this analogy is that the identification of the pigs with humans is restricted to humans who lack values yet can express them. The parallel is aided by the fact that the humans in the story are consistently 'types', overt fictional devices not pretending to any 'realism'. With this background the reader is left not negatively identifying the fate of both animals and pigs with directly comparable human fates, but recognising that each fails because they are different from humans; they lack qualities that humans can have, and humans should be able to overcome the failure.

In terms of genre conventions used in this chapter, the reader now also realises why they backfire. The fairy story reward system for good and bad cannot operate validly in a world where values are either arbitrary or cannot be expressed. Personal responsibility in linguistic interaction of argument and discussion is not a valid criterion for animals – the fairy story inevitably crumbles into melodrama and nightmare. The pastoral, biblical 'dignity' sought after by the animals backfires into nostalgia and melodrama because they cannot fit into the good/bad system in any other way than the falsely conventional. They cannot, not will not, personally effect the necessary changes; they are nostalgic not because they abdicate the responsibility but because they cannot express it and therefore cannot take it on. They turn to melodrama with its well-defined good and bad conventions of expression because it is the closest they can get to the expression of any value at all.

On the simplest level, if the scene is read as a true pastoral, then one must be blind to the manipulation of the pigs. It implies a blindness to expression similar to that of the animals themselves, and it is extremely doubtful whether anyone would read it in this manner. If it is read as nostalgia, the reader is continuing to read as if it were a fairy story in which the self-deception of the animals leads to punishment. This reading would have to dismiss the inter-commentary with the satire and all the elements of language and expression. A work cannot function as an allegory without reader participation. We have to be aware of the discrepancies ourselves before we can respond to them because the writer cannot present difference for us without defining it.

Here the vital connection with the satire is most necessary. The satire explicitly concerns rhetoric and its abuse. The reader cannot be blind to its workings unless he is reading it simply as a reproduction of the Russian Revolution. The satirical discussion of politics and language has by this point indicated that the pigs are abusing both powers, hence the pastoral reading is out. The discussion has also continually emphasised the problems of the animals with expression, so the ironic reading of simple self-deception is difficult to sustain. One is left with working out what should be going on. The barest recognition is that human beings are different from animals, have different abilities and responsibilities. What that recognition generates in interaction with the satire is unique to each reader, and provides the allegorical basis for a positive reading.

As well as being a crisis for the animals, the narrative situation is also a crisis for the reader. From this moment on he will either proceed to read the book negatively, unaware of the breakdown in conventions which present the positive allegorical elements; or he will always be aware of the further dimension involved. Concurrently, the narratorial stance will appear either cynical or constructive. The eighth chapter focuses once more on explicit fairy story techniques that may now seem incongruous. Here, repetitive structures are contained within the framework of the two rewritten commandments at start and finish, which provide the basis for a series of analogies. The politics, a new song, entrance of humans, the windmill and more chicken confessions, are all elements from previous chapters that we are seeing anew, through the gained perspective. The process of repetition within a circular action can be read as a negative cynical comment on the dead-end inevitability of political and linguistic corruption. On the other hand it can be read as a result of the lack of the animals' ability to rectify the situation, and further it raises the question of what human beings should do with their wider abilities.

The reintroduction of the fairy story elements now goes hand in hand not with the comedy of animals in their contrast to humans, but the black humour of the ridiculous things that they copy from them. This shift along with the continued ambiguity and confusion of the animals' response to the pigs, belies the conventional structure and self-deception that would underlie cynical reading. The clearest example is Napoleon's friendship with the farmers, and whether he allows the second destruction of the windmill to cover his mistake. The reader cannot know whether he does or not, and neither can the animals. The animals maintain their separation from the pigs through contrasting narratorial vocabulary. Napoleon is surrounded by formal and legal phrases while language around the animals is either uninvolved and passive or melodramatic.

The final drunkenness of the pigs combines both elements in the fairy story phrasing of 'Not a pig appeared to be stirring' along with the melodramatic 'cry of lamentation', 'with tears in their eyes' over Napoleon's hangover. The fairy story convention is only functional within a value system, and, since the pigs do not have one, they introduce arbitrary absolutes and superficial melodramatic response. The whole society is a mixture of artificial reactions within melodramatic conventions, and repressed personal expression. Again, for the animals, it is not just repression but inability. The reader is left entirely on his own by the narrator who returns to his techniques of juxtaposition and understatement. Yet now the lack of certain attributes leaves the humour against the animals rather sinister, as if someone were taking advantage of them unfairly. The reader reacts independently of the animals in this chapter; they do not understand, but we do. The discrepancies are cuttingly obvious. While it may be difficult to work out what their responsibilities are, it is not difficult to recognise that it is the human reaction that is more important and that it depends on us.

To start the ninth chapter the narrator removes himself again, gradually intruding more and more to present the melodrama of Boxer's death. Initially there are many analogies set up for the reader to actively discern. All the animals gain denser characters as if to emphasise that the melodrama is artificial, and also as if individual identity has become more important now that mass action has proved impossible. Benjamin's behaviour in particular becomes more effective and raises questions about why the events have happened. Since he is the character closest to the human reader in ability to express yet refusal to exercise expression, his activity may be some kind of hint.

The analogies gradually become more explicit. The reader, meanwhile, is alerted to changes by the great increase of analogy which asks us to assess for ourselves. The stance is moving away from speaking for the animals toward a human voice that intrudes with sarcasm and wit against the pigs. The apparent resumption of the voice when he mentions the 'dignity' of the animals alerts us immediately, and he follows it up with a clarification showing that they have no real choices. The deliberate pathos of their dreaming about warm mash is a restatement in curt physical terms of their own ambiguous and confused dreaming about retirement. Their 'spontaneous' demonstrations are organised and formal. The gradual intrusion of the narrator is not resented because he is speaking from the reader's human point of view on previously established events. Hence he uses a common knowledge that we are free to disagree with.

The chapter is then broken by the creation of the Republic and the return of Moses, both of which emphasise the animals' passivity, before it moves on to Boxer's accident. But any potential tragedy is undercut by reducing this event of greatest tension to the ridiculous. When the animals finally realise that Boxer is being taken to the knacker's yard they give a 'cry of horror'; they move 'In desperation' but 'Too late ...' Clover tries 'to stir her stout limbs to a gallop and achieved a canter'. The pathos and melodrama is not shocking because the reader has been exposed to it previously. Here though the conventions are used as if they are habitual second-nature to the animals, not because they must conform. Accepting conventions makes response easier. If at first one is forced into them, it gradually becomes more and more difficult to resist their seductive patterns; and eventually like the animals, one forgets that they are conventions at all.

Clover's pastoral over-view of the Major's initial utopian urge, is the last important recognition of the structure in which the animals now live. Active participation has been taken out of their hands. The narrator himself is outside the melodrama, detached and observing, no longer identifying with the animals. Neither does the reader identify. Writer and audience recognise the powerlessness, and the point made by intercommentary with the satire is that it arises from the animals' inability to express. The further point is that our recognition of their ineffectiveness makes us responsible for action.

The movement from fairy story to melodrama is carried out through their common dependence on authority. That the fairy story usually claims a magical or external source of authority whereas the authority of melodrama is man-made and man-imposed, is an interesting parallel that stimulates criticism of the latter toward a questioning of the former. But more obviously here the man-copied authority of the pigs is oppressive, negative, destructive and self-corrupting because it retains the elements of determinism and inevitability that the fairy story places beyond man's power. It is totalitarian. Melodrama is the genre of response within unquestioned man-made convention. It may be habitual as in the animals' reaction to Boxer's accident, or it may be actively destructive as in the responses demanded by the pigs. In both it is confined, not able to reason and assess, donning what is available. Anyone capable of a more active expression finds it unsatisfactory. The flickering in and out of fairy story and melodrama is a means of bringing to the reader's attention the inadequacy of all unquestioned convention including the one the narrator is using.

The final chapter begins once more in a narratorial detachment calling for the reader's involvement. The fairy story elements are present but now inextricably mixed up with the melodramatic response of the animals. Narratorial stance is not of a tale-teller within a society re-telling a story that backs up the cultural norms, but of a distanced narrator using fairy story conventions to comment on corrupt authoritarianism. The melodramatic elements that surface in the description of Clover during the final scene remind the reader of the inadequacy of the convention; but for Clover the ludicrous is unperceived. For the animals the fairy story becomes nightmare because the source of authority, the unassailable utopian vision, dissolves and is transferred to the pigs' new superiority. For the reader there is an additional question in the transformation of pig into human. Since they can do so because all their actions are implicitly human, humans are at the same time made pigs. The ambiguity of the situation is an essential strategic device that undercuts a negative reading. As noted earlier and as the text continually points out, these humans are not complete. They are limited 'types' who are as lacking in humanity as the pigs and the other animals. It is their lack that creates the ambiguity of their status.

Determinist and inevitable qualities of fairy story are brought back in full force during the opening paragraphs of the chapter. Recurrent motifs, lists and repetitions underline the pattern. The switch from a humour generated from animal and human contrasts, to the more barbed comedy of their similarities is continued in

Squealer's lists of responsibilities to 'files', 'reports' and 'minutes'. Extensive use of and/and constructions in, for example, 'neither pigs nor dogs produced any food by their own labour; and there were very many of them, and their appetites were always good', sets up the lack of actual connection between events in favour of the implied. The forced conjunction is emphasised by the liberal use of semi-colons. Three years previously in *Coming Up for Air* Orwell had tried to do away with the semi-colon. They, and colons, make it possible to omit the defining connections between separate parts of a sentence. Here he uses the device to point out that omission.

In relation to the bureaucratic jargon of the pigs, the animals' vocabulary continues to be vague and confused. Among themselves they retain the stirring phrases of the opening fairy story atmosphere. They are proud of owning the farm; they have a utopian belief that 'some day it was coming'; they use biblical phrases and allusions to stress that 'they were not as other animals'. The formal construction and use of recognised rhetorical devices such as balanced 'If/If/Then' statements that repeat and lead to their central belief that 'All animals are equal', indicate their dependence on classical convention. Many elements are directly from the Major's speech and their use here indicates what can go wrong with utopian visions, what was negative in his opening speech. His insistence on a unity achieved through acceptance denied the possibility of the animals learning how to reassess the situation. The promised utopia was another absolute that cut out concepts of bettering their lives. Because the animals did not actively participate in the direction their group was taking, because finally, they were not involved in the reasoning of the speech as well as its emotiveness, they are left with its phrases which can be repeated but which get them nowhere.

If we recall Orwell's discussion of politics and literature in the essays these are all the elements of truncated pastoral or fantasy; acceptance, self-satisfaction, refusal to question. But for the animals it is melodramatic because they know something is wrong, and gradually take on conventional responses because they cannot express themselves otherwise. The fairy story conventions that the animals hang on to are then completely undercut by the pigs walking on their hind legs, and the change in the last commandment to 'All Animals Are Equal/But Some Animals Are More Equal Than Others' (p. 87). The reader no longer experiences this as a reversal of expectation, but as a reinforcement of his different knowledge. Detached response is encouraged by the direct, knowing address 'Yes, it was Squealer' from the narrator about the pig on his hind legs.

Despite the undercutting that we perceive, the animals continue as before once their brief protest is thwarted by the sheep. When the humans come to visit, the animals are as afraid of them as they are of the pigs and stick closely to their usual jobs. They cannot understand the implications of the final scene between the farmers and the pigs, which centres on their linguistic similarity, but the reader can. Here he is faced with the idea that the pigs are actually human and vice versa. There is no longer contrast or similarity between the two, but identity. The linking concept of politics and language provided by the intercommentary with the satire, is that within these conventional authority-assuming speeches the other animals are recognised as 'lower animals'. Since the reader has spent much of his response identifying with these animals the definition is sinister rather than humorous. But one can evade the reflexive comment on the lower classes that is also contained in the concept. The narrator's third person reporting of the speeches indicates the detachment of the scene. And it all takes place in the comfort of a room, behind the glass of a safe compartment; it could be one of Orwell's train carriages.

By transmitting the scene through the 'old dim eyes' of Clover, the stance is trusted because of our response to her and because any perceived discrepancies are theoretically out of the narrator's hands. We also recognise her inability to understand which underlines our responsibilities. The resonance back to the phrase 'it did not seem strange' for anything to happen after the pigs had started walking on their hind legs, alerts the reader. Here something is again 'strange'. We question what this final change could possibly be, and although something 'seemed to be melting and changing' (p. 91), neither we nor the animals can identify it. Following this brief reminder of the animals' helplessness, the narrator reasserts himself and we discover that the pigs have become human. The final comment that it was 'impossible to say which was which' notes the ambiguity and confusion that the animals feel, at the same time as separating the reader from that confusion for he is aware of the implications. It is the separation that occurs through recognition of the differences that allegory conveys, and passes one back to the satire on politics and language with the hope that those differences will be taken up and learned from.

From Lynette Hunter, *George Orwell: The Search for a Voice* (Milton Keynes, 1984), pp. 178–90.

NOTES

[Lynette Hunter considers the limitations of satire and allegory as genres and how Orwell may transcend the limitations of the forms he employs to produce an interactive, internally and formally coherent text in *Animal Farm*. She examines the novel's subtitle, 'A Fairy Story', and the ways in which the narrator is gradually distanced from the conventions of 'telling' a fairy tale and manoeuvred towards a rhetorical position implicit in a satirical rendering of events. This essay is particularly useful on the reader's position *vis-à-vis* the text. Eds]

1.   George Orwell, *Animal Farm* (London, 1948), p. 10. All further references to this book will be included in the text.

3

Orwell's Political Persuasion: A Rhetoric of Personality

RICHARD FILLOY

George Orwell's writing was a response to the immediate issues of the age he lived in; and those issues, as he saw them, demanded writing that was clearly rhetorical. In his 1946 essay, 'Why I Write', Orwell commented 'Every line of serious work that I have written since 1936 has been written, directly or indirectly, against totalitarianism and for democratic socialism ...'[1] This commitment may seem to express an indifference to literary reputation, yet he also wrote that he wanted to 'make political writing into an art' (*Collected Essays*, I, p. 28). To judge from his subsequent reputation, he succeeded. In doing so, he faced and overcame two obstacles which all political non-fiction faces in achieving an enduring literary reputation.

First, political writing is usually written for immediate effect rather than long-term scrutiny. If political writers are to be effective with their immediate audiences, they must be topical. But if they are topical, interest in their writing is likely to fade with the issue's urgency. The writer who is to be remembered must find a way to overcome this dilemma. Second, the writer of non-fiction has to make his writing interesting without the mediation of a fictional world. Novels like *A Passage to India* or *Darkness at Noon* are certainly political and have kept their appeal beyond the time of the immediate topics they address. But such books have the advantage of fictional plots and characters to maintain an audience's interest even when their topicality has gone. The political essayist has only the subject matter and a perspective on it.

Certainly Orwell's reputation rests partly on his novels, but this explanation for his reputation is not sufficient. Of course *Animal Farm* and *1984* continue to be widely read and admired, but Orwell's four other novels (*Burmese Days, A Clergyman's Daughter, Keep the Aspidistra Flying*, and *Coming Up for Air*) have never enjoyed a great vogue and are not well known. On the other hand, essays like 'Marrakech' and 'Shooting an Elephant' and his books *Homage to Catalonia* and *Down and Out in Paris and London* have often been reprinted and are widely praised. Reflection suggests that the growth in Orwell's reputation as a writer depends largely on the rediscovery of and increasing admiration for his non-fiction.

To some extent admiration for Orwell's writing is based on the lucid and economical style he developed according to the ideas he put forward in 'Politics and the English Language'. Orwell's struggle to write 'less picturesquely and more exactly' resulted in an impressive stylistic accomplishment; yet even this, to his mind, was the result of his political intention (*Collected Essays*, I, p. 29). 'And looking back through my work, I see that it is invariably where I lacked *political* purpose that I wrote lifeless books and was betrayed into purple passages, sentences without meaning, decorative adjectives and humbug generally' (*Collected Essays*, I, p. 30).

If political purpose was the force behind Orwell's best writing, two important critical consequences follow. First, if we read Orwell's work in the spirit in which it was intended, his achievement depends on the power of his writing to persuade audiences of the worth of his political ideals. Long after his immediate political ends have been achieved or outmoded, his writing must still make audiences feel their importance at some level. Even his style, admirable for its own sake, is designed to help gain the audience's agreement and results from his sense of that purpose. Second and most important for the purposes of this essay, an understanding of Orwell's success as a writer must be based on an account of the rhetoric of his political persuasion. On what is it based? How is it constructed?

In proposing an answer to these questions, this essay focuses on Orwell's creation of an effective and enduring ethos in his writing. It argues that the character he created is different in important ways from the classical conception of an effective ethos for the rhetor and further that the creation of this character was not a natural outcome of Orwell's 'real' personality but the result of expert rhetorical and literary craftsmanship. In fact, the most important conclusion this essay urges is that Orwell's 'rhetoric of personality' is the artistic achievement most responsible for both Orwell's immediate success as a rhetor and his continuing popularity. In making these arguments, the essay aims at a clearer understanding not only of Orwell's political rhetoric but also of an important aspect of the rhetoric of non-fiction. In doing so, it proposes a revision of the classical theory of ethos, one which seems especially well suited, and perhaps limited, to the century of the common man.

This view can best be presented by returning to the question of the basis of Orwell's rhetoric. How did he go about persuading his audiences? To a great extent, he did it by seeming to be persuading himself first and foremost. Once again Orwell's words in 'Why I Write' are illuminating. 'I am not able, and I do not want, completely to abandon the world view that I acquired in childhood. ... It is no use trying to suppress that side of myself. The job is to reconcile my ingrained likes and dislikes with the essentially public, non-individual activities that this age forces on all of us' (*Collected Essays*, I, p. 28).

Good political writing for Orwell began with individual thoughts and feelings which were then adjusted, altered, even abandoned, to fit political principles. But as any reader of Orwell knows, that sense of the individual, of the person struggling with political necessity and social justice, is never lost. In a dust-jacket comment for *The Collected Essays*, Orwell's boyhood friend Cyril Connolly said of him, 'He was a man ... whose personality shines out in everything he said or wrote.' If we stop for a moment to consider those works of Orwell's which are best known, we will be forced to concur. In fact, Connolly's statement does not go far enough. Orwell's personality does not simply shine out; it is, in an important sense, always the subject.

In *Homage to Catalonia*, we do not merely see the Spanish Civil War through Orwell's eyes; we read the story of his commitment to and subsequent disillusionment with the republican cause. *The Road to Wigan Pier* is not merely a sociological study of miners' and workers' lives, nor is it simply reportage with the reporter's direct experiences incorporated; it is the story of Orwell's discovery of his feelings and attitudes toward these people and the system which controlled their lives. It is a recipe for creating personal political purpose. Similarly, 'Marrakech', 'Shooting an Elephant', 'Revenge Is Sour', *Down and Out in Paris and London*, and many other much-admired Orwell pieces are structured around a report of the narrator's personal feelings about his subject. Those feelings are not brought to the foreground for their own merits; they are there to serve Orwell's general purpose, political persuasion. Success or failure in that effort is proportionate to our ability to share those feelings. While Orwell seems to be self-absorbed, busily recounting his personal discoveries, changes, and conversions, he is also inviting the reader to partake of the same experiences and to change with him. The narrator's character thus becomes the chief means of persuasion.

The reliance on personal experience is even clearer if we pause to consider the basic arguments that Orwell advances in these cases. They are not new or startling. By themselves, they have little power to persuade most audiences. About the Spanish republicans he tells us that ends do not justify means which pervert those ends. About the British Raj he reports that empire is unjust and corrupts imperialists and subjects alike. Of the unemployed he says that they are not poor and dirty by choice but as the result of a system which forces those conditions upon them. Put in this way, it is easy to see why Orwell has no great reputation as an original political thinker. What makes these commonplaces of political argument appealing is the report of personal discovery. We see the reporter reconciling personal likes and dislikes with political necessity and social justice. We are persuaded insofar as we see that process validated and verified in Orwell's personal experience. The immediacy of experience is a kind of shorthand induction. One personal story well told may be more affecting than many a statistical sampling. It renders the commonplace generalisation it supports not only believable but appealing.

Argument from ethos is hardly new or surprising in political discourse. What should surprise us is the great intellectual currency Orwell has managed to lend it. Ordinarily, such argument is not well-regarded. It is considered the province of demagogues, a form of appeal well-suited to the masses but hardly likely to impress the educated, much less to endure, even be cultivated, among them. What should we make of this phenomenon? Why is Orwell's ethical argument persuasive and enduring while that of so many others is repugnant and ultimately ephemeral?

Before attempting to answer those questions in Orwell's case, we might profitably pause to recall the origins and development of the doctrine of *ethos* as an ingredient in persuasion. In doing so, we will be better prepared to note Orwell's departure from it. Aristotle originated the term as a rhetorical concept, along with *pathos* and *logos*, as one of the three artificial proofs, indeed the most important one. For him, a successful ethos was founded on three qualities: virtue, good sense, and goodwill. The first two traits, *arete* and *phronesis* in Greek, are exceptional characteristics connoting valour, wisdom, and ability which set the speaker above the audience and thus made him a good guide for their opinions and actions. Aristotle did note that common people are often more persuasive than their more educated fellows by reason of their understanding of the audience's beliefs and ways of thinking; but there is little doubt that his successful rhetor was a naturally superior sort, able to gain the audience's assent partly through a display of his personal superiority. From its beginnings, then, ethos as a means of proof depended on the speaker's ability to seem a special sort of person.[2]

This understanding was heightened during the rest of the classical period. In the Roman world, where orators were specially trained advocates in courts of law, the speaker's personality could be separated from the client's. Cicero emphasised that, whomever he represents, the orator must always appear to be a man of exceptional probity, civic-mindedness, and virtue (I, pp. 327–9, see also II, pp. 23–9). Quintilian captured both the importance and the essence of the Roman concept of ethos in his definition of the orator as 'a good man, skilled in speaking'.[3] When Augustine translated the pagan doctrine of rhetoric into a Christian context, it was even more obvious and important that the speaker, who served as an example to other Christians, must be an especially virtuous person.[4] There is in all these writers some recognition of the value of the common touch; but generally in the Western tradition, the speaker's or writer's character persuades by being especially good.

From that belief, indeed, springs much of the suspicion of arguments resting on the speaker's character. It is simply too easy to seem to be something one is not, and history is full of hypocrites and charlatans. Worse, one may be a genuinely attractive person with poor arguments. Because we are all attracted to some people's characters and because such characters can be counterfeited, it has come to seem especially dangerous to be persuaded by the character of a speaker or writer. To be swayed by character is to be distracted from the real issues; it is to make oneself vulnerable to demagoguery. The aim of the careful reader is to avoid such persuasion.[5]

Even in the face of such attitudes, Orwell's character has managed to have a great appeal to sophisticated readers and to form the basis of his persuasion. Why? That question may not be wholly answerable, but Orwell himself provided what seems a valuable insight. 'And yet it is also the truth', he wrote, 'that one can write nothing readable unless one constantly struggles to efface one's own personality' (*Collected Essays*, I, p. 29). At first glance that statement is at odds with both the earlier quotation about retaining one's world-view and the whole thesis of this essay. What keeps that from being the final import of the statement is the realisation that total effacement of personality is not possible. What these words suggest is not that personality should or even can be driven out of effective political writing, but that Orwell had a different use for ethos than that ordinarily associated with such appeals. Orwell persuaded not on the strength of an exceptional personality but on the ordinariness of a commonplace one. Self-effacement was an important persuasive strategy for Orwell. By making his reports those of an ordinary person rather than those of a great man, he allowed his audience to put themselves in his position without imagining the impossible. He made Aristotle's insight into the understanding common people have for their peers the basis for a different sort of argument from ethos. In the process of doing so, he turned the classical theory of ethos on its head. By offering us a character who is ordinary, Orwell not only allows the reader to share the perceptions of the writer, he also disarms our suspicion of an ethos which is so good and so intelligent that our training tells us to mistrust it. After all, we are not in the presence of an especially superior person, merely another poor soul like ourselves.

This technique can best be seen in a series of examples. Consider Orwell's ethical appeal in 'Shooting an Elephant'.

> In the end ... the insults hooted after me when I was at a safe distance, got badly on my nerves. ... [My job] oppressed me with an intolerable sense of guilt. But I could get nothing into perspective. I was young and ill-educated and I had had to think out my problems in the utter silence that is imposed on every Englishman in the East. ... Feelings like these are the normal by-products of imperialism; ask any Anglo-Indian official, if you can catch him off-duty.
>
> (*Collected Essays*, I, pp. 265–6)

Quite clearly Orwell reports his own feelings to support his point about the effects of imperialism; but, just as clearly, he seeks to make those feelings average and ordinary. He belittles his own mental processes and makes his personal experience unexceptional. His feelings of guilt and oppression, he implies, were merely common decency. Any decent person in a similar situation would share them. Nor is Orwell's response to his feelings exceptional. He gives in to pressure and shoots the elephant because it is expected of him, even though he knows it is wrong. Feelings and responses like this are likely to be familiar to his audience, even though the specific experience is not. The audience is thus encouraged to identify with the author's attitude toward imperialism by having first identified with the ordinariness of his perceptions and actions. More importantly, the audience is invited to conclude that Orwell's failure to act rightly is not a personal failing but one imposed upon him by the imperialist system. If the readers find Orwell a person like themselves and can identify with his discomfort under the circumstances, they are very likely to conclude that the circumstances ought to be changed.

The reader's ability to identify with the writer is crucial to the function of Orwell's ethical argument. It is perhaps no surprise that his ethical argument, a kind suited especially well to the egalitarian ideals of our century, is based in identification, a term central to the rhetorical theory of Kenneth Burke, who has done so much to recast rhetorical theory into terms fitting the twentieth century. Burke proposes, in fact, 'that our rhetoric be reduced to this term [identification] ...' and further urges that rhetoric must often be thought of as 'a general body of identifications'. By proposing identification as a basic human ideal, Burke validates the basis of Orwell's approach. He explains that the writer's character, insofar as it is the means by which the reader and writer are shown to be 'consubstantial', is basic to persuasion.[6]

The same process can be seen at work in this selection from 'Such, Such Were the Joys', Orwell's memoir of his early schooling.

> Whenever one had the chance to suck up, one did suck up, and at the first smile one's hatred turned into a sort of cringing love. I was always tremendously proud when I succeeded in making Flip [the headmaster's wife] laugh. I have even, at her command, written *vers d'occasion*, comic verses to celebrate memorable events in the life of the school.

> I am anxious to make it clear that I was not a rebel, except by force of circumstances. I accepted the codes that I found in being. Once, towards the end of my time, I even sneaked to Brown about a suspected case of homosexuality.
>
> (*Collected Essays*, IV, p. 401)

Orwell's point in this piece is that such schools used brutal psychological techniques to perpetuate a corrupt social order. Yet he makes this point not by showing himself as a strong-willed rebel but by stressing how easily he was influenced. Once again he makes his experience typical, demonstrating the vulnerability of the average, well-meaning, reasonable person in the face of strong social pressure. Once again the audience is encouraged to identify with Orwell's feelings, if not his precise experience, and to conclude that the system which imposes them is wrong.

A similar, but somewhat different, technique for rendering his own experience commonplace can be seen in this passage from 'Revenge is Sour', where Orwell describes his feelings on seeing a Nazi war criminal abused by a Jewish captor.

> So the Nazi torturer of one's imagination, the monstrous figure against whom one had struggled for so many years, dwindled to this pitiful wretch, whose obvious need was not for punishment, but for some kind of psychological treatment. ... Who would not have jumped for joy, in 1940, at the thought of seeing S.S. officers kicked and humiliated? But when the thing becomes possible, it is merely pathetic and disgusting.
>
> (*Collected Essays*, IV, pp. 20–1)

Here Orwell abandons the first person altogether as he uses the impersonal 'one' and 'who' to report his feelings. He has so far effaced his personality that his perceptions are not merely ordinary, they are not even individual. Yet few people were ever confronted directly with the situation Orwell reports and many who were did not find such abuse disgusting. In this passage, we are forced to agree not so much because Orwell's feelings are typical as because they are morally correct. Punishment, especially physical abuse, of 'pitiful wretches' ought to be disgusting; and therefore most audiences will not dispute Orwell's statement. But to report such feelings in the first person is to risk self-righteousness. By making them merely a moral commonplace, Orwell gains agreement from anyone who recognises that two wrongs don't make a right.

In *Homage to Catalonia* Orwell again employs this technique when he reports how he came to fight in the war.

> I had come to Spain with some notion of writing newspaper articles, but I joined the militia almost immediately, because at that time and in that atmosphere it seemed the only conceivable thing to do. ... When I came to Spain, and for some time afterwards, I was not only uninterested in the political situation but unaware of it. I knew there was a war on, but I had no notion what kind of a war. If you had asked me why I had joined the militia I should have answered: 'To fight against Fascism', and if you had asked me what I was fighting *for*, I should have answered: 'Common decency'.
>
> (*Homage to Catalonia*, 4, pp. 46–7)

Of course, most writers who came to Spain conceived of other things to do than join the militia, and many soldiers had a less naïve attitude about what they were fighting for. But by making his actions, even when they were exceptional and courageous, seem ordinary and common, Orwell demands that his audience identify his actions with general moral standards. Who can oppose common decency, especially if it seems the only conceivable course of action?

The extent to which Orwell used the techniques of generalising his feelings and experiences and belittling his own actions can be gauged by this series of short quotations from *Homage to Catalonia*.

> 1. A little while later, however, a bullet shot past my ear with a vicious crack and banged into the parados behind. Alas! I ducked. All my life I had sworn that I would not duck the first time a bullet passed over me; but the movement appears to be instinctive, and almost everybody does it at least once.
>
> (p. 22)

Here we see Orwell's denial of any special bravery and an equation of his actions with those of 'almost everybody'. Whatever he did in the war, this early passage assures us, was the action of an ordinary soldier.

> 2. It was the first time that I had been properly speaking under fire, and to my humiliation I found that I was horribly frightened. You always, I notice, feel the same when you are under heavy fire – not so much afraid of being hit as afraid because you don't know where you will be hit. You are wondering all the while just *where* the bullet will nip you ....
>
> (p. 44)

As in the preceding example Orwell reports his humiliation at finding himself no braver than average. Here he conveys his ordinariness by using 'you' to describe his own experiences. The technique reflects a certain daring since former soldiers among his readers must be willing to accept his description of the feeling of being under fire.

> 3. The few Englishmen I was among were mostly I.L.P. members, with a few C.P. members among them, and most of them were much better educated politically than myself.
>
> (p. 58)

Orwell here shows himself not only physically but intellectually undistinguished. As we read, we see him groping for a valid political understanding among men who must be his teachers as well as his fellow soldiers. Reading the book is thus designed to be a political education for us also, but one about which we are not made to feel inferior or patronised.

> 4. All this while I was lying on my side in the greasy mud, wrestling savagely with the pin of a bomb. The damned thing *would* not come out. Finally I realised that I was twisting it in the wrong direction. I got the pin out, rose to my knees, hurled the bomb, and threw myself down again. The bomb burst over to the right, outside the parapet; fright had spoiled my aim.
>
> (p. 90)

This passage reflects a commonplace: the effect of fear on physical actions. By saving the reason for his poor performance until the end of the experience, Orwell makes his readers see the whole action, which at first seems merely wretched and comical, as the result of fear. Once again, of course, Orwell shows us that he is not a hero.

> 5. Of course at the time I was hardly conscious of the changes that were occurring in my own mind. Like everyone about me I was chiefly conscious of boredom, heat, cold, dirt, lice, privation, and occasional danger.
>
> (p. 105)

Here again Orwell reassures us that he is not really an intellectual. He itches, fears, and is cold. The changes which he underwent and the political consciousness which resulted seem not the result of a superior mind or of hard thinking, they were almost imperceptible and natural to anyone who had these experiences.

6. Everyone who has made two visits, at intervals of months, to Barcelona during the war has remarked upon the extraordinary changes that took place in it. ... in December ... to me, fresh from England, it was liker to a workers' city than anything I had conceived possible. Now the tide had rolled back.

(p. 109)

Here Orwell casually reveals his naïveté upon arrival in Spain, but at the same time he makes his realisation of this naïveté a thing which 'everyone' who has had his experience notices.

7. And I remember feeling a vague horror and amazement that money could still be wasted upon such things in a hungry war-stricken country. But God forbid that I should pretend to any personal superiority. After several months of discomfort I had a ravenous desire for decent food and wine, cocktails, American cigarettes, and so forth, and I admit to having wallowed in every luxury that I had money to buy.

(p. 116)

Even after his experiences had changed him politically, Orwell insists, he was no saint, no self-denier. Being politically aware, he reminds us often, is not synonomous with giving up the personal desire for luxury.

It would be easy to double or triple the number of similar examples, but these should be sufficient to suggest the general point. By making his own actions and perceptions seem so ordinary, Orwell makes identification with his views easy.

If this interpretation of Orwell is correct, we may say that Orwell's literary persona persuades us by becoming a sort of hero, that is, he inspires admiration and agreement. Orwell's political persuasion is a rhetoric of personality in which the individual person is both the source of all political principles and the basis for persuasion to those principles. But clearly this persona is not a classical hero, a great spirit moved to great actions. Nor is it an antihero, an exponent of meaninglessness, of a senseless world where the individual is all that matters. Orwell's hero is that sort of person his audience might be at their best: decent, caring, and basically good, but fragile under pressure; often wrong, selfish, and confused, but capable of sacrifice for the general good. In Burke's terms, Orwell surrounds himself with properties which establish his identity, an identity in which the audience wishes to share and believes it can share because Orwell has rendered it an ordinary one (Burke, pp. 23–4).

By presenting his admirable properties as the ordinary and believable actions of one individual, Orwell achieves another important effect of ethical argument. He makes those properties real to the audience. Aristotle remarked that metaphor is the most persuasive of linguistic devices because it sets things 'before the eyes'.[7] Another way to characterise the immediacy of experience described above as shorthand induction is to call Orwell's personal narratives metaphorical presentations of the abstract principles for which he was arguing. Perhaps a better way of conceiving of this effect is to say that Orwell's ethical argument makes his principles present to his audience. Chaim Perelman considered presence an 'essential factor' of rhetoric and said that 'one of the preoccupations of the speaker is to make present, by verbal magic alone, what is actually absent but what he considers important to his argument ...'.[8] As we read Orwell's reports of his thoughts and actions, we are present at the formation of his principles and come to believe in their reality. Few sensations are more conducive to persuasion. But the critic must not confuse the feeling of reality, of 'presence', with reality itself. Perelman warns us, 'Presence, and efforts to increase the feeling of presence, must hence not be confused with fidelity to reality'.[9] What is true about this ingredient or effect of ethos must also be understood about ethos generally.

We have observed that seeing Orwell as a person like his audience inspires a belief in the rightness of his goals and the possibility of their attainment in all kinds of people, not just the already committed or exceptional. Lionel Trilling noted this characteristic when he remarked in his introduction to *Homage to Catalonia*, 'He is not a genius – what a relief! What an encouragement. For he communicates to us the sense that what he has done, any one of us could do' (*Homage to Catalonia*, p. xi). While this observation is correct as far as it goes, it is important for the rhetorical critic of Orwell and of political discourse generally to go beyond it. Orwell's literary ethos must be recognised for what it is. Like the presence of his first-person reports, Orwell's ethos is a rhetorical construct, achieved deliberately and through craft, with the same purpose as Orwell's lucid style: political persuasion. Trilling must be understood to describe not the writer but his rhetorical creation.

The temptation to equate the historical Orwell with his literary persona is strong. Few writers have done more to experience what they wrote about, and Orwell's rhetoric of personality was greatly aided by his breadth of experience. Indeed Orwell the writer and Orwell the man can be exceedingly hard to separate. After Eric Blair adopted the pen-name George Orwell, he increasingly abandoned his original identity in favour of the invented one. His second wife, Sonia, uses Orwell as her surname and always refers to him in her writing as Orwell. She notes that although he never legally changed his name, 'new friends and acquaintances knew him and addressed him as George Orwell' (*Collected Essays*, I, p. 20). Once he determined to become a writer, he seems to have lived his life largely for that purpose. Much of what he did was done in order to write about it, and still more was turned to literary account as an afterthought. Yet it is not these facts of time, place, and action nor the deliberate attempt to re-create himself as the political being whose experiences he reported that mark Orwell's persona as a construct; it is the way in which they are reported. This essay has repeatedly pointed out that the pose of ordinariness is an effective persuasive strategy. Incidentally it has shown how unreal that pose was. Orwell was not the average Anglo-Indian official, schoolboy, soldier, or reporter. His feelings and actions are made to seem commonplace, but they were not. They were the result of an exceptionally astute and sensitive observer of wide experience bringing a sophisticated intellect to bear on his situation. His very determination to experience the 'ordinary' lives of those he wrote about was exceptional – and sometimes mocked as an affectation. Those who knew Orwell and have remembered him in print, Cyril Connolly, Richard Rees, and Malcolm Muggeridge among others, do not recall an ordinary man but an extraordinary one who had exaggerated sensibilities and a morbid sense of class consciousness.[10] It took all of Orwell's literary craftsmanship to bury his Eton education and his intellectualism and to render his perceptions and thoughts ordinary.

The insistence that Orwell's appealing ethos be viewed as a rhetorical construct is not intended to demean him. On the contrary, it should enhance his literary reputation, for such an achievement bespeaks superb artistry. For this very reason, it is important not to accept Trilling's verdict at face value. If Orwell's ethos is not a genius, its creation may have been the work of one.

It is of further importance to insist on the artificiality of Orwell's character in his writing because it is only through recognising and studying the art of such an achievement that we will come to understand its role in the rhetoric of non-fiction. If we recognise it for what it is, Orwell's peculiar genius in creating an ethos of only average abilities may shed some light on how enduring political non-fiction is written. The careful manipulation of character may be seen as an important ingredient in the rhetoric of political writing. For such writing to survive the occasion which begets it, it needs an appeal which is not topical. The writer's character is just such an appeal: a good man is still admirable and interesting even when his specific context is gone. Such characters attract audiences by exemplifying values that transcend time and place: honesty, loyalty, empathy, and humility in Orwell's case. It is at this level that the writer can make an audience feel that long-gone political aims are still important: they are important because they are motivated by such transcendent values. Certainly not every writer will create a character like Orwell's; but Orwell's writing, at least, often depends, and perhaps survives, on his character's attractiveness.

The role of ethos in giving political non-fiction lasting appeal without sacrificing topicality seems worth further consideration. Writers from Edmund Burke to Joan Didion provide ample possibilities for further study; and the modern rhetorical theory of Burke and Perelman, among others, can provide both a basis and a vocabulary for undertaking such an investigation. This discussion of Orwell suggests that in modern writing the classical formula for an appealing ethos must be recast. A momentary reflection on Didion would seem to confirm that impression. One result of more extensive and historically varied investigation would be to discover to what extent an appealing ethos is a construct of particular historical circumstances.

The importance of the writer's ethos in creating lasting appeal in political writing also suggests an answer to the question of how the writer of non-fiction overcomes the novelist's advantage of a fictional world. Where the novelist creates interest in fictional characters and their story, the essayist may substitute his or her own character and personal experience. An author's perspective on a subject may be as interesting as a fictional character's – provided that the author can become as human and engaging. For, ironically, fiction often achieves greater presence than writing based in reality.

Thus, in elevating political writing to an art, the writer of non-fiction may need to borrow something of the fiction writer's rhetoric. Indeed Orwell's essays are often much like short stories narrated in the first person.

Following from the idea that the rhetorics of fiction and non-fiction need not be qualitatively very different is an intriguing possibility. Perhaps the basis of the distinction between fiction and non-fiction is best located in the audience's perception of the 'ordinariness' of the writers of non-fiction as opposed to the imaginative specialness of fiction writers. In announcing that a piece of discourse is fictional, writers set themselves the problem of convincing the audience that the worlds they create are sufficiently believable to compel the reader's attention. Thus, every novel or short story is a kind of *tour de force*, a demonstration and a celebration of the writer's imaginative and persuasive powers in creating and sustaining illusion. Non-fiction, on the other hand, must usually be content with the cloak of reportage. The writer of non-fiction is 'merely' reporting what is, not inventing new worlds. Writers of non-fiction are thus always comparatively 'ordinary'. Their subject matter, rather than their artistry, is always the focus. Yet the techniques of fiction and non-fiction may be very similar, and the craft required of the writers not very different.

This last point indicates how very fine the line between fiction and non-fiction or between political persuasion and literature may be. At the same time it shows why an avowedly political writer like Orwell may, without contradiction, be seen as a literary artist.

From *Literary Nonfiction: Theory, Criticism, Pedagogy*, ed. Chris Anderson (Carbondale, IL, and Edwardville, 1989), pp. 51–69.

NOTES

[Richard Filloy questions the construction and basis of Orwell's rhetoric of political persuasion. He argues that the power of Orwell's persuasive skills lies in his self-questioning and that Orwell's own personality and personal experiences are always the subject of his writing. Filloy returns to an Aristotelian definition of 'ethos' and of the 'good man' in order to exemplify that Orwell the man and the writer are inextricable. This last point is echoed in Stephen Ingle's essay (12). Eds]

1. Sonia Orwell and Ian Angus (eds), *The Collected Essays, Journalism and Letters of George Orwell* (Harmondsworth, 1970), I, p. 28. All further references to this collection will be included in the text.

2. See Aristotle's *Art of Rhetoric*, trans. J. H. Freese (Cambridge, 1926). The introduction of the three kinds of artificial proof and the claim that ethos is the most effective are at 1356a. The discussion of the constituents of ethos and their importance is at 1378a. The claim that the uneducated may be more persuasive than the educated is at 1395b. (References here and elsewhere in this essay are to the standard numbering of Bekker rather than to pages of an edition.)

3. This simple quotation from Quintilian, *Institutio Oratorio*, trans. H. E. Butler (Cambridge, 1920), 4, p. 355, while it is the familiar epitome of Quintilian's view, does not begin to convey the personal superiority of his ideal orator. Consider this passage: 'It is no hack-advocate, no hireling pleader ... that I am seeking to form, but rather a man who to extraordinary natural gifts has added a thorough mastery of all the fairest branches of knowledge, a man sent by heaven to be the blessing of mankind, one to whom all history can find no parallel, uniquely perfect in every detail and utterly noble alike in thought and speech' (4, p. 369).

4. This comment from Augustine, *On Christian Doctrine*, trans. D. W. Robertson (Indianapolis, 1958), gives a fair idea of Augustine's view of the importance of ethos, 'However, the life of the speaker has greater weight in determining whether he is obediently heard than any grandness of eloquence' (p. 164).

5. This attitude can be found in many places. The following passage, drawn from a textbook co-authored by one of the most distinguished contemporary theorists of argumentation, provides an illustration. 'Evidently an eloquent speaker writer can dress up his arguments in all kinds of ways so as to conceal their defects and make them attractive to his audience ... But in most cases, it is possible to separate the features that give our arguments genuine "rational merit" from those other rhetorical devices that have the effect of making them more attractive and persuasive than they deserve to be.' See Stephen Toulmin, Richard Rieke and Allan Janik, *An Introduction to Reasoning* (New York, 1979), p. 106.

6. Burke's discussion of identification is extensive and cannot be given full consideration here. For the present purpose, it is important because Burke makes identification and the ethical appeals which come from it central to persuasion rather than a feature we can or would want to separate from the 'rational merit' of a discourse. The quoted passages are from Kenneth Burke, *A Rhetoric of Motives* (Berkeley, CA, 1950), pp. 20, 26, 21.

7. Aristotle, *Art of Rhetoric*, 1405a and 1411b.

8. Chaim Perelman and L. Olbrechts-Tyteca, *The New Rhetoric: A Treatise on Argumentation*, trans. John Wilkinson and Purcell Weaver (South Bend, IN, 1969), pp. 116, 117.

9. Ibid., p. 118.

10. Cyril Connolly's memories of Orwell are contained in his book *Enemies of Promise* (New York, 1938); Richard Rees's in *George Orwell: Fugitive from the Camp of Victory* (Carbondale, IL, 1962); and Malcolm Muggeridge's in the Introduction to Orwell's *Burmese Days* (New York, 1962).

4

Orwell – Paterfamilias or Big Brother?

BEATRIX CAMPBELL

If we are to measure George Orwell's success in the durability of his two later novels, *Animal Farm* and *Nineteen Eighty-Four* then what we need to examine is his projection of Big Brother – the modern authoritarian state.

Big Brother has become *the* metaphor for the modern state, and, although its success is formidable, since the term has become part of our political vocabulary, it is also a problem. Orwell's state is not just a spectre of secrecy and surveillance, because the whole thesis also depends on a notion of absolute power which depends on the condition of mass powerlessness. In this context it is significant that Orwell feels comfortable in the temperate climes of English capitalism before the Second World War, only decades after the working class had won the franchise and before it was a major power in the land.

It is post-revolutionary power which inflames his nightmare of the future state – his critique of the modern state is unmistakably directed against the socialist state. But Orwell's equally nightmarish vision of absolute powerlessness derives not from some future defeat, but his own feelings about the working class who were his contemporaries. The horrors of *Animal Farm* and *Nineteen Eighty-Four* extend not only to the misuse of state power, but to the failure of politics itself. That failure derives from Orwell's big-brotherly view of the working class.

I want to argue, as Raymond Williams has in his excellent book *Orwell*, that the problem with Orwell is his representation, or rather misrepresentation, of the working class. More than that, there is also a problem in the way that masculinity, femininity and the family feature in his representations of class.

While Orwell's invincible edifice of the state may seem modern, his view of the working class isn't – it's the quaint, old-fashioned chronicle of a self-confessed snob. Despite his wish to invest his revolutionary optimism in the people, what he feels for the common people edges on contempt. Actually, he thinks they're dead common. He may *think* the working class is the revolutionary class, but he doesn't *feel* it.

Nowhere in Orwell do the working class *make* history. And in his quest for an authentic English socialism it is not the working class, but a sort of hybrid southern suburban species which becomes the revolutionary class – not because of its capacity to struggle, but because in some way it fits Orwell's notion of quintessential Englishness.

Throughout *Nineteen Eighty-Four* the off-stage appearances of the working class are remarkably resonant of *The Road to Wigan Pier*. The power of the state in *Nineteen Eighty-Four* seems perpetually stabilised in its very instability – but the instability is only a chimera. There is no real challenge to the state from its own people, and particularly not from the proles.

George Orwell's life and times with the proletariat began with *The Road to Wigan Pier* when, in keeping with a long tradition of English literature, the quest for the 'state of the nation', he set off on an expedition into the natural habitat of the working class. The tradition itself depends on a relation of otherness to this class. In the first place, normally such journeys could only be undertaken by people with the time and money to make them, in other words with resources not possessed by the working class itself. But more importantly, that relationship always inscribes the author in a relation of exclusion from the working class. The odd thing is that this quest for Englishness necessitates the discovery of that working class, as if it were hidden and mysterious. And of course, coming from Orwell's class position, that is exactly what they were. And remained. In *The Road to Wigan Pier*, Orwell depended on the activists for his access to the working class. But as Williams shows, Orwell insists on a separation between the working class and its activist intelligentsia. He cannot conceive of the working class itself as a *thinking* class with its own history, with a history of making itself. The result is the representation of a class which is thoughtless and leaderless, a class in its natural state.

Again, as Williams shows, Orwell's omission of working-class activists and organisations leaves him with the slate clean for his own observations. What Orwell brings to his journey is primarily himself, an observer who takes no counsel, an author with all the arrogance of innocence. Insofar as he is concerned with working-class politics as an organised force, he represents it as showing a flair for organisation but not for thinking. This separation is achieved because Orwell kidnaps working-class thinkers out of their class: 'I think, therefore I am' apparently doesn't apply to the proles; to think is to become middle class. It is this which enables us to track a continuity between *Wigan Pier* and *Nineteen Eighty-Four*. It is as if the documentary material of *Wigan Pier* provided him with his source material for *Nineteen Eighty-Four*: the proles are the same in both.

In *Wigan Pier*, Orwell seeks to sum up the working class in the archetypal proletarian group – the miners. For all that his description of miners' labour and their poverty is sympathetic, it is hardly radical. How does he describe these archetypal proletarians, and why did he single out the miners?

Orwell's graphic description of the work of miners facilitates his representation of workers as elemental creatures, work-horses. Williams reminds us that this is how they appear in *Animal Farm*, and so it is again in *Nineteen Eighty-Four*. As I have argued in *Wigan Pier Revisited*, I think Orwell's choice of miners is significant. As the mysogynist he is, it is not surprising that he has chosen the most masculinised profession.

Undoubtedly, his celebration of the miners was in part an attempt to restore them to a respected place in the ranks of the working class. He challenges the denigration of miners as noble savages because they are dirty by describing the conditions of their work and their bathless homes, and by establishing trenchantly the necessity of their work. For it is coal, he says, that makes the world go round. And at the same time he, too, casts them in the role of noble savages by his panegyric on their physique. He loves their lean, supple, black bodies. And so his celebration of the miners is both an affectionate discovery of their heroism *and* their masculinity – their work is a *man*ful struggle down there in the dark and dangerous abdomen of the earth. It is of course essentially physical work, and what Orwell is not concerned with is the history of that masculinisation of the work of miners. Mining is only men's work because women were banned from the work of hewing coal in the nineteenth-century struggle to expel women from hard physical labour. The feminisation of women demanded that expulsion. But that feminisation had an answering echo in the masculinisation of men. This is important for several reasons. The selection of the miners in this way as the most exotic martyrs of the working class is itself part of the process of masculinising the history of the working class.

Orwell visited Wigan in the 1930s when it was still one of the outposts of women's work in the mines. After the expulsion of women from the underground in 1842, there were campaigns throughout the late nineteenth century to purge women from the pit top, where it was believed by some that they were de-sexed by their strength. The campaign failed in Wigan, where women were only finally pushed off the pit top in the 1950s after nationalisation and a deal between the National Coal Board and the National Union of Mineworkers. Wigan was famous for its 'pit brow lasses'. Not as you'd know from *The Road to Wigan Pier*.

Wigan was also as much a cotton town as it was a coal town. Indeed, it is significant that Orwell spent a substantial part of his journey in Lancashire around the cotton belt, towns which employed women in the mills, towns which were the crucible of the English industrial revolution, towns where working-class history cannot be written other than as the struggles between men *and women* and capital. Not as you'd know that from *The Road to Wigan Pier* either.

So, women do not appear as protagonists in Orwell's working class. And neither does capital. And what we are left with is a sense of a class which suffers, but not of a class which struggles. And certainly not a class which wins. It's a class summed up in the anthem of the washerwomen in *Nineteen Eighty-Four*:

> They sye that time 'eals all things,
> They sye you can always forget;
> But the smiles an' the tears acrorss the years
> They twist my 'eart strings yet!

True to the tradition of such representations of the working class, the imagery contains pathos, isolation, inertia, defeat: it incites pity and philanthropy rather than protest and politics. The washerwoman in

Nineteen Eighty-Four has her parallel in *Wigan Pier* in a solitary image of an exhausted, but noble, woman, poking a stick down a drain. Both figures are used by Orwell to gather and focus his fondness for these poor people. But they are silent women, even when they are singing. They are sad, but above all they are solitary. And Orwell is about to entrench them in their solitude: in *Wigan Pier* he sees her as he is on his way, leaving town. In *Nineteen Eighty-Four* he discovers his affection for his washerwoman just before Winston is about to be arrested. The isolation of these figures in their proletarian landscape is about to be completed in both cases by the observer's departure. The only feelings we can be left with are grief and impotence.

Among the middle class and the upper class, women are targets of his acidic class contempt, expressed in the same vein as the mother-in-law joke. It's the 'Brighton ladies' and rich women lolling around in Rolls Royces whom he can't abide, presumably because they are the quintessence of the idle rich. They're an easy target, of course, given their unstated but enforced idleness as women.

It is women whom he identifies as the fifth column of the upper classes. In *Wigan Pier* Orwell briefly considers the lack of political solidarity among the middle class, not as a function of its dominance – for the upper classes are organised in a web of political associations of which there is no account in Orwell – but as an expression of women's backwardness.

> You cannot have an effective trade union of middle-class workers because in times of strikes almost every middle-class wife would be egging her husband on to blackleg and get the other fellow's job.

The unity of the working class, on the other hand, is assumed and cemented in the unity of the family, 'the fact that the working class combine and the middle class don't is probably due to their different conceptions of the family'. Orwell is clearly innocent of the tension within working-class households in precisely the case of that litmus test of intra-class solidarity, the strike.

The history of the working class is, however, a minefield of negotiated settlements between men and women, not least in the classic case of the strike. Men's strikes have always carried the proverbial risk of the complaining wife who was never consulted – it is classically represented in *Salt of the Earth*, an American film of a Mexican-American miners' strike in which the women's communal demands were never given political priority by their men. The men's strike is lived by women as an economic hardship that they were never consulted about. But when the women propose taking over the picket line after the coalowners take out an injunction against the striking miners, the men balk; the men vote against it, but the women – having first fought for their right to vote – all vote for it. The women's tenacity becomes the source of the strike's survival, demanded from them initially as individuals and yet opposed when it takes the form of a collective intervention. Individual solidarity, of course, is always in the service of the men. Collective action among the women always carries the threat of an organised power beyond the men's control. Orwell's observations about class loyalty between the genders are just another example of his unsubstantiated sentiments.

Take a look at the gender breakdown in voting patterns. The gender gap is dramatic within the working class. It is among middle and upper-class voters that there is a remarkable political symmetry. The fact is that the upper class is united across gender and class in ways that the working class isn't. It is conventional wisdom that the reason for this is that the labour movement and the Labour Party have faced women with a contradiction: it demands their class solidarity while it sanctions their sexual subordination.

Part of the problem is that Orwell's eye never comes to rest on the culture of women, their concerns, their history, their movements. He only holds women to the filter of his own desire – or distaste. We've already seen how he makes women the bearers of his own class hatred. In his avowedly political work the snarling innuendo he reserves for his 'Brighton ladies' and 'birth control' fanatics is rarely directed towards the figures of *real* power in capitalist societies – the judges, the parliamentarians and the capitalists. In fact, you are left with a sense of a society run, not only by the national family's old buffers, but of a society run by a febrile femininity, an army of doddering dowagers.

The point is that given his own centrality, and that of masculinity in Orwell's work, women are congratulated only when they stick to their men. The sexual filter surrounds all his female personae.

In *Nineteen Eighty-Four* we have working-class women represented by poor Mrs Parsons and a prole washerwoman. Mrs Parsons is a 'woman with a lined face and wispy hair, fiddling helplessly with the waste pipe', an infuriating person, always in the slough of a housewife's ruinous mess. And then there is the washerwoman whom Winston discovers during his fugitive flights into proletaria.

He only begins to reflect on her with any respect when he inexplicably discovers the revolutionary potential of the proles. Her 'indefatigable voice' sings on, as she endlessly hangs out her washing. He watches her 'solid, contourless body, like a block of granite', quietly admiring 'her thick arms reaching up for the line, her powerful mare-like buttocks protruded'. She's as strong as a horse, an image which has echoes in *Animal Farm*, where as Raymond Williams reminds us, 'the speed of his figurative transition from animals to the proletariat is interesting – showing as it does a residue of thinking of the poor as animals: powerful but stupid'.

As Orwell's Winston watches the 'over-ripe turnip' of a washerwoman reach for the line 'it struck him for the first time that she was beautiful'. Her 'rasping red skin, bore the same relation to the body of a girl as the rose-hip to the rose. Why should the fruit be held inferior to the flower?'

So we start with the strong but stupid work-horse and move to a vision of a woman in labour: both as she labours solitarily and stoically, and as a symbol of fertility. As Winston muses on how he and his lover Julia will never bear children he reflects on this washerwoman-mother: 'The woman down there had no mind, she had only strong arms, a warm heart and a fertile belly.' Just like Orwell's panegyric on the miners, all brawn and no brain, this quintessential proletarian woman is all belly and no brain. She has no culture and no consciousness worth contemplating.

His image of this woman echoes his more poetic representation of the miners as the archetypal proletarians, but there is more: her labour is solitary. Like the miners, her labour is elemental, basic: it is a fundamental, natural force. There is in these accounts no representation of subtlety, of craft and the consciousness associated with workers' combination. This representation of heroic manual labour is consonant with his celebration of her biology. It is only a short step from this to his formation of Julia's rebellion. Julia is Winston's sleeping partner in sedition. Her rebellion is essentially sexual. She's promiscuous, she's had hundreds of men and her subversion is sealed in an equation between corruption and sexuality. 'I hate purity, I hate goodness! I don't want any virtue to exist anywhere', shouts Julia. That's the extent of her opposition to totalitarian puritanism. 'I'm corrupt to the bones.' Winston loves that, not merely her capacity for love, 'but the animal instinct, the simple undifferentiated desire: that was the force that would tear the party to pieces'.

In a curiously sexual politics, he counterposes Julia's revolution-ary rapaciousness with his former wife Katherine's puritanism. Her party loyalty is expressed in her frigidity. Julia's delicious revolt is consummated in her illicit collection of make-up: throwing off the uniform of the party she dons the mantle of femininity.

But of course, the consequences of this reduction of Julia to her corrupt biology are to render her rebellion as something seething below the threshold of political consciousness. It is spontaneous only, and only so because it is only sexual. She's not interested in politics as such, even though she'll lay down her life for her revolt. When Winston finally gets his hands on Goldstein's bible of dissi-dence, he tells her urgently that they must read the forbidden text together. What does she do? She tells him to read it to her. And when he does? She falls asleep.

Women are akin to the proletarian man in Orwell's work, they are rendered natural rather than skilful, almost infantile in their un-consciousness rather than alert and organised. This facilitates the elision between work and politics – the workers work in their natural state and they have their social existence still in a kind of natural state. The working class is pre-conscious, tasteless and mindless, child-like in its quest for immediate gratification. Yet for some reason, which Orwell never explains, the working class is the material of revolution. Perhaps because of some quasi-religious notion that the meek shall inherit the earth. The people store in their hearts, muscles and bellies the power to change the world. All body but no brain – and yet without the collective brain of politics, the Machiavellian 'prince' of the party, how is their strength to turn into consciousness? This is perhaps the greatest lacuna in Orwell's work: Williams declares that 'in a profound way, both the con-sciousness of the workers and the possibility of authentic revolution are denied'. There is no sensitivity to the repertoire of tactics and strategies which the working-class movement, despite its many weaknesses, has deployed. The very absence of the problem of ideo-logy and consciousness produces an assumed leap from brute strength to the power of the *will*.

That leaves him without anything to say about working-class pol-itics as such, and its metamorphosis into revolutionary culture – you are always left with the feeling of contempt for 'the masses' and for the left intelligentsia. A thinking worker is never allowed to remain a member of the working class. It leaves him with insupera-ble contradictions – the workers are the revolutionary class and yet they aren't. Thinking workers are part of the intelligentsia and therefore irrelevant. It's as if, like so many members of his class, he can't forgive the working-class thinkers for their capacity to think. For all that Orwell in *Wigan Pier* owns up to the partiality of his class perceptions, he never shares the privilege of *thought* with his new class allies.

If the working class are the material of revolution, they are never the makers of revolution, despite his rhetoric. And so he compromises. Slumped in his own contradictions, he gives the middle class the ticket. They've been elbowed out of their revolutionary credentials by pansy intellectuals on the one hand and by their rough neighbours on the council estates on the other. They become the radical Englishness, WASPs to the last, moderate in all things. Not surprisingly, Orwell's revolutionary transition is a remarkably banal, anglo-saxon prospectus. Looking now at his Six Point Programme in *The Lion and the Unicorn*, it is hard to see how it really differs from militant social democracy. English socialism, he says, will nationalise, it will equalise incomes, it will have its own catchy tune, it will leave the Christians alone, it will be sensible. What his programme doesn't have, however, is any sense of *struggle*. The working class have created programmes like these, of course, but in Orwell's scenario they haven't produced his. At least, though, it would 'give the working class something to fight for'. He excludes the working class from history and fails to give it any place in the revolutionary cast, other than the supporting role, the proverbial extras.

In *Wigan Pier*, having exploited the services of the movement's activists, Orwell thanks them with:

> The English working class do not show much capacity for leadership, but they have a wonderful talent for organisation. The whole trade union movement testifies to this; so too the excellent working men's clubs – really a sort of glorified co-operative pub, and splendidly organised...

Elsewhere in *Wigan Pier* Orwell muses on the contradictions in English culture, between its polite respectability and its boozy, bawdy post-card culture. It all works towards an image of working-class men at play, training pigeons, swearing and gambling. Orwell thus summarises the working-class culture of 'the warm-hearted, unthinking socialist, the typical working class socialist' in a kind of bar talk. It produces a vision of the future, he says, 'of present-day society with the worst abuses left out, and with interest centring on the same things as at present – family life, the pub, football and local politics'.

The roots are already in *Wigan Pier* for Winston's shocking discovery of and disappointment in – the proles in *Nineteen Eighty-Four* when he sees a clutch of men peering at a newspaper, talking earnestly. Something must be up, thinks Winston. But no, they're only looking for the lottery results.

Orwell anchors his own anti-economism in a critique in *The Lion and the Unicorn* of the trade-union politics which dominate English Labourism. In this he was hardly original, as socialists and Marxists have always been preoccupied by this English disease. But in Orwell, anti-economism is associated with a sense of the working class as not only myopic but degenerate. Just as Orwell finds no point of resistance rooted in the working class itself in *Wigan Pier*, so is there none in *Nineteen Eighty-Four*.

There is more to say about the problem of economism, however. For Orwell is not alone in stumbling across it only to be mystified by it. As he eloquently suggests, for the working class men's movement, socialism is capitalism with the worst abuses left out. I have to confess that Orwell's own political prospectus, outlined in *The Lion and the Unicorn*, seems barely any different. What neither he nor the men's movement on the left seem to have registered is that this problem of economism may be associated with the masculinisation of working-class politics, its reduction to a men's movement. Orwell is a participant in this because he, too, writes women out of working-class history and politics. It isn't because working men are thick that they're economistic, as Orwell seems to suggest, but it may be that the historic settlement between capital and the men's labour movement over the role of women reinforces economic individualism and defuses the *social* dimensions of socialist struggle. Certainly, that economic individualism is associated with the economic subordination of women, and not surprisingly it produces a politics which evacuates the terrain of private life, on the one hand, and issues outside the parameter of the wage contract on the other.

Orwell argues for a cultural revolution as the necessary ignition to political revolution in England, and his great virtue is his attempt to anchor that vision in the continuity of commonsense culture. But far from that taking him towards the culture of those constituencies marginalised in the hierarchy of WASP socialism, he seeks to radicalise those components of consensus claimed by the right – the steadfast pillars of family and patriotism.

As Williams shows, Orwell's starting point is his quest to belong, a quest which leads him towards an attempt to produce a unity called England and Englishness. His metaphor for nationhood is the family, the collectivity in which all know their place in relation to each other, in which all are intelligible to each other. In the family, as in the nation, we all share the same concerns, the same interests and the same language. It is in the working-class family, above all, that we all come home to rest:

> you breathe a warm, decent, deeply human atmosphere which is not easy to find elsewhere ... His home life seems to fall more naturally into a sane and comely shape. I have often been struck by the easy completeness, the perfect symmetry, as it were, of a working class interior at its best...

It hangs together, he suggests, as a middle class family does, 'but the relationship is far less tyrannical'.

It is only in the context of feminist politics that the critique of the family clarifies it as a site of contradiction between men and women, as a settlement, always negotiated between unequals. Orwell's suggestive symmetry is exactly the simmering, seething volcano which has always, explicitly or implicitly, fuelled movements for women's economic, social and sexual independence. Feminism falsified the Orwellian romance with the proletarian family as an institution. It is not that feminism seeks to damn the strong bonds and loves lived within the family, but rather the *conditions* in which men and women negotiate their encounter with each other, their children and the rest of the world, based as they are on the principle of dominance and subordination. If, for feminism, that institution is challenged, then whither Orwell's appeal to patriotism?

Britain, however, was, and now is more than ever before, a richly cosmopolitan society. Orwell's 'patriotism' is an appeal to just one of those 'families', the English working class. In the aftermath of the family outing to the Falklands there is no guarantee that this patriotism would have a progressive hue.

There is an easy equation in his social democratic programme between *giving* the workers something to fight for and his sentimental construction of nationhood within the parameters of the family. His thesis of progressive patriotism works because his view of the nation is that of the family, an essentially unified whole, speaking the same language, united by kin, not divided by class. Because the socialist family would have the right people in control, the working class would presumably remain as they are – the children.

From *Inside the Myth: Voices from the Left*, ed. Christopher Norris (London, 1984), pp. 126–38.

NOTES

[In a socialist-feminist critique, Beatrix Campbell questions Orwell's representation of the working classes. This is a strongly argued position piece in which she follows Raymond Williams's lead but highlights Orwell's reluctance to include women in the wider context of working-class history and politics. Where women appear, she argues, they are presented as dysfunctional, infantilised, and their specific interests and claims disavowed. They often function simply as part of his overarching metaphor of nationhood as family. Eds]

5

The Inversion of Form: Deconstructing *1984*

ALAN KENNEDY

The year 1984 now recedes into memory and text, but it remains what we might call (using Lacan's term) a *point de capiton*, a buttoning-down point in the fabric of our interpretations of history as we come to conceive it through our experiences of literature. When we were in 1984 our experience was textualised in a different way, in that we were looking for the year to be a metaphor of itself, and sought identities between time and text. We tried to place the text by the time and the time by the text. If the year 1984 is (or was) better or worse than the fictional year 1984, then was Orwell right or wrong? Was he a prophet or a perceptive Cassandra or someone whose advice kept us off the terrible path to totalitarianism? Or, from the other side, can we find new value in Orwell's myth by looking at the terrors of our world and reading his novel as an allegory that gives us a frisson of recognition? All such readings (and they are part of the established atmosphere of Orwell criticism) assume a classic book rather than a text, a book whose meaning is determinable. The belief that the meaning of the novel is determinable is, I suspect, in perfect relation with the fact that so many people turned to the novel during the year 1984 with tremendous interest, an interest that led to massively renewed sales of the book, an interest fostered considerably by those market forces that stood to benefit from it. Public interest in the novel has now virtually disappeared, and is unlikely to reappear now that the year of the book has disappeared into history. The assumption that a novel can be equal to a particular moment in history would seem to be complicit both with a definition of the book as primarily a market commodity and with the related consumer attitude to literature as disposable once its moment has passed. So much perhaps for claims that literature must be seen to have determinable historical significance.

Now it so happens (as is well-known to critics) that the novel *1984*[1] is in fact hardly like the consistent and integral well-made book we should have to have were any of our comparisons of time and text to be workable. Now that we are positioned post-1984 (the year, but not the text), in a position which clearly signals that the novel *1984* differs from the year we are in, a new question of the relevance of literature can be raised differentially. How now to read *1984*? – and, if we come up with an answer, we may be able to project our analysis back into time and say that we should have been reading the novel differentially even when we were under the lure of the metaphorical identity of time and text. What I propose here, then, is a differential reading of *1984*, and by 'differential reading' I mean what might as well be called a deconstructive reading, although the signification of such a practice is still in doubt. Suffice it to say that I shall try to demonstrate that the text differs from itself, in a sense that should become clear as we proceed. My motive in doing so is double, at least. First, the issue raised by 1984 and *1984* is provocative enough in itself to move us to question again the mimetic notion of fiction and an unexamined theory of the relation of reading to writing. In the search for something other than a univocal reading of a text such as *1984*, we open ourselves to charges that one has heard in the air about deconstructive criticism often enough. The poststructuralist practice, by calling into question the legitimacy of the idea of the sign, apparently calls the whole literary enterprise (its relevance) into question. So I want to try to argue that the 'breaking of form', as Bloom calls it, need not mean the death of literature. Indeed, the differential breaking of form is the release of meaning. The text is found to have more meanings when the relation of form to meaning is broken. Clearly that is a claim that will take a lot of testing out, more than can be rehearsed here, but this might mark one opening.

Why desire more meanings and a differential sense of form though? Doesn't the whole thing reduce to textual frivolities? My second motive, then, is to argue that deconstructive readings need not be politically irrelevant. The multiplicity of meaning, or the release of new possible meanings by the unfolding of uncertainty operating in a text, might be thought of as one way of conceiving of the freedom of the text – or a way of preserving a sense of the literariness of literature precisely in the moment of breaking form. The resistance to form might then be thought of as an allegory of political activity. I think that deconstructive criticism will come increasingly to be seen as the art, and the politics, of resistance, of reading and writing as resistance. A deconstructive reading will be practising resistance at the same time as it is investigating it in the text. This will require us to take any formal inconsistencies and read them fully, drawing out their implications as if they were part of the canonical text, which of course they are. The result could be that kind of encounter with formalism, or an inversion of form, which allows for a discussion that both keeps within the formal constraints of art and at the same time exceeds them. For a discussion, that is to say, for which there is no beyond of politics or of art. Logically, three areas of attention are mapped out for us. The first is that of writing and reading, clearly invoked by our desire or intention to read resistantly. Second is the realm of desire itself, in which, as Freud still reminds us, the topic of resistance is central. This second realm takes us into an investigation of sexuality and into the problem of interpreting the dreams in *1984*. The third realm, of course, is that of politics, which is obviously central to Orwell's book; and, in that the topic is presented by way of a character such as O'Brien (who is so clearly a 'God' figure), politics also includes metaphysics. A useful coincidence for a deconstructive critic.

Let us consider Winston's experience of writing in his diary. He thinks of writing as recording, as recording the past, or the present as it is becoming the past. As soon as Winston puts himself in the position of acting as a responsible recorder of his thoughts and of events, he undergoes something very strange. His mind goes blank and he cannot write. His memory fails him. He is struck with a terrible recognition: although he might be able to write, he can never have an audience, and if he can't have an audience he can't write. Let me quote the passage:

> For whom, it suddenly occurred to him to wonder, was he writing this diary? For the future, for the unborn. His mind hovered for a moment round the doubtful date on the page, and then fetched up with a bump against the Newspeak word doublethink. For the first

> time the magnitude of what he had undertaken came home to him.
> How could you communicate with the future? It was of its nature
> impossible. Either the future would resemble the present, in which
> case it would not listen to him: or it would be different from it, and
> his predicament would be meaningless.
>
> (p. 10)

Are we, as readers, the future, or the past? Either way, is it possible
to comprehend *1984*? Isn't any knowledge we can get from the
book going to be useless? Of necessity knowledge of the past, which
cannot be changed? Knowledge that will be necessarily useless
because it is knowledge that nothing can be done, that there is no
rebellion possible, no way of reconstructing our stage, or of avoid-
ing death? Let us note more carefully what happens as Winston discovers what it means to engage in writing:

> For some time he sat gazing stupidly at the paper. ... It was curious
> that he seemed not merely to have lost the power of expressing
> himself, but even to have forgotten what it was that he had originally
> intended to say. For weeks past he had been making ready for this
> moment, and it had never crossed his mind that anything would be
> needed except courage.
>
> (Ibid.)

As it turns out, Winston just does begin to write – not to record,
not from memory, not to convey knowledge. He pours out a stream
of automatic writing, expressing his hatred of Big Brother. When he
has been writing for a while, something else strange happens to
him:

> Winston stopped writing, partly because he was suffering from
> cramp. He did not know what had made him pour out this stream of
> rubbish. But the curious thing was that while he was doing so a
> totally different memory had clarified itself in his mind, to the point
> where he almost felt equal to writing it down. It was, he now re-
> alised, because of this other incident that he had suddenly decided to
> come home and begin the diary today.
>
> (p. 11)

This is very unusual and very interesting: writing the diary can only
begin when the reason for writing it is forgotten. The ignorant
writing of the diary leads to the discovery of another memory
which was the origin of the intention to write the diary. So the past

is here really created (re-created) by writing; it is not a matter of recording it at all. In fact it is a bit like inventing the past, or history, by writing it. Winston himself, in 'correcting' the official record in his job at the Ministry of Information, invents at one point a character who takes on a life of his own. Winston comes close to behaving like a novelist. At least, memory does not direct writing. Writing creates memory. Writing is not a documentation. So the creative process of writing is: forgetting – writing – memory – writing. Which makes us wonder just what reading can be. Is the goal of reading knowledge, or forgetting?

Our discussion of writing led us directly into thinking about doublethink. Let us continue our discussion of doublethink by seeing it at work in the Established Language of 1984, Newspeak. The purpose of Newspeak is to limit consciousness (and therefore power) by limiting words and concepts – by fixing language so that the meaning will be 'in the words'. 'Every concept that can ever be needed will be expressed by exactly one word, with its meaning rigidly defined and all its subsidiary meanings rubbed out and forgotten' (p. 45). One can notice first the ahistorical aim of this goal, and second the ahistorical notion of language that would give rise to the belief that language can be limited by law – short, that is, of actually murdering all the speakers of it. In Orwell's time there appeared the first edition of the *New English Dictionary*, which shows that not only is the history of meaning constantly rewritten, but so is the meaning of history. So a legislative dictionary seems impossible – barring, as I said, universal tongue surgery. But Orwell would apparently have us believe that it might be possible to have one word for one meaning.

One consideration about the nature of language shows us that this is impossible. We could simply refer to metaphors and leave it at that. Consider, though, this syntactical, metonymical example: 'John ducked his sister in the pool. John's sister ducked when she saw him coming. John then ducked all responsibility.' What one concept applies to the word 'duck'? Take a more complex possibility, one where the two intentions of the word are suspended in ambiguity: 'John's sister ducked.' Did she hide in fear of her brother, or did she retaliate against her brother by drowning him; or by hiding herself under water; or by committing suicide? Words change meanings figuratively (which is what our word 'ducked' has already done) and they also change function and meaning by changing position in the sentence: transitive becomes intransitive, subject becomes object, noun can be verb. Unless we assume that Big Brother will outlaw syntax and therefore the structural possibilities of ambiguity as well as all tropes, then we cannot expect him to be successful.

So little is Big Brother aware of the problem that he apparently actually encourages contradictions, since he allows metaphors and double meanings, as in the word 'duckspeak':

> 'There is a word in Newspeak,' said Syme, 'I don't know whether you know it: duckspeak, to quack like a duck. It is one of those interesting words that have two contradictory meanings. Applied to an opponent, it is abuse; applied to someone you agree with, it is praise.'
>
> (p. 47)

Gone, it seems, is the rule of one word for one meaning. Are we meant to read this as an inconsistency on Orwell's part? Or are we meant to read it as Orwell's indication that Big Brother is a logical impossibility? And, if Big Brother is a logical impossibility, what are we to do with a novel in which the characters are so much living in fear of him? If the duckspeak principle is a qualification of the earlier 'one to one' position, then it means that one must tailor meanings to situations, which is of course what we always try to do with language. Except, of course, in cases in which the situation is not only not clear, but unspecifiable; as in the case of the writing of Winston's diary, which has no proper audience, and in the case of a novel, which also seems to have no proper audience – at least if our own inability to read it means that we are therefore not the proper audience.

Big Brother's principle of altering the language is applied also to all the timebound environment of Oceania. One must not be allowed to read the past in any language of architecture. Trying to remember a nursery rhyme – is Orwell hinting that the familiar and familial teaching of nursery rhymes is also a source of orientation? – Winston speculates about the history of church buildings: 'One could not learn history from architecture any more than one could learn it from books. Statues, inscriptions, memorial stones, the names of streets – anything that might throw light upon the past had been systematically altered' (p. 82). Orwell, and Big Brother, seem to recognise with Barthes and others that what we think of as external to text, the whole fabric of our social lives, is itself textual. When he is to meet Julia in Victory

Square, Winston gives us the following description. First we get a view of a statue of Big Brother, then this detail: 'In the street in front of it there was a statue of a man on horseback which was supposed to represent Oliver Cromwell' (p. 94). What are we to make of this, especially of that unreliable and unspecifiable phrase 'supposed to represent'? Was Winston merely mistaken in his first claim that all statues and names of streets have been systematically altered and that apparently no one can read history from them? Does he forget that he made it and are we supposed to have an example of the dangers of faulty memory, since his memory failure disorients us? Has Orwell forgotten? Are we to believe that Big Brother has deliberately put a badly made statue of Cromwell near his own for some obscure purpose? A joke perhaps, a cheeky test of perceptions, a trap?

Consider another example of this sort. When Winston is first taken to the Ministry of Love, we are given his reaction this way:

> He did not know where he was. Presumably he was in the Ministry of Love. ... His cell might be at the heart of the building or against its outer wall; it might be ten floors below ground, or thirty above it. He moved himself mentally from place to place, and tried to determine by the feeling of his body whether he was perched high in the air or buried deep underground.
>
> (p. 181)

Since we are not told that he was brought in unconscious, we might wonder why he didn't notice at that time. Our puzzlement deepens: 'At each stage of his imprisonment he had known or seemed to know, whereabouts he was in the windowless building. Possibly there were slight differences in the air pressure' (p. 227). Once again we seem to have a fault in Orwell's memory of his own narrative, a deliberately planted inconsistency, or a necessary doublethink. So, if we suspect Orwell's memory to be faulty, what trust can we place in the claim that one needs to have an accurate memory in order to have a sense of personal orientation? What can we make of the fact that so many people feel that they have a clear orientation to Orwell's novel? Is forgetting (of its inconsistencies) crucial to a comfortable feeling of order? In order to appreciate the possibilities of art and pure form, is it required of us to cultivate ignorance of such 'flaws'? Or is it possible to doublethink them, by means of an inversion of form, into part of the novel (which they are)?

Forgetting and remembering are central elements in dreams, of course, so let us briefly look at one of the dreams that Winston has. One of the things dreams do is to restore or represent the past. We can account in psychoanalytical terms for one central dream that Winston has: a dream of his mother and sister sinking into green water in the saloon of a boat. Did Winston duck his sister? Has he been ducking the recognition for years? He certainly lives for years with the belief that he had killed his mother. Just after receiving the message (the first contact) from O'Brien, Winston has a dream which is 'comprehended by ... a gesture of the arm'. 'Comprehended' means 'made up of in total', but it also means 'understood by'. Could we understand the gesture of an arm, we should understand the dream. If *1984* is an anxiety dream, then perhaps it too is comprehended by a gesture of the arm (perhaps the gesture of writing). The gesture of the arm is a protective gesture (maybe writing also is a protective, defensive gesture). Perhaps we are meant to recall this dream gesture when Winston receives a crippling blow on the elbow from O'Brien's troops when they first begin to torture him. Whatever the case, the result of his dream is that Winston comes to a realisation: '"Do you know," he said, "that until this moment I believed I had murdered my mother?"' (p. 131). In the dream he had remembered his last glimpse of his mother, and within a few moments of waking the cluster of small events surrounding it had all come back. It was a memory he must have deliberately pushed out of his consciousness over many years.

Somewhere in the family, then, in its history or structure, there is a source of guilt that makes memory falter, acts as a memory hole. In forcing memory to falter, then, Big Brother is acting just like a member of the family (as his name really ought to have told us), and not at all like a political figure. The political theme of the novel begins to look like an allegory of an Oedipus complex. Winston recalls, with remarkable narrative clarity, the details of the time and place of his crime. He recalls his father's disappearance, and then scenes in which 'he would grab bits from his sister's plate' and an occasion on which he had stolen her share of chocolate. With father gone, the only other rival for mother's attention comes in for attacks of deprivation. Then his mother and sister disappear, never to be heard of again; as if it were the appropriate punishment for a greedy boy who tried to possess too much – at least he feels guilty for her disappearance, as if his competition for treats from the mother led to her disappearance. Winston is about to explain 'the real point of the story' to Julia when she falls asleep. Who can blame her when it turns out that all he wants to do in bed is read her stories from Goldstein's book or tell her about his dreams? In the absence of his audience Winston cannot proceed, so the narrator explains the story by giving us a general commentary: the real point is that the mother had private feelings 'that could not be altered from outside'. This leads to some reflections on the Party, the Proles, confessions, and a conclusion on Winston's part that the Party had not 'mastered the secret of finding out what another human was thinking', and that 'the inner heart remained impregnable'.

It is no wonder that he comes to such a conclusion, since he remains blind to the contents of his own heart, even when they are revealed. For what is remarkable is that the real main points of his story do not figure at all in the explanation. One of these points is that he was (and is?) a greedy child, probably responsible for his mother's and sister's starvation: 'He knew that he was starving the other two, but he could not help it; he even felt that he had a right to do it. The clamorous hunger in his belly seemed to justify him' (p. 132). At this point we are supposed to universalise the principle and say forgivingly that hunger brutalises people – a conclusion that allows us to forget the brutality of those who are not hungry as they contemplate the starving of the rest of the planet. In his earlier dream of his mother's drowning, his unconscious has already begun to make rationalisations and justifications for him, by arranging for his mother to drown in the dream with a look of forgiving understanding on her face: 'There was no reproach either in their faces or in their hearts [!], only the knowledge that they must die in order that he might remain alive, and that this was part of the unavoidable order of things' (p. 27). What a novelist's understanding Winston shows in his awareness of what is in the hearts of his 'victims', even though it is also impossible to know what is in the secret heart of anyone. Let us now restore more of the passage that presents us with the idea of the gesture of the arm:

> The dream had also been comprehended by – indeed, in some sense it had consisted in – a gesture of the arm made by his mother, and made again thirty years later by the Jewish woman he had seen on the news film, trying to shelter the small boy from the bullets, before the helicopters blew them both to pieces.
>
> (p. 131)

I have heard Vietnam invoked with reference to this passage. It makes more sense to see Winston's dream, the one that frees him from the guilt of his mother's death, as Orwell's wish, and ours, to be freed from the guilt of the mass murders of the Second World War. Unlike his mother, he was incapable of making a protective gesture for his sister. His final failure is that he cannot make such a gesture for Julia, nor she for him. So we can perhaps regard Winston's dreams of rebellion against Big Brother as nothing more than a greedy child's attempts to have more chocolate, or to have his mother to himself. He plots with the inconsistency of a child and because of his inadequacy we are supposed to believe in the strength of the Party. His childishness is evidenced when O'Brien is gloating over having broken him. Winston immediately says, but I haven't betrayed Julia. This is like a child, who has hidden some chocolate in the cupboard, saying to his parents, I don't know where it is, but don't look in the cupboard. It betrays a need to be caught and punished.

Of course, another remarkable thing about the dream sequence is its evidence that the individual memory does work. Things can be repressed and then they can return; the mind can store and restore the past with great accuracy. What then of the Party's claim to control both record and mind? Orwell seems to have forgotten the dream sequences, and yet they are of central importance to any understanding of the novel. The book seems increasingly like Orwell's dream, or nightmare. There is actually a second part to his first dream of the drowning of his mother and sister. It is a dream that seems 'a continuation of one's intellectual life'. The scene shifts suddenly to the place that Winston calls the 'Golden Country', where he seems to be standing alone. Then there is a confusion about whether Winston is actually alone or is in a family group with his mother and sister, as indicated by the plural pronoun in this passage:

> The girl with the dark hair was coming towards them across the field. With what seemed a single movement she tore off her clothes and flung them disdainfully aside. Her body was white and smooth, but it aroused no desire in him, indeed he barely looked at it. What overwhelmed him in that instant was admiration for the gesture with which she had thrown her clothes aside. With its grace and carelessness it seemed to annihilate a whole culture, a whole system of thought, as though Big Brother and the Party and the Thought Police

could all be swept into nothingness by a single splendid movement of the arm. That too was a gesture belonging to the ancient time. Winston woke up with the word 'Shakespeare'[2] on his lips.

(p. 28)

This dream, amongst other things, represents a foreknowledge of the meeting with Julia. Perhaps we have here Orwell's indication that the past controls the future. It would be safer for him to conclude that dreams create the future, therefore conscious dreams, like novels, have a special role and perhaps responsibility. The girl in the dream makes an obvious sexual gesture, but Winston does not desire her, neither in his dream nor when he actually meets Julia in the Golden Country (at least, not at first: he has to talk for an hour first – perhaps another clue to the importance of writing, language, and its relationship to sexuality). This beautiful body that can be looked at and not desired comes in a dream of his mother's death and her look of forgiveness. Which makes one suspect that the revealed body that must not be desired is in fact that of the mother; or that the dream is at first one of wish-fulfilment: if my mother desires, then sexual desire for her is possible, followed by a further wish-fulfilment in the appearance of a naked woman, and by the reappearance of the incest prohibition (Winston does not desire), a reappearance that allows the desire to continue precisely because it will not culminate, will never end, because it cannot be fulfilled. The sexual gesture made by the dream 'Julia' is one that would 'annihilate a culture'. Julia's later sexual revolutionism makes us read this in one particular way, as Orwell's advocacy of sexual liberation and identification of sexual repression with tyranny. As it turns out in the book, though, sex does not have the power to annihilate tyranny. The sexual threat of this gesture of the arm is not specific to Big Brother after all; it could annihilate any whole culture.

Let us read one passage again: 'all could be swept into nothingness by a single splendid movement of the arm. That too was a gesture from the ancient time.' And we cannot help recalling the other arm gestures, the ones that are protective (if futile) as opposed to this one which is destructive, but only potentially so, and then of all culture, not only of tyranny. We know that there is only one universal ('natural') prohibition in culture, and that is the prohibition of incest. So we can conclude that in *1984* we do indeed have a version of what Freud called the Oedipus complex in operation.

Winston has seen the convenient disappearance of his father; with a twist he seems to be responsible for the death of mother and sister (but is not really guilty of that, even though he has guilt dreams about something); he dreams of possessing his mother in the form of Julia (when he touches Julia her body is like water) but finds that he is a being of culture and cannot desire her in fact and so awakens to recover from the displaced guilt of the mistaken belief that he had killed her. He had only desired her too exclusively and too selfishly, with a desire, in being selfish, that does destroy cultures. He becomes somehow secretly intimate with a surrogate father-figure called either O'Brien or Big Brother, and seems oddly anxious to give in to this surrogate's power in order to be punished. His failure to escape the Oedipus complex is an index of his inability to save his culture.

What can we make of all this? We can conclude that Winston is a special case, and not take his plight too seriously, not take Orwell's nightmare vision of the totalitarian state seriously (which is not the same as not taking totalitarianism seriously, of course). We can conclude that Orwell's conscious purpose is undercut and exceeded by an unconscious one. We might even suspect that he was conscious enough of this unconscious purpose to leave the obvious (but unnoticed) inconsistencies in the book (although perhaps he did so unconsciously). The unconscious purpose demonstrates tellingly the way in which the family structures our relationship to the state and to political power.

One of the most distressing aspects of Oceania is one readily forgotten, one that is not much stressed by the narrative. The Party trains children to spy on parents. This just seems an unpleasant fact, but the dream analysis allows us to see it as a terrible perversion. If children are really led into betraying their parents, if they really act out the negative elements of the Oedipus complex, then they become willing victims of the state. They become willing participants, psychologically, in a state that disorients the past because they themselves, in dream, must disorient their own pasts in order to protect their psyches, or souls, from the truth. Even when the truth is restored to them in dreams they will of necessity misread it – and so doublethink will have been achieved naturally. They will, like Winston, have no real sexual drives and therefore no desire to create the future. They will seek surrogate parents in the state or in Big Brother figures. So all the complex apparatus of Oceania, all its repressive mechanisms, are laughable; they are satirically undercut by the unconscious of the novel, since all that is needed is the slightest push of a finger: just disorient a little the incest prohibition, or upset the natural-cultural order of children to parents, and everything else follows. Unconsciously, differentially, Orwell has once again demonstrated that guilt and its controls, the necessary discontents, are central to the building of human civilisation.

Now, let us take a quick look at the subject of sexuality in the text. If reading comfortably is not possible, perhaps we can contrive a process of unsettling, of desedimentation, of the ways in which the role of women and the nature of power have been written into *1984*. Probably the most unusual passage in the novel, the one that sticks in the memory in one way or another, is the following one. It is the summary comment on the significance of the lovemaking between Winston and Julia:

> In the old days, he thought, a man looked at a girl's body and saw that it was desirable, and that was the end of the story. But you could not have pure love or pure lust nowadays. No emotion was pure, because everything was mixed up with fear and hatred. Their embrace had been a battle, the climax a victory. It was a blow struck against the Party. It was a political act.
>
> (p. 104)

This passage seems a natural continuation of Winston's earlier thoughts: 'And what he wanted, more even than to be loved, was to break down that wall of virtue, even if it were only once in his whole life. The sexual act, successfully performed, was rebellion. Desire was thoughtcrime' (p. 58).

As we have seen, however, desire can hover between crime and fulfilment; can direct one's energies either into the past or into the future. The two quotations above, taken together, especially in our time (well, that is clearly out of date: our time is now the time during AIDS, and the sexual revolution is on hold waiting for a vaccine to herald another new age of liberation), are probably read by most people in a simple manner, a romantic manner: the state equals repression, which is bad, and sexuality equals freedom. We can raise doubts about this simplistic reading by noticing that Winston actually says that there is no pure love or lust left nowadays; fear and hatred, the political emotions, are part of things. Which suggests that, if we take him literally, his own loves and lusts are not pure, but his desires also are ideologically infected. So one can wonder if it is pure sexuality, or politicised sexuality, corrupted sexuality, that is rebellious. Or are we to think that it is only when pure sex has been corrupted by political emotions, only when it is willed as opposition, that it becomes rebellious? Which leads us to wonder if sex can ever be opposition if it is really fear and hatred that are the source of opposition.

That consideration leads us to read the description of their lovemaking more closely and to notice that it is not made up of either the look that used to suffice, or merely an embrace and a climax, but a battle and a victory. Which makes us think that Winston is deluded in his belief that the sex act is a political act of rebellion against the Party, because it is the Party that politicises all private life, and anyone who willingly allows political motives to drive his sexuality is already doing the Party's work for it. Which means that Winston, in his futile sexual affair, is opposing himself and not Big Brother. No wonder he is such an easy victim for O'Brien. Clearly the Party has some interest in sexuality as an important force that has to be controlled, since it conceives of 'pure' desire as thought-crime.

Julia, we are told, refers everything to her own sexuality, and so has a profounder insight into both sex and Party policy:

> Unlike Winston, she had grasped the inner meaning of the Party's sexual puritanism. It was not merely that the sex instinct created a world of its own which was outside the Party's control and which therefore had to be destroyed if possible. What was more important was that sexual privation induced hysteria, which was desirable because it could be transformed into war-fever and leader-worship.
>
> (p. 109)

At first sight this makes a kind of sense. Before trying to unsettle that sense, let us note that a casual slander on Julia is allowed to pass unnoticed here with the claim that introduces the passage: 'With Julia, everything came back to her own sexuality.' One suspects, rightly, that the narrator has the blindness of the male point of view. When O'Brien is apparently introducing them into the secret Brotherhood, the underground opposition group – and what is a sexual hedonist doing entering into a political conspiracy, after all? – he asks, '"You are prepared, the two of you, to separate and never see one another again?" "No!" broke in Julia.' Winston hesitates for ages before he uncertainly follows her lead and then also answers no. Clearly, she has formed the stronger attachment, is more capable of love and loyalty, at least at this point. Where then is her single-minded sexuality? Surely she could just dump Winston, and find an endless string of other lovers to satisfy her sexually.

Back to the analysis of hysteria. A second glance makes us wonder if in fact it is desirable for the Party to induce hysteria as a means of control. Hysteria is a condition of unpredictable wandering, a highly energised and dangerous condition. One wonders if a drugged and docile population wouldn't be easier to control. Let us hear more of Julia's analytic commentary:

> 'When you make love you're using up energy; and afterwards you feel happy and don't give a damn for anything. They can't bear you to feel like that. They want you to be bursting with energy all the time. All this marching up and down and cheering and waving flags is simply sex gone sour.'
>
> (Ibid.)

So now perhaps we understand what keeps protesters against nuclear arms, US foreign policy, or whatever, going: it is sexual deprivation. And we can do an easy survey amongst our fellow citizens, whenever their energy flags, give them some practical advice. What we might not be able to do is to explain where Don Juan, or Casanova, found the energy to carry on. Nevertheless, Winston is persuaded: 'That was very true he thought. There was a direct intimate connexion between chastity and political orthodoxy.' One might wonder, and want to ask Orwell about this, what the Romans, Pontius Pilate say, would have said about Christ's chastity? Winston's analysis continues, 'For how could the fear, the hatred, and the lunatic credulity which the Party needed in its members be kept at the right pitch, except by bottling down some powerful instinct and using it to account.' This claim too has a kind of validity, until one asks, if diverted sex energy is the driving force then won't political meetings have the same effect as sexual activity? Certainly the two-minutes-hate meetings are presented as exactly the inverse of two minutes of love. But, then, after hate, as after sex, the population should have the same lassitude and satisfaction, the same attitude of not giving a damn for anything. Hate, sexually driven, ought to have the same periodicity and the same political futility as pure sex.

In fact, we might begin to wonder if the Party itself has not intuited some kind of a problem. The Junior Anti-Sex League, to which Julia belongs, 'advocated complete celibacy for both sexes. All children were to be begotten by artificial insemination (artsem, it was called in Newspeak) and brought up in public institutions.' Winston does note that this idea is not 'meant altogether seriously', whatever that may mean. He goes on to add that 'The Party was trying to kill the sex instinct, or, if it could not be killed, then to distort it and dirty it' (p. 56). He adds further that this effort has been largely successful amongst women, and the lack of evidence of this in the book makes us believe once again that we may be in the hands of an author with an unusual view of human sexuality.

Winston's wife, Katharine, is perhaps Orwell's example of deadened and dirtied female sex, since we are told that to 'embrace her was like embracing a jointed wooden image'. She 'submits', we are told. But she cannot be submitting to Winston's importunate sex drive, since he tells us that 'he could have borne living with her if it had been agreed that they should remain celibate'. So she is not submitting to Winston – at least, not to his desire not to desire. Further:

> curiously enough it was Katharine who refused this. They must, she said, produce a child if they could. So the performance continued to happen, once a week quite regularly, whenever it was not impossible. She even used to remind him of it in the morning, as something which had to be done that evening and which must not be forgotten.
>
> (p. 57)

She refers to this performance either as 'making a baby' – a phrase that horrifies Winston for some reason – or as 'our duty to the Party'. I think we can suspect a feminine wile here, in her regular use of the phrase 'making a baby', unless we want to think of Katharine as well as Winston as totally ignorant of the periodicity of human conception. What can a woman do with such a man but try to trick him into living, and when she sees him obstinate give up and end it? How can we account for the strange contradiction in the fact that all conception is apparently supposed to be by means of artsem and yet Katharine reminds Winston daily of their duty to the Party? We may have an amusing inverse invocation of Walter Shandy and his monthly clock here; we certainly seem to be in the presence of another inconsistently rational and sexless male. Does

Katharine deliberately forget artsem and the facts about conception in order to stage her daily performance? Is she the missing sexual heroine and underground founder of the family and of the only true resistance to the state? (Enough of rhetorical questions: yes, I think she is.) Does Winston's rejection of her again mark him as not a sexual rebel at all, but a willing accomplice of the Party's policy of desexualisation?

Questions to which there can be no final answers. Our analysis has been hovering around the subject of power and we might hope a close consideration of power will clear up all the confusions we have been encountering. In fact we can construct a satisfying hypothesis that goes something like this. The novel wants to demonstrate that the lust for power is an absolute, an ultimate and therefore ultimately inexplicable desire. It is all-mastering, and irreducible to reason. Power is desired not for any reason, not for any end, not as a means. Power is desired for its own sake. In that sense it is like God, beyond reason. Since power lust is inexplicable, then it doesn't make sense to try to make sense of the ways in which the power-hungry seek to maintain their power. Such a commentary seems totally inadequate on the surface, and there are other, more satisfactory theoretical accounts of power.

If we could discover that the account of power in *1984* is itself inadequate, then we might be able to conclude that the novel does indeed fail to achieve its conscious intention. We can reach such a conviction, in fact, simply by denying that power can be treated as an absolute in human society. It turns out that selfishness is not the driving power of human society as we know it. Anthropologically speaking, human beings are successful for the same reasons as animals such as coyotes are successful: the sex drive is powerful, in the general sense. That is, people like to reproduce themselves. Which is to say that their deepest drives are directed towards the continuation of the species; or that in fact individual needs are overcome by the needs of the group. Our success now is a result of the selflessness of evolutionary forces. And, of course, we have to recognise that we live in paradox, and that our success in building societies is what gives us the technological mastery to destroy ourselves.

The conundrum of power as conceived by O'Brien can perhaps best be grasped by the image he gives of the future: 'a boot stamping on a human face – for ever'. Now, it is very difficult for O'Brien to avoid the master/slave paradox: that the master is bound to his slave; or that, for the boot to feel power, it is dependent on the existence of the face. This fact I want to interpret to mean that even power is not self-sufficient: in order to exist, power needs to be perceived. O'Brien himself makes this point indirectly: 'We control matter because we control the mind. Reality is inside the skull' (p. 212). In his period of acceptance, Winston begins to echo this 'truth': 'What knowledge have we of anything, save through our own minds? All happenings are in the mind. Whatever happens in all minds, truly happens.' O'Brien's final word on the matter is, 'Nothing exists except through human consciousness' (p. 213). Which of course means that power exists only through human consciousness. If power is a kind of God, then it requires the consciousness, as Winston indicates, of all human minds for it to 'truly happen'. 'We are the priests of power', says O'Brien. 'God is power' (p. 212). So it seems that, for God to exist, for God as power to exist (especially since he is an idea), he and it must be perceived.

If God is power, then we can comprehend that he had to create the world so as to be perceived. Which leads us to consider the logic of the Party's repressive methods. The Party is superior to Stalinist Russia, to Hitler, we are told, because it refuses to make martyrs. It requires rebellious individuals to become conscious of its power, and O'Brien is at the height of his voluptuous enjoyment when he can see Winston squirming in the agony of consciousness of O'Brien's power. The boot is never happier than when it is recognised as a boot by the face. Then, of course, when the individual freely submits to the Party, he is killed. The brain is to be made perfect before it is blown out. Which means that, with the elimination of the rebellious individual, the Party needs another one; it needs to create another dissident consciousness, in order to be able to put the boot in again and reaffirm the reality of its power by creating consciousness of power. So the Party itself is caught in a dangerous double game of having to survive by creating opposition to itself. No wonder it does not see the only logical way to perpetuate itself (by means of radicalising the Oedipal rebellion).

Which makes one wonder why the Party stops short of making martyrs. O'Brien notes that previous totalitarian regimes failed by making martyrs and so creating crystalline centres of opposition, and, since the Party cannot stand opposition, it will not make martyrs. Which contradicts the need of the Party to have opposition, or at least to have general consciousness of its power for it to exist. If the Party is never openly perceived as exercising its power, then it will not be perceived as having power. As Canetti[3] so tellingly shows, those in genuine human societies have power only because they are perceived as having the power of death over members of a society. In societies in which power is clearly recognised, there is a regular public demonstration of the power of the ruler by means of death (which could lead us to speculate on the return to capital punishment in the United States and its recently reaffirmed abolition in Canada). Hence the importance of capturing enemies and bringing them back to the home village before slaughtering them. So, it turns out that perhaps O'Brien, while he is a better metaphysician than Winston, is not in fact the best metaphysician, or at least not the most astute analyst of the real nature of power. Which of course makes us think again that perhaps Orwell's novel is not at all a prophecy or a warning, but a challenge: a challenge to our reading ability; a challenge to become a better metaphysician than O'Brien; a challenge to question O'Brien's claim that all reality is in the mind, or that all reality is available in the form of knowledge.

We have already said that our knowledge of the book is for ever uncertain, since it takes us into the realm of the unconscious, or dreams, where we have as our guide only the uncertainty of interpretation, which is always going to be organised around a kind of blindness. And we have perhaps only this much knowledge: that what we know is likely, as is the case in this book, to be undermined by what we have called the unconscious. Which is to say that reality is perhaps that part of us which we precisely cannot know. At the end of his life, we think we see Winston as simply defeated. In fact, he seems to come close to developing a Derridean possibility, that of keeping a mental reserve, a residue.

> He set to work to exercise himself in crimestop. He presented himself with propositions – 'the Party says the earth is flat', 'the Party says that ice is heavier than water' – and trained himself in not seeing or not understanding the arguments that contradicted them. It was not easy. It needed great powers of reasoning and improvisation.
>
> (p. 224)

He learns how to repress all indications of rebellion and plans to become the apparently perfectly willing victim. In fact, however, he is creatively practising doublethink; he is consciously indulging in repression and this skill has its inverse positive side:

> For the first time he perceived that if you want to keep a secret you must also hide it from yourself. You must know all the while that it is there, but until it is needed you must never let it emerge into your consciousness in any shape that could be given a name. From now onwards he must not only think right; he must feel right, dream right. And all the while he must keep his hatred locked up inside himself like a ball of matter which was part of himself and yet unconnected with the rest of him, a kind of cyst. One day they would decide to shoot him. You could not tell when it would happen, but a few seconds beforehand it should be possible to guess. It was always from behind, walking down a corridor. Ten seconds would be enough. In that time the world inside him could turn over. And then suddenly, without a word uttered, without a check in his step, without the changing of a line in his face – suddenly the camouflage would be down and bang! would go the batteries of his hatred. ... They would have blown his brain to pieces before they could reclaim it. The heretical thought would be unpunished, unrepented, out of their reach for ever. They would have blown a hole in their own perfection. To die hating them, that was freedom.
>
> (p. 226)

What he is aiming for is one instantaneous act of rebellious rejection at the moment of death, at the instant that the bullet crashes into the skull. He knows he must not know anything contrary to Party wishes; just as he knows that he does still think in opposition, and can do that precisely by forgetting his knowledge, only to recover it at the instant of death. By facing death so directly, and by using the strategies of deconstructive doublethink, Winston makes an unstated claim to being a better metaphysician (by not being one) than O'Brien. But this resolution is made before Room 101, and we must assume that when he is waiting at the end of the novel he no longer has this inner capacity for resistance. But that is not surprising. What we have been arguing is that resistance is a quality of the mind, and if the mind is destroyed then there can be no further resistance.

Perhaps *1984* is a good novel in spite of itself – in spite of its 'flaws' and in spite of its obvious claims to meaning and the standard readings. If this is true, however, it means that reading is best described as resistance to the text, just as writing itself is a matter of resisting a given text in the act of writing another. If asked whether reading and writing are coherently complementary activities, we would have to say yes, in that they are mutually resistant; or that their self-identity is their *différance*.

From Alan Kennedy, *Reading, Resistance, Value* (London, 1990), pp. 129–48.

NOTES

[Alan Kennedy applies a deconstructive reading of *1984* whereby he explores the aporias and inconsistencies within the relation of meaning to textual form. He chooses to examine how deconstructive criticism that focuses on the acts of reading and writing may be a form of resistance to texts. Kennedy exemplifies his ideas through a specific reading of Winston's diary-writing and the dream sequences in *1984* and he proposes a number of links between the Oedipus complex, and the imperative of sexual desires and freedom, and Big Brother's powers within the mechanisms of totalitarianism. Eds]

1. George Orwell, *1984* (Harmondsworth, 1954). References will be given parenthetically in the text.

2. Possibly Orwell intends the reference to Shakespeare here to be a deliberate warning to the reader against an unresistant literary reading of the text, since Winston's reaction seems so absurdly inappropriate.

3. Elias Canetti, *Crowds and Power* (Harmondsworth, 1981).

6

Character, Progression, and Thematism in *1984*

JAMES PHELAN

What Murray Sperber said in 1980 about the criticism of *1984* remains true today: despite all the attention Orwell's novel has received, its detailed structure has yet to be sufficiently analysed.[1] For this reason, my account of the progression will be fairly detailed. One of the striking features of that progression is that after Orwell introduces the first major instability in Chapter 1 – Winston's thoughtcrime, his beginning his diary – he does not significantly complicate that instability until the eighth and last chapter of Book One, when Winston returns to Mr Charrington's shop, the place where he bought the diary. This feature is made all the more striking because, with the exception of the segments given over to *the book* of the brotherhood, the remainder of the narrative rather tightly follows the line begun with that crime and continued with Winston's developing relationships with Julia and O'Brien. Analysing how the narrative progresses in Book One will also illuminate the relationship between Winston's mimetic and thematic functions.

Apart from the introduction of the first instability, the narrative in the first book progresses largely by the introduction and partial resolution of a significant tension. 'It was a bright, cold day in April and the clocks were striking thirteen.'[2] This first sentence creates a gap between the narrative audience that already knows the year of the action and is already familiar with clocks striking thirteen and the authorial audience for whom these facts are either unknown or unfamiliar. Mark Crispin Miller's discussion of this first sentence[3] points to the significance of April in the British literary tradition from Chaucer to Eliot, a significance which further emphasises the peculiarity of the weather for the season. Since the authorial audience would be presumed to know that tradition while the narrative audience, located in time after the Party's alteration of the past, would not, the mention of April further emphasises the gap between the two audiences. This gap also signals a tension of unequal knowledge between author and authorial audience: he and his narrator surrogate know all about this world but plunge into the narrative without orienting us. The tension is heightened as the first few paragraphs work in this gap between narrative and authorial audiences and make references to a poster of someone called Big Brother; a preparation for something called Hate Week; a telescreen; INGSOC; Thought Police; the Ninth Three-Year Plan; and the Ministry of Truth. Our reading is driven in part by a desire to reduce this tension.

Of course the experience of beginning a narrative and being asked to read as if we shared knowledge that we do not actually possess is a common one. Such an experience does, I think, always produce a mild tension, but that tension is often quickly resolved. My claim about 1984 is that the initial defamiliarisations emphasise the tension (the difference between it and other narratives that carry the illusion of occurring in our world is a matter of degree) and that this tension is not – indeed cannot be – quickly resolved. It functions to propel us forward in the narrative, but because of other signals we are given about Winston as a mimetic character, it orients us toward the acquisition of information that will influence our judgements, expectations, desires, and attitudes about the characters and the instabilities they face. In general, cognitive tension functions in this way in narratives with a strong mimetic component. In narratives like the classic detective story, where the mimetic component is restricted, cognitive tension can be the primary source of the progression. (Of course in such narratives, the cognitive tension does not manifest itself in a gap between authorial and narrative audiences but between both of them and the author.) Ethical tension is typically a sign that the narrative has a strong mimetic component; it is itself one mechanism through which authors induce readers to form judgements, set up expectations, develop desires, adopt attitudes, and so on.

After introducing the major instability of Winston's thoughtcrime (an incident to which I shall return), Orwell's narrative progresses by reducing the tension: rather than immediately showing how the first thoughtcrime leads Winston into a related series of actions, Orwell shows us Winston going about his business in his world, occasionally punctuating the accompanying disclosures about that world by returning to scenes of Winston writing in his diary. By the end of Book One, Orwell has reduced much – though not all – of the tension and simultaneously complicated our understanding of the major instability. In addition, through his references to Julia and O'Brien he has laid the groundwork for further development of the instability.

One of the major ways in which the progression by tension complicates the initial instability is to affect our expectations about Winston's success in eluding the Thought Police. By the end of Book One, we certainly still hope that he will, but we have strong reason to think that he will not. In addition, through maintaining the technique of the opening paragraphs and through representing Winston in numerous contexts, Orwell has also revealed most of Winston's major attributes. The narrative then returns to the progression by instability.

More specifically, before Book One is over, Orwell shows us Winston with his neighbours, Mrs Parsons and her rabid children; Winston submitting to the morning exercises (Physical Jerks) beamed over the telescreen; Winston working at the Ministry of Truth, where his job is to alter records, especially those contained in newspapers; Winston undergoing the trials of eating lunch in the Ministry's cafeteria; Winston reflecting on the Party's control of the past through its handling of the counter-revolutionaries Jones, Aaronson, and Rutherford; Winston roaming about the proles' quarter of the city until he once again finds himself in Charrington's shop. Through these various scenes Winston frequently reflects on the social and political organisation of his world as it impinges on – or indeed, determines and controls – the particular activity he is engaged in; occasionally, Orwell gives us Winston's thoughts about incidents in his own past life such as his vague memory of his mother sacrificing herself for him, and his unhappy marriage to Katherine, who despised sex but thought of procreation as their duty to the Party.

The world revealed through these scenes and incidents is a curious mixture of efficiency and inefficiency, a world with sophisticated technology and a poor standard of living. Telescreens can both transmit and receive, and individuals can be watched vigilantly by the Thought Police, but elevators frequently don't work and food is barely palatable. Winston can rewrite newspaper articles and the historical record can be swiftly altered, but the streets don't get cleaned, and decent medical care for such things as Winston's varicose ulcer seems to be non-existent. Above all, Oceania in 1984 is a world dominated by the Party and the social structure it has imposed on the province. The basic principle of this structure, we soon learn, is state control over the individual. The relatively poor standard of living signifies both one way of exerting control – it keeps the Party members extremely dependent – and one way the system is execrable.

The telescreens, the enforced Physical Jerks, the ubiquity of Big Brother, the ritual of the Three Minutes Hate, the existence of the Spies and the Thought Police, the creation of Newspeak, the abolition of written laws without the abolition of punishments: all these Party innovations testify to its elaborate – and largely successful – efforts to control the lives of its members. Mrs Parsons's fanatically loyal children terrorise her. Winston's thought that his friend Syme, a dedicated worker on the new edition of the Newspeak dictionary, will be vaporised simply because he understands the intended effects of the impoverished language points to the truth that, ironically, Syme has himself articulated: 'Orthodoxy is unconsciousness.' Winston's memories of his mother and his wife indicate how the Party has destroyed the most intimate relationships: Winston thinks that the kind of sacrifice his mother made 'had been tragic and sorrowful in a way that was no longer possible. Tragedy, he perceived, belonged to the ancient time, to a time when there were still privacy, love, and friendship, and when the members of a family stood by one another without needing to know the reason. … Today there were fear, hatred, and pain, but no dignity of emotion, no deep or complex sorrows' (p. 22). He was not able to develop any deep emotions in his own marriage because Katherine had been so unconsciously orthodox that she could not experience such emotions. Finally, Winston's excursion among the proles illustrates how the Party keeps them occupied with work on the one hand and bread and circuses on the other.

The extent – and success – of the Party's control is sketched more fully in the information about Winston's job, in his remembrance of what happened to Jones, Aaronson, and Rutherford, and in his attempt to find somebody who can remember the time before the Party was in power. As we see Winston at work, we see how the

Party controls history. Winston's remembrance of the three counter-revolutionaries dramatises the consequences of that effort: to control history is to control reality. Although Winston's photograph of the three counter-revolutionaries is concrete evidence that the official version of their history is false, he could not do anything public with that evidence. Furthermore, thinking back to his brief possession of the photograph, Winston muses that the 'photograph might not even be evidence'. Finally, the impossibility of recapturing history is dramatised in Winston's futile attempt to get the old prole to answer his questions about the past.

By the end of Book One, our knowledge of Winston's world is not complete, but the tension between Orwell and the authorial audience is greatly diminished: we know the kind of world we are reading about, and this knowledge has significant consequences for our understanding of the initial major instability and of Winston's character. We come to understand that to begin the diary is to rebel against the Party, not merely because the diary contains exclamations like 'DOWN WITH BIG BROTHER!' but also because the act of writing is an act of individual consciousness and autonomy. Simply by sitting down to write, indeed, by contemplating that act, Winston is guilty of thoughtcrime; he is asserting his selfhood against the Party, which wants to deny that selfhood. The central issues of the whole narrative are gradually defined in the course of Book One: can Winston elude the Thought Police and go on writing the diary, and more important, can he have any sustained existence *as an individual* in this totalitarian society? As the form of the second question indicates, the progression of Book One leads us to read Winston thematically: he comes to represent the individual citizen, and what he does and what happens to him matters to us because of what these things imply about the possibility of individual freedom in totalitarian society. This movement of Book One gives thematic prominence to certain of Winston's attributes, even as Orwell's handling of the point of view emphasises his mimetic function.

By the end of Book One, the most salient attributes of Winston's character to emerge are his name, his age, his habit of thinking by subconscious association, his intelligence, his concern with the past, his love of beauty, his hatred of the Party, and his optimism; furthermore, though Winston is distinguished from his associates by his intelligence and his resistance to the Party, he is not given any great powers of action – he is a man more ordinary than extraordinary. The first chapter of the novel, indeed its first three paragraphs, establish Winston's name and age – and as noted above in a somewhat different way, they immediately signal to the authorial audience that his world, despite its similarities to our own, is a synthetic construct. Our awareness of the fictionality of the world naturally brings the synthetic component of Winston's character into the foreground of the narrative. This foregrounding combines with other aspects of Orwell's presentation to emphasise some of Winston's thematic dimensions. When we learn in the sixth paragraph that he lives in London, and when the later progression encourages us to regard him thematically, his name and age take on further associations. Combining the extremely common British surname with the first name of England's greatest hero of the 1940s identifies him as what a typical male British citizen of 1984 would be – if there were still a Britain. Since he is thirty-nine, he was born in 1945, and, we can infer, was named for Churchill. The last name, though, emphasises his ordinariness: this is not Winston Churchill, but Winston Smith. I shall return to the significance of this point after discussing the way Orwell handles the conclusion of the narrative.

Later in the narrative, after Orwell reveals how the Party is destroying the past, and especially after Winston becomes involved with Julia, his age takes on a thematic significance that further defines his representative status. His conversations with Julia indicate that the next generation simply cannot envision life without the Party. Having grown up with the Party as a fact of life, Julia takes it so much for granted that it constrains her ideas of rebellion; until she meets Winston, her goal in life is to manipulate the Party's system rather than overthrow it. She, for instance, pretends to be a rabid member of the Junior Anti-Sex League so that she can have a cover for her various sexual liaisons. Winston, in contrast, with his dim memories of life before the Party, can envision life without it. His response is to do whatever he can – keep his diary, get involved with Julia, attempt to join the Brotherhood – to resist the Party's repression of individuals. His optimism allows him to hope that such resistance may eventually lead to the Party's overthrow, even as his intelligence reminds him that such an outcome is unlikely. This disparity between Winston and Julia clearly marks him off as a member of the last group of citizens to remember life without the Party, the last group that could use that connection to the past as a motive for rebellion. 'Who controls the past controls the future.' As the narrative progresses, Winston's name and age combine to make him a figure of 'the last man in Europe', a phrase that Orwell considered using as the book's title.[4] Consequently, the stakes of the instabilities are raised: Winston's story is not just an exemplary case of what happens when the individual rebels against the totalitarian state but also an account of how the Party responds to one of its last apparently serious threats.

Despite the elements of the opening chapter that foreground its synthetic status, and despite the movement of Book One that places Winston's actions into a broad thematic context, Orwell's initial treatment of Winston himself is directed toward emphasising his mimetic function. Orwell's own statement about the book aptly describes the effect of the opening pages: 'it is in a sense a fantasy but in the form of a naturalistic novel'.[5] Orwell relies greatly upon the manipulation of point of view to establish Winston's mimetic function. Winston is consistently the focaliser in the narration; we see things as Winston sees them, though frequently the voice used to express Winston's vision is the narrator's.[6] 'Outside, even through the shut window pane, the world looked cold. Down in the street, little eddies of wind were whirling dust and torn papers into spirals' (pp. 3–4). It is Winston who is up at his window looking 'down' at the 'little eddies of wind', but it is the narrator who describes the wind in those terms. In addition to emphasising the mimetic function of Winston's character, this technique has other important effects in the progression, but these can be better understood after we look at the progression in Book Two.

At the end of Book One when Winston returns to Mr Charrington's shop, Orwell begins to shift the main principle of movement from the resolution of tension to the complication of instabilities. Winston builds on his initial 'crime' of buying the diary by buying the hundred-year-old glass paperweight, and he begins to think about returning again and again to the shop, even about renting the upstairs room. Book Two opens with Julia's approach to him, and soon they are in love with each other and united against the Party. In addition, O'Brien makes his approach to Winston, and the lovers soon join the Brotherhood. Meanwhile Winston rents Charrington's upstairs room, and he and Julia begin meeting there. With each step, the magnitude of their rebellion and the exercise of their individual freedom (one equals the other) increase, and so of course does the danger that they will be captured. 'We are the dead', they remind themselves without fully believing what they are saying. Having established the overarching thematic background in Book One, Orwell here designs the trajectory of the main action around our mimetic interest in Winston and his struggle. And as Orwell confines us to Winston's vision through the point of view, he has us participate in the trajectory of Winston's own emotions in the main action: Like Winston, we not only take pleasure in his relationship with Julia and in his finding an apparently kindred spirit in O'Brien, but we also come to desire deeply the total overthrow of the Party.

At the same time, from the information in Book One about the power of the Party, we develop a strong sense that this positive outcome is not possible. When Winston and Julia are arrested by the Thought Police, we share his feeling that such an event was inevitable, but our knowledge offers no solace for the disappointment we feel. Moreover, even the appropriate surprise of discovering Mr Charrington to be a member of the Thought Police does not fully prepare us for the new developments of the progression in Book Three, developments that are dependent in large part on Orwell's management of the point of view and that in turn contribute to the emphasis on Winston's mimetic function. Book Three resolves the instabilities by tracing the conversion of Winston's rebellion into his total defeat. Although such a resolution has been implicit in the narrative from early on, Orwell is able to maximise its power by suddenly showing us that the tension between his knowledge of the world and ours has not been resolved as fully as we thought. In consistently restricting us to Winston's vision, Orwell does not give his own authority to Winston's conclusions about the world; we need to recognise that those conclusions are always subject to later revision. In fact, it is because he handles the technique this way that Orwell can legitimately 'surprise' us with the truth about Charrington and O'Brien. At the same time, Orwell counts on our erroneously accepting some of Winston's conclusions. For example, in Chapter Two Orwell depicts Winston thinking about the ubiquity of Big Brother: 'Even from the coin the eyes pursued you. On coins, on stamps, on the covers of books, on banners, on posters, and on the wrapping of a cigarette packet – everywhere. Always the eyes watching you and the voice enveloping you. Asleep or awake, working or eating, indoors or out of doors, in the bath or in bed – no escape. Nothing was your own except the few cubic centimetres inside your skull' (pp. 19–20). Although we are still clearly being given only Winston's vision here, we are inclined to share it and Orwell does nothing to alter that inclination. The inviolability of one's mind is one of the supposed truths of our world, Winston's thoughtcrime has not yet brought down any punishment on him, and the rhetoric of the passage makes the final sentence a mere concession. We are being told by both Winston and Orwell about the limited freedom the individual has; we accept what we are told, including what the passage regards as the single small exception. Although the rest of Book One tells us a great deal about Winston's world and about the power of the Party, it is not until the very end of the narrative that we learn that even those few cubic centimetres are not one's own. Indeed, the Party's power extends far enough to control not only what one does, not only what one thinks, but also what one feels.

I shall return to discuss the resolution in some detail but even here we can recognise some important effects of the delayed resolution of the tension. In relieving so much of the tension in Book One, Orwell gives us the illusion that we know the worst. When we learn that even our extensive knowledge of the Party's mechanisms of control has underestimated its power, our revulsion from such a totalitarian state becomes even greater – and so too does the effectiveness of the narrative as a warning. In this way the tension is crucial to the mimetic (and emotional) effect of the ending, which in turn Orwell uses to reinforce the thematic point about the threat of totalitarianism.

In general, Orwell's handling of Winston's character follows the pattern outlined here: he emphasises Winston's mimetic function, increases our involvement with his progression toward his fate as itself an emotionally affecting experience,[7] and then ultimately subordinates that function and our involvement to his communication of a larger thematic point. The relation between the mimetic and the thematic is fairly clear for such attributes as Winston's concern with the past and his love of beauty;[8] perhaps the least obvious and most dramatic illustration of the general pattern occurs in what Orwell does with Winston's attribute of associative thinking, which is itself a significant part of his psychological portrait. Here Orwell immediately establishes this attribute as a significant mimetic trait, but he does not develop its full thematic significance until the final pages of the narrative.

Winston's attribute of associative thinking is established simultaneously with the introduction of the first major instability. Winston's first diary entry describes his trip to the 'flicks' the previous night. During the war films, which were depicting various people being shot or hit with bombs or otherwise violently obliterated to the great approval of most spectators, one proletarian started shouting her objections to the film. Winston breaks off his account after saying that the police turned her out; then we are told, 'He did not know what had made him pour out this stream of rubbish. But the curious thing was that while he was doing so a totally different memory had clarified itself in his mind' (p. 8). That memory turns out to be a look from O'Brien during that morning's Two Minutes Hate, a look that Winston interprets as a signal that O'Brien is on his side. Winston never figures out the connection between the two events, but Orwell expects his audience to recognise that the scene at the flicks clarifies the scene during the Two Minutes Hate because in each an individual acts in opposition to the hysterical mob surrounding him or her. Orwell never does anything else with Winston's instinctive connection between the two events; and consequently, the association becomes significant largely for the way it adds a psychological complexity to Winston's character. Furthermore, at this stage of the narrative, this important attribute does not have any thematic function.

As the narrative develops, Orwell places this attribute in a rather complex relationship with Winston's optimism. When Winston begins his diary, he tells himself that he is thereby making himself one of the dead; but as I noted above, this admission does not become a conviction until he is actually captured. Instead, he goes on with his acts of rebellion, becoming more and more hopeful about the possibility of eventual success with each passing day. Yet Orwell shows us, through Winston's habits of associative thought, that in another part of himself Winston senses that his optimism is based upon a denial of certain perceptions. In Chapter 7 of Book One, for example, Winston gazes at a portrait of Big Brother which forms the frontispiece of a children's history textbook: 'The hypnotic eyes gazed into his own. It was as though some huge force were pressing down upon you – something that penetrated inside your skull, battering against your brain, frightening you out of your beliefs, persuading you, almost, to deny the evidence of your senses' (p. 55). Then he consciously resists these conclusions as his optimism gains the upper hand: 'But no! His courage seemed suddenly to stiffen of its own accord.' And then: 'The face of O'Brien, not called up by any obvious association had floated into his mind' (p. 55). Although the vision of O'Brien comes hard upon the heels of his renewed courage, the narrator's comment about the absence of any obvious association directs the audience to supply that association: Winston subconsciously links O'Brien and Big Brother.

In case we have lingering doubts, Orwell shows us at the end of the next chapter that the association can also move in the other direction: Trying to think of O'Brien, whom he now regards as the eventual audience for his diary, Winston focuses on the memory of O'Brien's saying in a dream, 'We shall meet in the place where there is no darkness.' The nagging presence of the telescreen interferes with his thoughts, and then 'The face of Big Brother swam into his mind, displacing that of O'Brien' (p. 70). This reinforced association of the two occurs in the last paragraph of Book One, and thus provides an ominous backdrop to the apparently positive developments of Book Two. Again, though, the general point is that Orwell is using the attributes to increase the psychological realism of his treatment of Winston and thereby to increase the extent of our emotional involvement in his unfolding story.

Before I turn to how Orwell makes the attribute of associative thinking function thematically, I need to expand on my earlier assertion that this attribute is part of Orwell's attempt to create a realistic individual psychology for Winston – even as Orwell leaves it to us to piece together the workings of that psychology. Recall Winston's initial thought after breaking off his first diary entry: 'He did not know what had made him pour out this stream of rubbish' (p. 8). Later in the narrative Orwell supplies us with the answer: in recounting the scenes where the mother in the movie vainly tries to protect her child who burrows into her and where the proletarian mother in turn tries to protect her children from having to watch such a movie, Winston is recalling his own mother's attempts to protect his sister – and more generally himself as well. The first time he sleeps after beginning the diary, he dreams of watching his mother and sister sink in the bottom of a ship while he is able to stay up and out in the light; later, when Julia brings chocolate to their first tryst, it stirs up 'some memory which he could not pin down, but which was powerful and troubling' (p. 81). Still later, during one of his visits to the room above Charrington's shop with Julia, he dreams of his mother again and this dream allows him to pin down the earlier memory: it is a memory of the last time he saw his mother, and how on that occasion his own ravenous hunger drove him to take for himself his sister's lesser share of chocolate.

What is most vivid in the memory is how Winston's mother embraced and tried to protect his sister, and how even after he snatched her chocolate, his mother went on trying to protect and comfort her. Winston draws a very significant moral at that point: 'he did not suppose, from what he could remember of [his mother], that she had been an unusual woman, still less an intelligent one; and yet she had possessed a kind of nobility, a kind of purity, simply because the standards that she obeyed were private ones. Her feelings were her own, and could not be altered from outside. ... If you love someone, you loved him, and when you had nothing else to give, you still gave him love. ... The terrible thing that the Party had done was to persuade you that mere impulses, mere feeling were of no account, while at the same time robbing you of all power over the material world' (pp. 109–10).

Yet the significance of Winston's dreams and memory for the narrative are not exhausted in this moral, because they reach beyond these insights to affect our understanding of what happens in Book Three.[9] The whole sequence – journal entry, dream, dim memory, second dream, clear memory – works like the associative thought processes to emphasise Winston's realistic psychology. The particular nature of the dreams and memories adds a significant dimension to our understanding of how and why Winston's betrayal of Julia breaks him. When, faced with imminent attack from the ravenous rats, Winston shouts 'Do it to Julia!' he violates something at the core of his values because it is at the core of his own existence: the feeling that he is alive because the woman who brought him into the world and loved him had sacrificed herself for him. Both the power and the repulsiveness of the Party are emphasised by our understanding that Winston had no choice but to act as he did.

The ending of the narrative then takes these attributes of Winston's character that have been working to emphasise his mimetic function and converts them into thematic functions. In the last chapter, Winston has become a figure reminiscent of Jones, Aaronson, and Rutherford. In Chapter 7 of Book One, Orwell describes Winston's recollection of the day he saw the three of them in the Chestnut Tree Café.

> It was the lonely hour of fifteen. ... The place was almost empty. A tinny music was trickling from the telescreen. The three men sat in their corner almost motionless, never speaking. Uncommanded, the waiter brought fresh glasses of gin. There was a chessboard on the

table beside them, with the pieces set out, but no game started. And then, for perhaps half a minute in all, something happened to the telescreens. The tune that they were playing changed, and the tone of the music changed too. There came into it – but it was something hard to describe. It was a peculiar, cracked, braying, jeering note; in his mind Winston called it a yellow note. And then a voice from the telescreen was singing:

'Under the spreading chestnut tree
I sold you and you sold me
There lie they, and here lie we
Under the spreading chestnut tree.'

The three men never stirred. But when Winston glanced again at Rutherford's ruinous face, he saw that his eyes were full of tears. And for the first time he noticed, with a kind of inward shudder, and yet not knowing *at what* he shuddered, that both Aaronson and Rutherford had broken noses.

(pp. 52–3)

In the last chapter, Winston sits in the same café, and again it is almost empty at 'the lonely hour of fifteen'. From time to time, an 'unbidden' waiter comes and fills Winston's glass with gin, which has become 'the element he swam in', while he fitfully plays a solitary game of chess and listens to the telescreen. He recalls his last, cold, painful visit with Julia, a visit in which they confessed that they had betrayed each other. And then:

Something changed in the music that trickled from the telescreen. A cracked and jeering note, a yellow note, came into it. And then – perhaps it was not happening, perhaps it was only a memory taking on the semblance of sound – a voice was singing:

'Under the spreading chestnut tree
I sold you and you sold me –'

The tears welled up in his eyes.

(p. 195)

The expected inferences are clear: the song is the Party's way of mocking Winston for betraying Julia, just as it had been mocking Jones, Aaronson, and Rutherford for their own versions of mutual betrayal. More generally, what has happened to Winston in the Ministry of Love is just a variation on what always happens to thought-criminals. Winston has come to represent the inevitable failure of the individual to resist the totalitarian state.

Nevertheless, at this point the instabilities created by Winston's rebellion and the Party's response to it are not entirely resolved: the tears are a sign that he is still attached to his former attitudes, that he regrets his betrayal of Julia. If he were to die now, he would die hating Big Brother – and thus, by his own earlier definition, achieve some measure of victory. Orwell works toward the resolution of the instability by following the progress of Winston's thoughts.

First, he gives us one more instance of Winston's associative thought process. Winston's thoughts of the alleged war in Africa – 'He had the map of Africa behind his eyelids. The movement of the armies was a diagram: a black arrow tearing vertically southward, and a white arrow tearing horizontally eastward, across the tail of the first' (pp. 195–6) – trigger a subconscious association with a childhood memory. He thinks of an afternoon spent playing with his mother a game called Snakes and Ladders, a game in which the tiddlywinks move vertically and horizontally. 'Soon he was wildly excited and shouting with laughter as the tiddlywinks climbed hopefully up the ladders and then came slithering down again. ... His tiny sister, too young to understand what the game was about, had sat propped up against a bolster, laughing because the others were laughing. For a whole afternoon they had all been happy to- gether, as in his earlier childhood.' Then Winston's training at the Ministry of Love takes over: 'He pushed the picture out of his mind. It was a false memory' (p. 196).

This reaction to the memory is sharply different from Winston's reactions to his previous memories. As we have seen, those lead him to reflect on the Party's elimination of the human bonds that develop in a social order that allows privacy, friendship, and love. His pushing the memory away signifies a very crucial step in his defeat: under the pressure of his training, he is betraying not only his own prior belief in the integrity of the past but also the bonds that were part of his early private life and part of his identity. His rejection of the memory is also crucial because it represents his own conscious attempt to control his subconscious. In presenting the memory, Orwell is reminding us that Winston's mind has worked in ways that were beyond his control. In presenting Winston's first memory of a happy time during this afternoon of his own dull unhappiness, Orwell is showing us again the power of Winston's subconscious. But when Winston reacts by denying the validity of the memory, his defeat is all but complete.

The final steps come with the telescreen's announcement of Oceania's victory in Africa. In representing Winston's response here, Orwell indicates that Winston's memory is not so easily pushed away; instead, it is perversely transformed and applied to Winston's present situation. Wildly excited in memory, he becomes wildly excited in the present: 'in his mind he was running, swiftly running, he was with the crowds outside cheering himself deaf' (p. 197). Happy and content in memory, no longer at odds with his mother and sister, he becomes happy and content in the present, no longer at odds with the Party:[10]

> Ah, it was more than a Eurasian army that had perished! Much had changed in him since that first day in the Ministry of Love, but the final indispensable, healing change had never happened until this moment ... sitting in a blissful dream, he was back in the Ministry of Love, with everything forgiven, his soul white as snow. He was in the public dock, confessing everything, implicating everybody. He was walking down the white-tiled corridor, with the feeling of walking in sunlight, and an armed guard at his back. The long-hoped-for bullet was entering his brain.
>
> (p. 197)

He is ready for the last step of his transformation, the final perverse twist the Party's training produces on his specific memory and his general consciousness.

> He gazed up at the enormous face. Forty years it had taken him to learn what kind of smile was hidden beneath the dark moustache. O cruel, needless misunderstanding! O stubborn, self-willed exile from the loving breast! ... But it was all right, everything was all right, the struggle was finished. He had won the victory over himself. He loved Big Brother.
>
> (p. 197)

This passage appropriately closes and completes the narrative because it not only signals the end of Winston's rebellion but also indicates the extent of the Party's ability to control the individual. It is able to manipulate not just behaviour, not just thoughts, but also emotions. It is even able to control the workings of the subconscious mind. In achieving this completion, the narrative transforms the thematic dimension accompanying Winston's trait of associative thinking into a major thematic function. That trait now exists not only to give Winston mimetic plausibility but also to demonstrate the extent of the totalitarian state's power. If it can effect such a transformation in a mind like Winston's that frequently operated in a way that was beyond his own conscious control, its power is enormous indeed. The narrative's warning about totalitarianism becomes even more urgent.

Orwell's handling of vision and voice in the final pages sheds further light on the relation between the mimetic and the thematic functions of Winston's character there. Previously, as the narrative has presented the world of 1984 through Winston's vision, the authorial audience has been asked to share virtually all of Winston's evaluative comments. Here for the first time, our evaluations are diametrically opposed to his. Indeed, since we have been travelling with Winston so closely throughout the narrative, if Orwell had not been so insistent on the state's control over the individual, we ourselves might have felt betrayed by Winston in this passage. Even within the final passage Orwell takes steps to block that response. In the sentence represented by the ellipsis above, the narrator leaves Winston's vision and describes him from the outside: 'Two gin-scented tears trickled down the sides of his nose' (p. 197). The outside view provides a comment on his internal elation; we see him not as triumphant but as pathetic. The emotions generated by our vision work to support our own opposition to the totalitarian system that reduced Winston to this state. Again, in short, Orwell develops the mimetic response and then subordinates it to his thematic purpose.

This reading of the ending and the way it affects both the previous mimetic characterisation of Winston and the indictment of totalitarianism suggest a further conclusion about Orwell's use of mimetic and thematic elements of Winston's character. At first glance, it may seem surprising that Orwell does not make Winston a man with greater powers of action. If he is to be a figure of the last man in Europe who succumbs to the power of the state, and if his losing struggle is to be as tragic as possible, then, we might argue, Orwell ought to have made him more formidable. Although I believe that such a strategy might have also been effective, I think that Orwell was constructing the narrative along different lines – and toward a different kind of effectiveness. For Orwell the greater power of the totalitarian state is finally a foregone conclusion. He builds some suspense about whether Winston can succeed in his rebellion by restricting us to Winston's point of view for most of the narrative and by not fully resolving the tension about the nature of the totalitarian state until

Book Three, but the greater emphasis in the narrative is on what the state does to the individual, common man. In this respect, Winston's mental life is of more significance than his powers of action. By showing us what the state does to an individual with such a mental life, an individual who finally is not a serious threat to the Party, Orwell places the burden of his indictment precisely on the dangers that the totalitarian state poses for Everyman.

In conclusion, the narrative progression of *1984* eventually gives the greatest weight to the thematic functions of Winston Smith's character, but the effects of those functions also depend crucially on Orwell's ability to make Winston function as an effective mimetic character. At the same time, the progression develops different thematic functions from different attributes: his age and his ordinariness make him a certain kind of representative figure; his love for the past is used to develop the thematic point about the connection between the Party's control of the individual and the Party's control of history; his associative thinking is used to develop the thematic point about the Party's control over the thoughts and feelings of the individual. Moreover, all these separate functions work together as part of the narrative's exploration of the threat of totalitarianism. In this respect, we might say that the separate functions eventually run together in a Grand Central Function as Winston becomes the embodiment of individual actions and desires that the totalitarian state seeks to crush. The narrative of *1984*, in other words, presents one form that the mimetic-thematic relationship can take. More generally, it presents one remarkable example of how one component of character can be subordinated to another without that subordination restricting the component, for Orwell can only communicate the full thematic significance of Winston's character through his extended development of his mimetic component.

From James Phelan, *Reading People, Reading Plots* (Chicago, 1989), pp. 28–43.

NOTES

[James Phelan notes the tendency on the part of even those critics who advocate structuralist and deconstructionist critical positions, to concentrate on the themes in a literary work. He reads Orwell's *1984* as a novel where the mimetic and thematic functions of the character of Winston

Smith are essential to an understanding of how the text itself operates. Phelan interprets the structure and narrative progression of *1984* and explores the cognitive tensions that arise for the reader, in an effort to reveal and foreground the literary strategies Orwell deploys. This is a detailed literary analysis that is less concerned with Orwell's political stance than others in the collection and it is interesting to read it against Richard Rorty's differently emphasised philosophical reading (essay 8) of *1984* and *Animal Farm*. Eds]

1. Much of the commentary has instead focused on the novel's ideas and politics and sometimes is less concerned with interpretation than with assessment of the ideas stipulated by the commentator. Nevertheless, Orwell has had many good critics, especially Alex Zwerdling, *Orwell and the Left* (New Haven, CT, 1974), Jennie Calder, *Chronicles of Conscience: A Study of George Orwell and Arthur Koestler* (London, 1968), and more recently, many of those represented in four collections: Irving Howe (ed.), *1984 Revisited: Totalitarianism in Our Century* (New York, 1983); Peter Stansky (ed.), *On Nineteen Eighty-Four* (Stanford, CA, 1983); Ejner J. Jenson (ed.), *The Future of Nineteen Eighty-Four* (Ann Arbor, MI, 1984); and Charles Klopp (ed.), *1984: Vision and Reality, Papers in Comparative Studies*, 4 (1985). Especially noteworthy in these collections are Mark Crispin Miller, 'The Fate of *1984*', in Howe; Zwerdling, 'The Psychopolitics of *1984*; in Jensen; and Calder, 'Does the Past Matter? Orwell's Glass Paperweight', in Klopp. Sperber's essay, '"Gazing into the Glass Paperweight": The Structure and Psychology of Orwell's *1984*', *Modern Fiction Studies* (1980), 213–26, differs from my analysis of the progression not only in particulars of interpretation but also in overall focus: Sperber wants to connect the book to Orwell's psychology and so is concerned, for example, with separating the author and character at the end of the novel. Orwell's novel has also come in for its share of negative evaluation. Among the most vigorous attacks are Louis Kampf, '*Nineteen Eighty-Four*: Why Read It?', in Klopp; and Patrick Reilly, '*Nineteen Eighty-Four*: The Failure of Humanism', *Critical Quarterly*, 24:3, (1981), 19–30.

2. George Orwell, *1984* (New York, 1982), p. 3. Hereafter citations will be given by page numbers in parentheses in the text.

3. See Mark Crispin Miller, 'The Fate of 1984' in Howe, *1984 Revisited*.

4. In a letter to F. J. Warburg, 22 October 1948, Orwell says, 'I haven't definitely fixed on the title but I am hesitating between "Nineteen Eighty-Four" and "The Last Man in Europe".' Howe, *1984 Revisited*, p. 284.

5. Letter to F. J. Warburg, 31 May 1947. Quoted from Howe, *1984 Revisited*, p. 283.

6. I follow Gérard Genette here in my use of the terms 'vision' and 'voice'; the first identifies 'who sees', the second 'who speaks'. See Gérard Genette, *Narrative Discourse: An Essay in Method*, trans. Lane Lewin (Ithaca, NY, 1981).

7. Indeed, I think that this emphasis in the narrative helps explain why the space given over to Goldstein's book, despite its clear thematic significance in setting forth much of the totalitarian philosophy behind the Party's operations, seems excessive. In that space we lose – or at least suspend – the mimetic involvement that Orwell has been developing, and we do not learn enough new information to make up for that loss.

8. For a fuller discussion of Winston's concern with the past, see Jenni Calder, 'Does the Past Matter? Orwell's Glass Paperweight', in Klopp, *1984: Vision and Reality*.

9. For a different reading of the significance of these scenes, see Patrocinio Schweikart, 'Why Big Brother: The Maternal Subtext of *Nineteen Eighty-Four*', *Papers in Comparative Studies*, 4 (1985), 69–80.

10. Zwerdling's discussion of the 'Psychopolitics of *1984*' in the Jensen anthology cited in note 1 perceptively traces the transfer of Winston's feelings for his mother to Big Brother, a transfer now about to be completed.

7

Nineteen Eighty-Four: The Insufficient Self

PATRICK REILLY

Orwell's debt to Swift is plain even to an inattentive reader – *Animal Farm* is so clearly a levy upon the comic treasury of the *Travels* – but a reading of the essay on Swift reveals the full extent of the reluctant admiration wrested by the genius of the great Augustan from his twentieth-century descendant.[1] While barely willing to allow the *Travels* as a work falling just on the right side of sanity, Orwell nevertheless simultaneously ranked it as one of a handful of irreplaceable masterpieces produced by western man, a test of our trusteeship, to be preserved whatever else we might be forced to relinquish. The Swift connection is by now a commonplace of Orwell criticism; what is still not, however, sufficiently recognised is the degree to which *Nineteen Eighty-Four* is shaped by Swift's great fable; how, specifically, in wrestling with the central problem of *Gulliver's Travels* – the hunt for the human being – Orwell came to create his own dark masterpiece.

Both texts pursue the truth about man, seeking the true self, the authentic person, who will at last be found beneath the accretions of culture and the drapings of mythology; both end in a kind of conversion in which once sacrosanct dogmas about human identity are exposed as totally untenable superstitions. Gulliver travels to all those strange places and meets all those remarkable peoples to confront, not the truth of the external world, but the reality within – he is his own greatest, most appalling discovery. What he finds shatters the complacent assumption enshrined in the logic books:

homo est animal rationale. The pool in Houyhnhnmland reveals a very different, nauseating reality. Winston is likewise taken to Room 101 not to penetrate the truth of Oceanic society, to add the 'why' to the already mastered 'how', but to be broken with the revelation of his own turpitude; Big Brother remains a mystery, it is Winston himself who is shockingly uncovered. In each case the reaction is the same: after such knowledge, what forgiveness? That the one investigation is conducted in the mode of comic satire while the other, depressingly humourless, confines its reader to a pessimistic prison, should not obscure the basic underlying similarity. The search for the self ends for each in catastrophic success; the chill disclosure of human corruption occurs in Houyhnhnmland and Oceania alike.

It has long been recognised that intimidation is the prime objective of Swift's satire, that the 'Digression on Madness' and Gulliver's last voyage strive to induce in their reader a sense of demoralisation, a fearful questioning of what it means to be human, verging upon a panic-stricken intuition that it may mean nothing at all. No one who reads the *Travels* can miss the theme of conditioning and entrapment that informs the whole fiction. For many centuries we in the west have celebrated the autonomous self as the highest of all our values, so precious that we continue, even yet, to reject solutions to our grievous social problems when such remedies threaten the sanctity of individual rights – the earthly paradise itself come too dear if the cost is the suppression of the self.

Gulliver's Travels shockingly proposes that this exalted idea of the self, self-justifying and inviolable, cornerstone of Christianity and humanism alike, is mere delusion. As Gulliver moves from society to society, to be moulded anew to each fresh set of cultural assumptions, the nihilistic speculation becomes increasingly insistent: perhaps there is ultimately no self at all, no central human core, beyond the reach of manipulation, perhaps there is nothing essentially human to withstand the coercions of culture? Such satire puts on trial the very existence of the self as an entity independent of the social system in which it acquires awareness. What is so unnerving about Gulliver as average, everyday man is that he changes with every change of environment, seems ominously deficient in any fixed or permanent characteristics, is short or tall, clean or unclean, only by comparison; he is a relative creature – giant among Lilliputians, Lilliputian among giants, Yahoo among Houyhnhnms, horse among men. Man, in the sense of some irreducibly human core, some residual quality transcending cultural control, resisting or modifying environmental omnipotence, is shown as fiction and sham, the belief that there is a human *given* exposed as the most pathetic of delusions.

The scandal of Swift is his suggestion that man is merely a mechanism, a function of his environment, imprisoned in a system which he evades, if at all, only to enter another, forever exchanging captivities. All the different peoples of the book live locked into their own structures, unaware or contemptuous of other life-styles, refusing to credit what they have not been programmed to believe. Gulliver moves from culture to culture, demonstrating that the same belief can be invincible or ludicrous depending on its social context and that what we call truth is what others call prejudice; demonstrating, too, just how easily man can be re-conditioned to abhor what he once revered, to regard as normal what was formerly bizarre. But if man is so infinitely malleable, so much a moral and intellectual weather-vane, what becomes of the boasted freedom of the mind, the inviolable sanctity of the self? What makes the *Travels* so chillingly modern is its anticipation of a major theme of structuralism in suggesting that man is simply the sum of his codes, programmed like a computer to follow instructions, incapable of change until re-programming occurs. There *is* no self apart from society, no nature but only culture, no answer to the question, 'Who is Gulliver?', except in terms of the particular cultural context where he temporarily chances to be.

Yet this is not the whole truth about the *Travels* and can, in fact, taken in isolation, be misleading. Far from putting down the book in the conviction that all is contingent and relative, the reader is only too disturbingly conscious that the search for the self has ended in an absolute fact, namely, the brutal reality of Yahoo man. Only those who believe that Swift's chief target is Gulliver himself, that Gulliver is a gull precisely in falling so foolishly for the Houyhnhnm propaganda that equates man and Yahoo, will be able to treat Gulliver's final disclosures as the delusions of a disordered mind. For such readers Yahoo man is Gulliver's ultimate blunder, *not* Swift's concluding accusation. But those who decline to use Gulliver as a lightning conductor for Swift's contempt have to acknowledge that the Yahoo is a fact of the *Travels* and not just a fool's hallucination. The book which seemed to discredit all truth ends by advancing the hideous truth of Yahoo man. *That* is where

Gulliver's search leads, for, back in England, he adheres to the truths of Houyhnhnmland, refusing, as so invariably in the past, to alter his beliefs with the altered environment. We have no right to speculate beyond the book's covers to imagine a new Gulliver, transformed yet again and re-dedicated to the possibility of human goodness. The *Travels* insist that the Yahoo is real; it is the rational qualities we pride ourselves upon that are exposed as spurious.

This is the truth that Swift sends Gulliver travelling to learn. He sets out on his final voyage convinced of certain unimpugnable truths: that England is the queen of nations and man the crown of creation, that society, with all its institutions and artefacts, is the incontestable sign of human excellence. In Houyhnhnmland he is made aware of the frauds that have been practised upon him: man is not *animal rationale* but Yahoo; society exhibits not the glittering evidence of human achievement but the proof of human depravity. Winston Smith is engaged on a similar search which culminates in a similar disaster. Like Gulliver, he, too, strives to fathom the mystery of his own existence – by ransacking his memory, by treasuring every scrap of evidence from the abolished past, by involving old proles in pub conversations in the vain hope of deciphering history. He desperately seeks the evidence that will confirm what he already knows is true; that truth is objective, existing regardless of the fears and wishes of men, that love is stronger than hate, that the skull is an inviolable realm, a no-go area to the strongest conceivable tyrant, that the past is unalterable, with yesterday's event beyond the possibility of recall or revision. These are the adamantine truths upon which Winston relies as he initiates his challenge to Big Brother. From the outset he is prepared for the worst, and the worst is that he will be caught, tortured and executed. But he knows, too, that the truths he cherishes are insuperable and that when his body is dead his ideals will have triumphed.

Nineteen Eighty-Four records an education as Winston is taught, painfully, to discard mistaken views of the world in favour of harsher, more correct ones. His final transformation is as shocking as Gulliver's; Gulliver changes from lover of humanity to misanthrope, Winston from freedom-fighter to power-worshipper, rebel to lickspittle. The full enormity of this metamorphosis can be gauged only by someone familiar with Orwell's political views as expressed repeatedly throughout his essays and reviews. The easiest way to clarify all this is to consider the great change we experience in passing from the world of Conrad to that of Orwell. Much more

important than the forty-odd years are the two world wars that separate *Heart of Darkness* from *Nineteen Eighty-Four*. Orwell's
dismay in the face of the atrocities left no corner of him where even
a scintilla of an earlier romanticism could lodge; consequently, his
attitude to evil is closer to Swift's icy disdain than to Conrad's ambivalent fascination confronting Kurtz. If the keynote of *Heart of
Darkness* is horror, that of *Nineteen Eighty-Four* is disgust. It is a
book dense with disgust, relieved only momentarily by the excursion to the Golden Land or by the brief, anachronistic marital com-
panionship of the room behind the antique shop.

Otherwise there is an atmosphere of terror and tedium, of
squalor forever on the brink of nightmare, disgust competing with
fear: urine, sour beer, crumbling cigarettes, firewater gin, the reek
of sweat, stew like vomit, broken bones, smashed teeth, bloody
clots of hair, gorilla-like guards, public executions. Oceania is a dull
hell, with O'Brien's elegant apartment the one oasis of beauty in a
squalid, crumbling city. Orwell's intense loathing for totalitarianism
kept him immune from any tendency to admire, however obliquely,
the men of power who had brought such things to pass.

There is at least a hint of hero-worship in Marlow's attitude to
Kurtz – it is, after all, Kurtz's diabolism that has made him a
significant man as well as a lost soul, raising him above the mean-
ness of the other pilgrims; Marlow feels that it is better to be
damned like Satan than dismissed as dross, better to be wanted for
murder than wanted for nothing. There is, similarly, more than a
trace of admiration in Winston for his torturer, O'Brien, as a being
so much greater than himself. Power extorts even from its victims
not merely reverence but also gratitude: the Lord giveth and the
Lord taketh away – blessed be the name of the Lord; though he slay
me, yet will I trust in him. The difference is that while we suspect
Conrad as sharing, at least in part, Marlow's romantic view of the
great criminal, we know from his own words that Orwell abomi-
nated the power-worshipper, especially when he was revealed as
lurking, perhaps even unknown to himself, beneath the disguise of
freedom-fighter.

Orwell's reaction against the glamorisation of evil that surfaces
fitfully in *Heart of Darkness* included a contempt for the cult of the
heroic malefactor, the criminal superman who proves his manumis-
sion from mediocrity by stepping over the trivial codes of petty
men. Repeatedly throughout his writing, in his review of Carlyle,
his comments on Stalin, his essays on Burnham and Hadley Chase,

he showed his complete antipathy to any element of the Great Man syndrome.[2] Power – his Burma experiences are ample testimony – made Orwell feel ashamed and guilty. When, in *Down and Out in Paris and London*, an old man is humiliated in a pawn-shop and his fellow-victims, waiting their turn to be served, laugh dutifully at his discomfiture, Orwell is sickened more by the sycophancy of the power-worshippers than by the inhumanity of the tyrannical clerk.[3] No other twentieth-century writer has campaigned more strenuously to purge the minds of his fellows of this revolting ailment.

It is all the more shocking that the hero of his last book should end up as the most despicable of power-worshippers, truckling disgustingly to what has unmanned him. It is worse still that Winston should have initially offered himself as Prometheus, defier of unjust power, champion of freedom and individual integrity, the last man in Europe. To choose to be Job is allowable, perhaps even commendable; to suffer unresistingly like Christ or Billy Budd is not necessarily the badge of inferiority. But to be changed into Job after aspiring to be Prometheus is a transformation so great as to provoke unease in the minds of its spectators – it is difficult to believe that the substitution of roles has been achieved by anything other than disgraceful means.

Winston is like Gulliver in that each is finally shown as denying the values once expressed, renegade to all they had previously held dear. The problem is that in each case the writer makes it impossible for us simply to repudiate the renegade as a traitor to the great tradition to which we still unswervingly belong – it would neuter these books to present them as serene affirmations of the values which their protagonists scandalously renounce. If, as we hope, Gulliver and Winston are wrong, they are so in a way that makes it very difficult to eschew their company. The beliefs they reject are ours too, among our most prized possessions, and it is inconceivable that their creators expect us to follow these defectors all the way, abandoning wives for stables and loving our violators. But why, then, do Swift and Orwell impede the reader when he understandably tries to extricate himself from a compromising involvement with the renegade? At what point in these narratives can we, without incurring the charge of Pharisaism or smugness, dissociate ourselves from their heroes' aberrations?

When Gulliver gazes into the pool and sees staring back the face of the Yahoo, he is not just a harmless lunatic inviting our pity or derision – he is clearly commissioned by Swift as our delegate to

Houyhnhnmland and it would be altogether too facile to pronounce him insane for daring to call us Yahoos. When Winston cracks so shamefully, yet so inevitably, in Room 101, we witness not just an individual lapse but the fall of man. To jib, however justifiably, at the vulgarity and sensationalism of the rats is beside the point. Not the individual instance but the general psychological law is what concerns Orwell; Room 101 contains the worst thing in the world, represents the unendurable trial. For anyone to claim that he would have overcome Room 101, hence that Winston's capitulation proves only his own personal cravenness, is to make nonsense of Orwell's intention. Our relationship to Gulliver and Winston is far more problematic than a simple rejection of kinship; they are our brothers, even if the relationship gives no cause for celebration. The fact that we are ashamed and discomfited does not entitle us to pretend that they are strangers.

Throughout the *Travels* but especially in Part IV we have only Gulliver to identify with – we know, as does Swift, that there are no rational horses, so that our choice is between Yahoo and human being. When we learn that they are really the same, we feel (and are meant to feel) helpless, for there is nowhere else in the book to go. Our spokesman having deserted to the enemy, we can either follow him across or abuse him as fool. Swift's cunningly contrived trap is that we cannot do the first and should not do the second. Gulliver scores too many hits to be a mere fool. If, within the text, he is unassailable, that is what Swift intends, since it is outside the text, and nowhere else, that he must be proved wrong. Anyone who dislikes being called Yahoo has a simple defence: stop behaving like one.

Nineteen Eighty-Four springs a similar trap. Winston begins as our spokesman, upholding the same pieties that we revere. When, aping Gulliver, he rejects these pieties, his recantation poses a problem. We are not to join him in craven capitulation to Big Brother, but neither, at the risk of being Pharisees, can we dismiss him as a weakling who has fallen miserably below our own high standard. To imply that Big Brother's good fortune was not to have us for opponents smacks of presumption. The book asks us to identify with Winston and to say honestly how we would fare in his place. Orwell's mortifying intention within the text is to extort the humiliating confession that we would do no better. The logic of Oceania is that the last man is doomed to defeat, simply because in such a dark finale any hope of individual resistance has vanished.

The book is a grim warning not to let things get so bad or else we are forever lost. Swift wishes his readers to act *outside* and *after* his text, to stop being the Yahoos we are; Orwell wishes his readers to act *outside* and *before* his text, lest we become the slaves of his prophecy. Prevention is Orwell's aim, and not simply because prevention is better than cure, but for the far more terrifyingly urgent reason that there must be prevention because there *is* no cure – Oceania is too late for salvation.

We can, of course, if we wish, dismiss Oceania as a bugaboo, a nightmare existence which our waking state will never countenance, and deny that things can ever become so bad because there are certain inbuilt guarantees – epistemological, psychological, moral – which preclude the possibility of such degradation. But Winston has already said all this and has been shown as disastrously wrong. Not only, liberal protestations notwithstanding, can the worst thing in the world happen, but its probability increases in proportion as it is derided as merely a bad dream – Room 101 is built with the inadvertent planning permission of those who glibly deny its possibility. Orwell was not so foolish as to write a warning against something he believed impossible. Winston's threshold of apprehension at the book's beginning is shown to be far too sanguinely high – he fears capture and death, but not subjugation. But he 'knows', too, that certain other things can never happen, that certain nightmarish speculations cannot survive in the light of day; his punishment is to see the nightmare become fact in the place where there is no darkness.

Winston's dogmas turn out to be delusions, a series of blunders in epistemology and morality. He believes in the existence of truth and the inviolability of love, thereby challenging what Orwell had denounced as the two most monstrous of modern iniquities – the denial of objective truth and the growth of power-worship. Power itself is impotent in the realms of truth and love: $2 + 2 = 4$, whatever Big Brother says to the contrary; Winston loves Julia, and there is nothing Big Brother can do to change it. In mind and heart man is invulnerable. These granite assumptions crumble like clay when put to the test. Winston's root error, the sandy foundation of all his other convictions, is his belief in the sufficiency of the self, his confidence that, however coercive the environment, the individual has it within him to tame experience, to master the external threat and discipline the internal depression. Man is the lord of life and consciousness is his infallible guard against the menace of being.

Nineteen Eighty-Four records the last dispiriting encounter in the conflict between being and consciousness, a problem with which Orwell had had a life-long tussle. What is the relationship between the pressure of external reality and the response of the critical intellect? Does man shape the world or the world man, or is there reciprocal formation with the outcome dependent on which fights harder and endures longer? Orwell clearly rejects the vulgarisation of Marx prevalent in his own time, the view that man is passive before the economic facts of his existence: 'Life is not determined by consciousness but consciousness by life.'[4] Equate life with the productive process and it becomes easy, if not inevitable, to regard human history as essentially the history of changing means of production – the tools that men use are the determinants of human evolution.

'All I know is that I am not a Marxist.'[5] Marx's own words suggest a position more complex than the dogmatic simplicity of some of his followers. He sees man, paradoxically, as at once free and conditioned: 'Men make their own history, but they do not make it just as they please; they do not make it under circumstances chosen by themselves, but under circumstances directly encountered, given and transmitted from the past.'[6] He is not above rebuking crude materialism as a sophomore fallacy: 'The materialist doctrine concerning the changing of circumstances and upbringing forgets that circumstances are made by men and the educator must himself be educated.'[7] Marx's newest exegetes are concerned with promoting the true, original, humanist champion against Kautsky's distortion of the historical fatalist, the iron determinist who saw man's life as just another part of natural history; the oppressive scientific ogre gives way to a man with an open, tentative and inquiring mind, at once provisional and innovative, humanist and fallible. Thus Marx avoids the twin errors of 'voluntarism' and fatalism: men make themselves but not just as they please; the world is given but not determined; circumstances make man but man makes circumstances; there is a dialectical unity of structural change and changing consciousness.

To rescue Marx from the iron law of History and from a determinism erroneously derived from natural history entailed a more subtle reassessment of the relationship between consciousness and being than the vulgarians of materialism were prepared to allow. Orwell's surprising exegesis of the famous opium allusion shows his own preference for the humanist champion above the infallible scientific realist.[8] In identifying the essence of true Marxism as a refusal to live by bread alone, Orwell deliberately brackets Marx with Christ and praises socialism in the language of traditional religion. Marx is arrestingly ranked alongside Christ as another hero resisting the first satanic temptation: to turn stones into bread, thereby electing man's belly the ruling organ and material welfare the aim of his being.

Orwell's Marx is created in his own image and likeness, manifesting Orwell's own brand of ethical socialism and endorsing his reiterated insistence that man's paramount problem is spiritual rather than material, that a lack of money is minor when set beside a lack of meaning. Bread is important since without it there can be no life, but a sufficiency of bread is not the one thing needful: 'The belly comes before the soul, not in the scale of values but in point of time.'[9] Not every human problem is a derivative of economics. Flory in *Burmese Days* is troubled by a lack of meaning, not a lack of means; the slums imprisoning him are those of the spirit – on any spiritual means test he lines up with the wretched of the earth. Not till Winston Smith will we meet another Orwellian protagonist for whom money counts so little. Flory and Winston are alike in that their difficulties are never financial – they crave significance, not cash, are victims of ontological rather than material deprivation. Flory's problem is not *how* but *why* to stay alive, and his failure to solve it reveals a bankruptcy that is existential rather than financial.

Unlike Flory, Dorothy Hare survives but in a curiously inconclusive way. Materially speaking, the book is a circle, ending where it began: a harassed drudge is once again making costumes for a fête, just as she was when her breakdown occurred. What *has* changed is her consciousness, not her being, for the book enacts an interior journey from Christianity to atheism – Dorothy returns to her father in Suffolk but not to her father in heaven. She starts out confident as to the *why* of life, worried only about the *how*; with enough money to pay the bills she might have staved off breakdown and gone to the grave impervious to doubt. It is the breakdown that takes her to otherwise unknowable worlds where religious faith withers away. She begins the book worrying about money and ends it worrying about meaning – money, she finally perceives, is important but secondary. Her loss of faith notwithstanding, she is still the same earnest, ascetic, industrious puritan she was, simply more lugubrious now that she knows 'the deadly emptiness ... at the heart of things'.[10] She has learned, crucially, that 'all real happenings are in the mind';[11] concluding, like the rebel Winston, that what truly matters is internal, she espouses consciousness, the primacy of the indomitable mind, as her defence against the wasted world. A bleak stoicism, an almost narcotic absorption in the task to hand, no matter how petty that be: these are the weapons of consciousness against a brutal, inane being. Consciousness holds being at bay, as Dorothy confronts the world with the stoic assumption that the mind is master of experience, that the resolved intelligence can shape even calamity to its own requirements. It is a victory when contrasted with Flory's suicide, though not of a kind to make the heart spring with joy.

Such a triumph over circumstance fails to inspire in us a sense of human transcendence or pride in man's nobility, for it lacks the exhilarating ring of Milton's Lady routing the enchanter: 'Fool, do not boast, thou canst not touch the freedom of my mind.'[12] Dorothy, by contrast, grits her teeth and soldiers on. Orwell discovers this sense of exuberant invincibility, paradoxically, among the apparent deadbeats of Paris and London. He finds, elatedly, that the slum corrupts but does not denature: man is greater than his environment, with the power to triumph over his external conditions. The spirit, though shackled to matter, can, nevertheless, soar free of its chains; being limits consciousness, yet consciousness can overcome being. Material conditions matter, but are not everything. It is life that shapes economics and not economics life. To accept the latter is to be an idolator. The English are particularly prone to economic idolatry in their assumption that money measures life and that to be poor is to be sinful. That is why Bozo, the crippled pavement artist, is so bravely nonconformist in rejecting guilt – why should he be ashamed of a beggary he did not choose and cannot help? Unlike Flory and Winston, he repudiates the oppressor's degrading valuation. The worst degradation, as the organisers of the extermination camps realised, is that which is appropriated and internalised, when the victim sees himself as vermin. Conversely, no person is completely victimised until he annuls himself. Bozo will not annul himself. Doubly penalised, lame and poor, he challenges the sinfulness of poverty, will not agree that he is worthless because he is poor. Through his interest in astronomy, he succeeds, though penniless, in maintaining intellectual standards; scorning environmental servitude, he taps his forehead and insists, 'I'm a free man in here'.[13]

This triumph over the world is the more inspiring when we recall that it was beyond Flory as it will be beyond Winston. Winston's belief in the indomitable mind is exposed as a pathetic delusion that shrivels when tested. Bozo, by contrast, stands out like an Abdiel in an army of tramps too broken to dispute their manifest iniquity. 'There was, clearly, no future for him but beggary and death in the workhouse';[14] he is, nevertheless, the freest man in the book. Down in the depths Orwell discovers nobility as well as degradation: the Russian waiter, Boris, the old man who gallantly finds the money for a shave from his meagre weekly income, the little Glasgow tramp who runs after Orwell to pay a debt – each in his own way testifies to the spirit of the unconquerable poor, the nobility of the human being.[15] Even in a prison Orwell finds the free spirit, in the *cloaca* delightedly detects pure crystal. It is a conviction that touches its Everest point in the figure of the Italian soldier in *Homage to Catalonia* – 'no bomb that ever burst shatters the crystal spirit'; nor no slum either.[16]

Man is greater than his environment – hence the obscenity when his environment insults his dignity. But no matter how vile the world, man need not be its helpless victim, far less its accomplice, for resistance is always his privilege. Even in the most unpropitious circumstances – Parisian slum and English dosshouse, the stricken North of England with its poor huddled in apathetic desolation, the nightmare city of Barcelona given over to witch-hunt – Orwell finds the proofs of man's invincible nobility. Even in Spain where the first intimations of totalitarian horror announced themselves, the triumph of consciousness over being is simultaneously present. In the brave little officer and the decent Civil Guard, Orwell pays homage to human transcendence. Man is the master of society, lord of politics and economics, not their helot. And so, despite the atrocities and betrayals, Orwell returns from Spain assured of the unbreakable crystal spirit, 'with not less but more belief in the decency of human beings'. Far from feeling cheated, he is elated: 'I have seen wonderful things and at last really believe in Socialism which I never did before.'[17]

Man is both decent and insuperable; when the world does its worst, he does his best, and his best is always good enough. The decency of ordinary folk is the epiphany that illumines the close of *Keep the Aspidistra Flying*, the blessed permanence of London is the redemptive vision at the end of *Coming Up for Air*. 'The bombs aren't made that could smash it out of existence.'[18] The pool at Lower Binfield is irreprievably polluted but London is reassuringly indestructible. To London add man. Consciousness is the master of being; the self is always sufficient whatever the challenge.

No wonder that Orwell's readers are perplexed and dismayed when they engage *Nineteen Eighty-Four* – how to account for so shocking a recantation of all that had been so previously cherished? The confidence in unconquerable man is as shattered as the shattered paperweight and consciousness is now the terrified thrall of being. The tradition of heroic resisters linking the earlier books finds no successor in the humiliated, failed rebel of Airstrip One. Here is no Flory refusing to tolerate an intolerable existence, no Dorothy stoically measuring reality against her own resolute mind. If, as Boris says, victory goes to him who fights the longest, then it is, scandalously, O'Brien, and not Winston, who has the staying power.[19] If, as Bozo says, external repression is futile against the brave spirit, that spirit is now dismissed as the discredited dogma of an outworn mythology. Gordon Comstock's reverence for the tree of life is an anachronism – the Party is about to abolish the orgasm and commence *in vitro* fertilisation. George Bowling's assurance that human nature is too massively, solidly established to be altered is a delusion; there *is* no human nature, simply a substance malleable as putty in Big Brother's hands.

All Orwell's reiterated rebukes and warnings to the optimists and liberals are now embodied as real, unexorcisable horrors. He had urged the English not to trust the deceptive legacy of liberalism: the empty guarantees that truth must prevail, that persecution must defeat itself, that mental freedom is inviolable – all those beliefs of the nursery which surprise us when still cherished by the political adult.[20] He had identified as a major weakness of English culture the 'sentimental belief that it all comes right in the end and the thing you most fear never happens'.[21] Whatever appals the mind cannot happen: first article of the liberal creed. By contrast, *Nineteen Eighty-Four* nerves itself to imagine the worst and then enacts the horror. From the outset Winston fears that his rebellion is the act of a lunatic and the book verifies his fears. Room 101 is the harsh school where the defects of a liberal education are corrected.

Why, for example, is H. G. Wells so foolish as to believe that only good men can be good scientists?[22] ... The liberal assumes that the human spirit is a constant throughout history, forever threatened but, like Dryden's hind, destined never to die. It is a belief that rests ultimately upon the anti-historical conviction that human nature is an unalterable datum, unvarying from age to age, superior to history and immune to event. From the Enlightenment assumption of a constant human nature to Bertrand Russell trusting to the spirit of man as an insuperable check to totalitarianism, this belief has been the cornerstone of western optimism, shared, as the crystal allusion shows, by Orwell himself.

But what if it isn't true? What if man is not a constant, what if love of liberty is merely a cultural artefact, a conditioned reflex that fades as the matrix alters? Slavery cannot endure, declares the liberal; Orwell points to the great slave states of antiquity which lasted for millennia and asks how we can be so sure that they cannot return, this time the more permanently because they will have science and technology to support them.[23] Men bred for servitude is a nightmare that an innocent liberalism will not contemplate, but does that mean that it cannot happen? 'What sickens me about left-wing people, especially the intellectuals, is their utter ignorance of the way things actually happen.'[24] *Nineteen Eighty-Four* rubs the intellectuals' noses in the dirt they will not see, even when it is sometimes of their own making. 'The thing you most fear never happens.' What Orwell most feared was the shattering of the crystal spirit; that the speculation was abhorrent was no reason for banning it.

Hence the deliberate affront to the optimists as Orwell goes to the other extreme: they had said such horrors *cannot* happen; Orwell's text shows that they *must*. Winston as dissident intellectual is defeated and it is a blunder to believe that this is simply due to O'Brien's controlling the dials of torture, for Winston is defeated in the mind, precisely where Milton's Lady, taunting the torturer, denied he could reach. The past is unchangeable, truth is objective, words have fixed meanings, love is invincible – all of these precious axioms are revealed as hanging on the slenderest filaments; the book shocks because in it every one of these propositions is refuted. 'It is quite possible that we are descending into an age in which two and two will make five when the Leader says so.'[25] Suspense comes, if at all, not from wondering whether Winston can elude, far less overthrow, Big Brother, but whether he can sustain defiance to the modest extent of dying for the faith, winning the martyr's crown: 'the object is not to stay alive but to stay human'.[26] Even covert martyrdom, a secret defiance carried to the grave, a purely internal heresy, will be enough to keep a man human. No need for Winston to join Spartacus, More and Bonhoeffer provided he can die, privately hating Big Brother; let being win every argument so long as consciousness has the last word. But even this limited victory is a fantasy, as much a piece of wish-fulfilment as Jack the Giant Killer. The Giant wins; the dissident loses everything except his life in the book's appalling conclusion, the more appalling in that he is still alive.

The privilege of heroic death is as obsolete as Shakespeare and the paperweight, and humanism is denied even a martyr. What

Winston most fears as lunatic, heretic, minority of one, is that there *is* no truth to die for, and the book confirms his dread. Relying on the spirit of man, Winston might just as well have trusted in Poseidon or Thor or the exploded God of Christian mythology. The freedom of the mind is as gross a superstition as the flying house of Loreto, excusable in Milton's Lady, blessedly ignorant of Pavlov and brainwashing, but unforgivable in the residents of Oceania. Not the heavens but the cellars of Miniluv testify to the omnipotence of the new god. Man's palimpsest existence deprives him of any irreducible human core, any inviolable consciousness, to defend him against the reality in which he lives, moves and has his being.

Winston's dilemma is the same in ethics as in aesthetics: the things he admires have no place in the life of Oceania. Like diary and paperweight, love and friendship, even tragedy itself, are simply fading memories of a bygone ethos, belong to 'a conception of loyalty that was private and unalterable. Such things, he saw, could not happen today.'[27] Even the traditional gestures of sacrificial love have become a target for realist derision – the nonsensical act of the lifeboat woman in trying to shield the child from the bullets makes the cinema audience laugh. 'We live in an age in which the autonomous individual is ceasing to exist – ceasing to have the illusion of being autonomous.'[28] Once man believed himself a free and separate being; the twentieth century has taught him better. *Nineteen Eighty-Four* rounds off his education by showing that love, generosity and friendship are equally pipedreams.

The twin nightmares of *Nineteen Eighty-Four* are verified in the end. The first is the epistemological dread of being locked within the self with no access to objective truth and, consequently, no way of knowing if such truth exists. The associated moral horror is to be walled within the self with no outlet to generosity or love. Winston starts out fearing the epistemological nightmare and ends up trapped in the moral one. 2 + 2 are whatever Big Brother decides and the whole world, Julia included, can perish provided Narcissus lives. There *is* no truth, epistemological or moral, to live or die for. The paradox is that Winston's self-love is yoked to self-contempt. A person sinks to the pit of degradation when he internalises the humiliator's judgement. Such was the strategy pursued in the camps. The aim was not simply to make Auschwitz *das Arschloch der Welt* (the world's arsehole) where human beings were transformed into waste product, but to bring the victims to regard themselves as excrement. The victim's sense of his own value must be

destroyed within the citadel of his own mind, since, whoever har-
bours his own worth, has thwarted the totalitarian enemy. To
retain even a scintilla of self-respect is to possess a power to resist
which Big Brother cannot tolerate.

Consciousness determines being, despite what the Marxists say;
the man who believes in his own value continues to have it – the
last man in Europe remains so as long as he wills it. Orwell was in-
trigued by the snobbish tramp he met in the spike: 'in the sight of
God ... he was not a tramp. His body might be in the spike, but his
spirit soared far away, in the pure aether of the middle classes.'[29]
The tone is amused, almost derisive; what Swift calls self-deception
and Sartre *mauvaise foi* is discernible in this superb exhibition of
essence prevailing over existence, consciousness over being. Orwell
pokes fun at the self-deceiver, yet there is also something admirable
in this no-surrender attitude, this brave resolve not to be submerged
in tramphood or permit matter to dictate to spirit.

Winston depressingly fails to match this resolve. In the Ministry
of Love spirit cravenly capitulates to matter when Winston finally
accepts himself as the bag of filth which the mirror reveals. He
cannot sustain the amphibian existence, the ability to inhabit simultaneously the diverse worlds of being and consciousness, which
enables the snobbish tramp and the pavement-artist Bozo to live in-
vincibly in degradation. The tramps and deadbeats of Paris and
London are filthy *and* generous, foul-mouthed *and* loyal, still,
however incredibly, temples of the Holy Ghost, hosts to the crystal
spirit. *Nineteen Eighty-Four* appals to the degree that it fulfils
O'Brien's vow to drain man of all redemptive nobility. Gone is the
sense of comradeship that shines through the vilest environment,
the sense of self-respect that exalts the frequenters of gutters; only
the Yahoo remains, squalid, mean, lost to all possibility of heroism
or self-transcendence. Winston is not the man he thought he was or
tried to be, not dissident nor rebel nor lover – what possible bearing
could *his* thoughts or strivings have upon his destiny? He is the
wretch of O'Brien's deciding, the mere commodity of the system
within which he transiently functions. Being rules, O.K., is the dis-
maying graffito scrawled over Orwell's last communiqué.

The world is barren of truth and love, a dual dispossession which
provokes very different reactions. It is shocking to learn that there
is no truth because it leaves one feeling cheated; man is mistaken
about the universe, but, far from being responsible for its unrea-
son, he may well feel betrayed by the world's failure to match his

rational demands. But it is sickening to learn that there is no love, because, if true, that *is* man's fault and his shame – this time the deficiency is internal, with man compelled to see himself as traitor rather than victim. In an absurd world where he alone has value, man can continue to regard himself as victim or even as tragic hero. Hence the importance of Room 101 as the appropriate climax of Orwell's despondent text; it exists to exhibit man as insufficient, even vile, to reveal him as a bag of filth, thereby denying him the tragic status which has hitherto always been his consolation for defeat. Orwell defined tragedy as a destruction in which man nevertheless shows himself greater than the forces that destroy him; Big Brother refuses Winston the privilege of tragedy, for the defeat in Room 101 is immitigably abject.

Winston is demolished along with his humanist hopes. We can, if we wish, soften this conclusion by treating it as the débâcle of a very flawed individual whose failure leaves the true doctrine intact, thus wrenching the text away from the despair-of-a-dying-man view to that of a cautionary tale for progressives, an optimistic exhortation to those who share the faith not to repeat the blunders. The temptation then is to import into the text a tougher strain of humanism (our own, naturally) which would have sustained Winston if only he had found it. The related fallacy is to pity poor Winston for not being like us and it is the graver because he *is* like us, is intended by Orwell as the universal representative, his defects not those of an individual or a group, but, at crucial points, of humanity itself. The quotation from Lermontov's preface to *A Hero of Our Time*, annexed by Camus to describe his own 'hero' in *The Fall*, could just as appositely precede *Nineteen Eighty-Four*: 'It is in fact a portrait but not of an individual; it is the aggregate of the vices of our whole generation in their fullest expression.' It is much too facile to condemn Gulliver as madman or Winston as coward and think thereby to evade the criticism of ourselves – impossible to believe that Swift and Orwell meant us to escape so easily.

The pool in Houyhnhnmland and the mirror in Miniluv are alike in forcing man to confront his true self, and in each case physical loathing parallels inner corruption. The *philosophes* may prate about *animal rationale* but Yahoo is the revolting reality. Similarly, Winston's noble rhetoric about the spirit of man collapses when set against the incriminating tape-recorder and the accusing mirror. Winston's faith in man, however attractive, crumbles when tested.

Neither Gulliver nor Winston can protect their consoling dreams against the hideous truth.

Yet Room 101 is the necessary final disclosure because, even after listening to the tape and looking at the mirror, Winston still clings to the possibility of self-transcendence through love. To love another person better than oneself is a provocation that the totalitarians of Oceania cannot abide. Winston still regards himself as such a lover, and with large justification, for the same tape that condemns him as a terrorist exalts him as a lover. He hates Big Brother so much that he is ready to commit any atrocity that may help to overthrow the tyrant, but, even for so blessed a consummation, he refuses to part with Julia – great as is his loathing for Big Brother, his love for Julia is greater still. In *The Devils* poor, foolish Stepan Verkhovensky achieves on his deathbed the key Dostoevskian insight: 'Love is higher than existence. Love is the crown of existence. And how is it possible that existence should not be subjected to it?'[30] It is not Winston's idiom but it is his sentiment. He makes the same commitment to Julia as Milton's Adam to Eve – 'Our state cannot be severed; we are one,/One flesh; to lose thee were to lose myself.'[31] The tape tells Big Brother what Winston regards as the best thing in the world, hence what must be destroyed so that O'Brien's vow to drain Winston of everything redemptively human may be fulfilled. The stage is set for the novel's final contest: the best thing in the world versus the worst thing in the world, love versus Room 101.

That is why Winston's final self-discovery is so appalling. He savours the full shame of his selfhood, acknowledging the humiliating truth – that his stinking, rotting carcase is the most precious thing in the universe, that he will grovel to any abomination, sacrifice any love, if only the panel between his face and the rats stays closed. 'If you want to keep a secret you must also hide it from yourself.'[32] Room 101 is the confessional where every secret is laid open and the self admits the truth. That is why O'Brien refuses to tell Winston what he must do to save himself. No other agent must intervene and such help is, in any case, redundant, for the self always, infallibly, knows what to do. O'Brien, pedantically discoursing on the antiquity of the torture, is deaf to Winston's frantic appeals, supplies only the simple assurance: 'You will do what is required of you.' Without tuition.

This moment of shameful self-recognition is almost a trademark of modern literature, though its pioneer is the Swift of Gulliver's last voyage. All of those travels culminate in the resolution of an identity crisis when Gulliver at last discovers who he truly is, and in this Swift fathers a tribe of parallel revelations in our own time from Conrad and Mann to Camus and Golding. What Kurtz learns in the jungle, Aschenbach on the lido, Jean-Baptiste Clamence on a Seine bridge, is the same harsh lesson enforced on Winston in Room 101. Our forbears, in their ancient terminology, would have called it a conviction of sin, the sudden, shattering awareness bequeathed by Adam to all his sons of a shamefully indefensible nakedness. The spirit is willing but the flesh is weak: in some such terms they would have explained the sense of failure. In Orwell even this unequal contest has become a fiction, for there is, finally, no spirit to challenge matter, only a flesh reliably feeble and a self dependably insufficient: 'you *will* do what is required of you'.[33]

How does a man respond to this revelation of disgrace? There are a number of competing strategies and the choice defines the man. Othello opts for heroic, Flory for squalid, suicide, Kurtz for horrified despair, Gide's immoralist for defiant self-assertion, Clamence for cynical malevolence, Parolles for equable acceptance: 'Simply the thing I am/Shall make me live.' Winston is at once more anguished and depressing, for he cannot die nor justify himself nor live in amnesic insouciance. The worst thing in the world is that there is no death in Room 101, neither heroic nor expiatory; Winston is condemned to life, a life drained of value or virtue. He survives (that is what is so appalling) to suffer an unbearable antinomy: he has behaved shamefully and he could not help it. An inexpiable guilt, a sense of personal vileness that locks the door to any remedial action – this (it is Clamence's discovery too) is the worst torment of all.

In their final books Orwell and Camus address the same ethical dilemma: how can man recover innocence? Confessing one's guilt brings, in itself, no absolution and Orwell's faithless lovers agree. Each admits the fact of betrayal, but in such a way as to intensify self-disgust rather than bring relief or pardon. Comedians like Parolles may pardon themselves, but where can a failed Prometheus or a perjured Romeo find absolution? The only confessional belongs to the enemy and one goes there to be degraded, not redeemed. Swift, Camus and Orwell all explore the humiliation of man: Gulliver looks in the pool and knows himself, Clamence hears the cry from the river and hurries on, Winston learns in Room 101 whom he truly loves.

'Do it to Julia'; Winston screams out Big Brother's triumph and his own abasement – much more worrying, our abasement too.

Having sided with him in his rebellion, it is difficult to extricate ourselves from his defeat. At what point did he go wrong? At which test would we have done better? The trap is as cunningly malicious as any set by Swift, for we have been manoeuvred into a distressing complicity which we cannot easily repudiate without appearing to adopt the self-righteousness of the Pharisee. It is a representative defeat, with all men falling in Winston as they did in Adam. Even in the *Travels* Gulliver exempts his sextumvirate of moral supermen from the general indictment, but Orwell is much more ruthless in denying that anyone, however heroic, can overcome Room 101. Winston knows in his dream that his mother and sister must die so that he may live, for this is 'part of the unavoidable order of things'.[34] Egoism is the law of life. When, no longer dreaming, he remembers his mother beseeching him not to be selfish, he remembers too the futility of her appeal: 'it was no use':[35] How can decency resist an empty belly? He snatches all the food and condemns his sister to death. The shame afterwards is just another pointless crucifixion, for it is the shame of being human – we are all bags of filth and there is no more to be said: 'all you care about is yourself'.[36] Hemingway makes of the self a cornerstone for stoic fortitude: 'you have only yourself', but if you are Santiago what more do you need?[37] Winston is no Santiago; the peculiar anguish of *Nineteen Eighty-Four* is that there is only the self versus Big Brother, and the self is, cruelly, not enough.

It strikes Winston that 'in moments of crisis one is never fighting against an external enemy, but always against one's own body',[38] and it is the pain-shunning body, swelling to fill the universe, that betrays the would-be idealist. In battle the great, noble issues give way to brute preservation; only those ensconced in cosy armchairs dream of self-transcendence, just as only those companioned by fear and want know the untameable strength of the animal desire to survive. Well-fed people have no problem in conquering the pangs of hunger. Once again there is an almost despicably easy escape for any reader determined to evade the accusation in Orwell's text, namely, to insist that the insufficient self in *Nineteen Eighty-Four* is simply Winston's and that his failings are no index of our fortitude; his collapse is a purely personal one – when *we* reach Room 101 we shall show him what he should have done.

Yet the text will not allow us to arraign Winston as the sole culprit or isolate him as a sad exception. On the contrary, he is, all too distressingly, the universal representative. In the Ministry of Love a skull-faced man, clearly dying of starvation, is given some bread by a fellow-prisoner who is at once brutally beaten by a guard for his act of charity. The skull-faced man, ordered to Room 101, begs obscenely for reprieve, and, searching frantically for a substitute victim, fixes naturally upon his benefactor, hysterically accusing him of having whispered treason as he gave the bread. Orwell's modern rendition of the parable focuses less upon the charity of the Good Samaritan than upon the degrading ingratitude of the recipient. If the ultimate proof of love is to die for another, the nadir of self-love is to use the benefactor's body as a shield.

Nor is the skull-faced man to be regarded as a monster of depravity, for, within the text, he is a normal man acting as all men do when put to the test, as the Good Samaritan will act too when *he* is summoned to Room 101; we may feel ashamed only on condition of recognising the guilt as universal. Room 101 is where humanity is found lacking, not where cowards are separated from heroes. In *Nineteen Eighty-Four* there are no Sydney Cartons or Thomas Mores, no heroes or martyrs, for these are simply the mistakes of an inefficient penology, of blundering executioners who take them at their word that they prefer death when they are really fake suicides, inadvertently killing themselves in an obstinate attempt to make it look real. It is essentially a matter of chronology, of being on hand at the inevitable moment when the hero has seen through his own sham and the martyr is screaming to be saved from himself. Nothing is finally more important than one's own skin. 'All you care about is yourself', says Julia, explaining her treachery as a single instance of a universal law, and Winston, the betrayed betrayer, taught by his own experience, agrees.[39] Orwell's characters do as they must and despise themselves for it. They are in the desperate condition described by St Paul, quoting from the *Psalms*, in his *Epistle to the Romans*: 'There is not one just man. ... All have gone astray together; they have become worthless. There is none who does good, no, not even one.' Paul, however, has a remedy where *Nineteen Eighty-Four* offers none. Oceania's God is no redeemer but the guarantor of man's degradation. O'Brien predicts Winston's future: 'We shall crush you down to the point from which there is no coming back. ... Everything will be dead inside you. Never again will you be capable of love, or friendship, or joy of living, or laughter, or curiosity, or courage, or integrity. You will be hollow. We shall squeeze you empty, and then we shall fill you with ourselves.'[40] It is a promise devastatingly kept. At the end of Orwell's dark prophecy the self has not only ceased to be sufficient – it has ceased to exist.

From Patrick Reilly, *The Literature of Guilt* (London, 1988), pp. 92–113.

NOTES

[Patrick Reilly examines what he sees as an interesting intertextual relationship between *1984* and Swift's eighteenth-century satire *Gulliver's Travels*. He perceives an inter-reliance that has at its base the deconstruction of a liberal-humanist search for the sanctity of the self, for universal truths and for authenticity.

In an essay that derives its thesis from intertextual connections, Reilly also draws Conrad's *Heart of Darkness* into his framing of *1984*. He notes the significance of the two world wars that take place between the publication of Conrad's and Orwell's texts and detects a shift from a Conradian fascination with an 'insufficient self' to an Orwellian disgust in *1984* with the bellicose and brutal realities of man, that echoes Swift's much earlier preoccupations. Reilly explores the reader's identification with, and entrapment within, the guilt and discomfiture inherent of both Gulliver and Winston, an atrophy that the reader is steeled to challenge outside of the text and beyond it via an active engagement with Orwell's ethical Socialism. Eds]

1. Sonia Orwell and Ian Angus (eds), *The Collected Essays, Journalism and Letters of George Orwell* (Harmondsworth, 1970), IV, p. 257 and p. 261. Hereafter cited as *CEJL*.

2. *CEJL*, I, p. 56; III, pp. 246–60; IV, pp. 201–2, 203, 205–6, 214–15.

3. George Orwell, *Down and Out in Paris and London* (Harmondsworth, 1963), p. 20.

4. Lewis S. Feuer (ed.), *Marx and Engels: Basic Writings on Politics and Philosophy* (London, 1969), p. 288; see also p. 84.

5. Quoted in Peter Singer (ed.), *Marx* (Oxford, 1980), p. 38.

6. 'The Eighteenth Brumaire of Louis Napoleon' in *Karl Marx and Friedrich Engels: Selected Works in Two Volumes* (Moscow, 1950), I, p. 249.

7. L. S. Feuer (ed.), *Marx and Engels*, p. 284.

8. *CEJL*, II, p. 33; III, p. 121.

9. *CEJL*, II, pp. 304–5.

10. George Orwell, *A Clergyman's Daughter* (Harmondsworth, 1964), p. 258.

11. Ibid., p. 240.

12. *Complete Shorter Poems of John Milton*, ed. John Carey (London, 1981), p. 209.

13. Orwell, *Down and Out*, p. 147.

14. Ibid., p. 148.

15. Ibid., pp. 22, 27, 48, 120; *CEJL*, I, p. 66.

16. *CEJL*, II, p. 306.

17. *CEJL*, I, p. 301.

18. George Orwell, *Coming Up for Air* (Harmondsworth, 1962), p. 224.

19. Orwell, *Down and Out*, p. 22.

20. *CEJL*, IV, p. 465.

21. *CEJL*, II, p. 297.

22. *CEJL*, II, p. 170.

23. *CEJL*, I, p. 414.

24. *CEJL*, I, p. 395.

25. *CEJL*, I, pp. 413–14; II, p. 297; III, p. 177.

26. George Orwell, *Nineteen Eighty-Four* (Harmondsworth, 1958), p. 136.

27. Ibid., pp. 27–8.

28. *CEJL*, II, p. 161; III, p. 160.

29. *CEJL*, I, p. 64.

30. Fyodor Dostoevsky, *The Devils*, trans. David Magarshack (Harmondsworth, 1967), p. 655.

31. John Milton, *Paradise Lost*, ed. Alistair Fowler (London, 1976), p. 494.

32. Orwell, *Nineteen Eighty-Four*, p. 225.

33. Ibid., p. 229.

34. Ibid., p. 27.

35. Ibid., p. 132.

36. Ibid., p. 235.

37. Ernest Hemingway, *The Old Man and the Sea* (St Albans, 1976), p. 43.

38. Orwell, *Nineteen Eighty-Four*, p. 85.

39. Ibid., p. 235.

40. Ibid., p. 206.

8

The Last Intellectual in Europe

RICHARD RORTY

Orwell's last two novels are good examples of what Nabokov thought of as 'topical trash', for their importance is a result of having made a big practical difference. We would not now be reading and admiring Orwell's essays, studying his biography, or trying to integrate his vocabulary of moral deliberation into our own unless he had written *Animal Farm* and *1984*. *Lolita* and *Pale Fire* will survive as long as there are gifted, obsessive readers who identify themselves with Humbert and Kinbote. But even Irving Howe, who wrote one of the earliest and best discussions of *1984*, admits that Orwell is one of those writers 'who live most significantly for their own age'.[1]

Orwell's best novels will be widely read only as long as we describe the politics of the twentieth century as Orwell did. How long that will be will depend on the contingencies of our political future: on what sort of people will be looking back on us, on how events in the next century will reflect back on ours, on how people will decide to describe the Bolshevik Revolution, the Cold War, the brief American hegemony, and the role of countries like Brazil and China. Orwell thought of our century as the period in which 'human equality became technically possible' and in which, simultaneously,

> ... practices which had long been abandoned, in some cases for
> hundreds of years – imprisonment without trial, the use of war pris-
> oners as slaves, public executions, torture to extract confessions, the

use of hostages, and the deportation of whole populations – not only became common again, but were tolerated and even defended by people who considered themselves enlightened and progressive.[2]

Someday this description of our century may come to seem blinkered or shortsighted. If it does, Orwell will be seen as having inveighed against an evil he did not entirely understand. Our descendants will read him as we read Swift – with admiration for a man who served human liberty, but with little inclination to adopt his classification of political tendencies or his vocabulary of moral and political deliberation. Some present-day leftist critics of Orwell (e.g., Christopher Norris) think that we *already* have a way of seeing Orwell as blinkered and shortsighted. They think that the facts to which he called attention can already be put in a context within which they look quite different. Unlike Norris, I do not think that we have a better alternative context. In the forty years since Orwell wrote, as far as I can see, nobody has come up with a better way of setting out the political alternatives which confront us. Taking his earlier warnings against the greedy and stupid conservatives together with his warnings against the Communist oligarchs, his description of our political situation – of the dangers and options at hand – remains as useful as any we possess.

Nabokov thought aiming at this sort of inevitably temporary utility betrayed the lack, or the waste, of the gifts which were essential to a figure called the 'writer'. Orwell, too, had views about this mythical figure, pretty much the opposite of Nabokov's views. Different writers want to do different things. Proust wanted autonomy and beauty; Nietzsche and Heidegger wanted autonomy and sublimity; Nabokov wanted beauty and self-preservation; Orwell wanted to be of use to people who were suffering. They all succeeded. Each of them was brilliantly, *equally*, successful.

Orwell was successful because he wrote exactly the right books at exactly the right time. His description of a particular historical contingency was, it turned out, just what was required to make a difference to the future of liberal politics. He broke the power of what Nabokov enjoyed calling 'Bolshevik propaganda' over the minds of liberal intellectuals in England and America. He thereby put us twenty years ahead of our French opposite numbers. They had to wait for *The Gulag Archipelago* before they stopped thinking that liberal hope required the conviction that things behind the Iron Curtain would necessarily get better, and stopped thinking that solidarity against the capitalists required ignoring what the Communist oligarchs were doing. Whereas Nabokov sensitised his readers to the permanent possibility of small-scale cruelties produced by the private pursuit of bliss, Orwell sensitised his to a set of excuses for cruelty which had been put into circulation by a particular group – the use of the rhetoric of 'human equality' by intellectuals who had allied themselves with a spectacularly successful criminal gang.

The job of sensitising us to these excuses, of redescribing the post-World War II political situation by redescribing the Soviet Union, was Orwell's great practical contribution. What Howe calls the combination of 'desperate tenderness and desperate topicality' in *Animal Farm* and in the first two-thirds of *1984* sufficed to accomplish this limited, practical goal. But in the last third of *1984* we get something different – something not topical, prospective rather than descriptive. After Winston and Julia go to O'Brien's apartment, *1984* becomes a book about O'Brien, not about twentieth-century totalitarian states. This part of the book centres on the citations from *The Theory and Practice of Oligarchical Collectivism* (co-authored by O'Brien) and on O'Brien's explanation of why Winston must be tortured rather than simply shot ('The object of torture is torture'). It is a vision of what Howe calls 'post-totalitarianism'.[3] It is no longer a warning about what currently is happening in the world, but the creation of a character who illustrates what might someday happen. Orwell was not the first person to suggest that small gangs of criminals might get control of modern states and, thanks to modern technology, stay in control forever. But he was the first to ask how intellectuals in such states might conceive of themselves, once it had become clear that liberal ideals had no relation to a possible human future. O'Brien is his answer to that question.

I want to discuss separately the two jobs Orwell did in his last two novels – redescribing Soviet Russia and inventing O'Brien. I shall begin with the first, returning to O'Brien later. Orwell's admirers often suggest that he accomplished the redescription by reminding us of some plain truths – moral truths whose obviousness is on a par with 'two plus two is four'. But they are often made nervous by his second accomplishment, and tend, as Howe says, to discount the 'apocalyptic desperation' of *1984* and instead to 'celebrate [Orwell's] humanity and his "goodness"'.[4] This goes along with a tendency to suggest that Orwell was not really a particularly accomplished writer, but that he made up in goodness what he lacked in artistry. Here, for example, is Lionel Trilling: 'Orwell's native gifts are perhaps not of a transcendent kind; they have their roots in a quality of mind that ought to be as frequent as it is modest. This quality may be described as a sort of moral centrality, a directness of relation to moral – and political – fact.'[5]

Trilling's way of speaking is echoed by Orwell himself. In a much quoted passage at the end of 'Why I Write', Orwell says, 'One can write nothing readable unless one constantly strives to efface one's own personality. Good prose is like a window pane.'[6] Earlier in the same essay, he lists as one of the four possible motives for writing books the 'historical impulse', defined as a 'desire to see things as they are, to find out true facts and store them up for the use of posterity' (CEJL, I, p. 4). These passages, and others like them in Orwell's essays, are often read together with the following passage from 1984:

> The Party told you to reject the evidence of your eyes and ears. It was their final, most essential, command. [Winston's] heart sank as he thought of the enormous power arrayed against him, the ease with which any Party intellectual would overthrow him in debate. ... And yet he was in the right! ... The obvious, the silly, and the true had got to be defended. Truisms are true, hold on to that! The solid world exists, its laws do not change. Stones are hard, water is wet, objects unsupported fall towards the earth's centre. With the feeling that he was speaking to O'Brien, and also that he was setting forth an important axiom, [Winston] wrote: 'Freedom is the freedom to say that two plus two make four. If that is granted, all else follows.'
>
> (p. 790)

Emphasising these passages (and others like them)[7] has led many commentators to conclude that Orwell teaches us to set our faces against all those sneaky intellectuals who try to tell us that truth is not 'out there', that what counts as a possible truth is a function of the vocabulary you use, and what counts as a truth is a function of the rest of your beliefs. Orwell has, in short, been read as a realist philosopher, a defender of common sense against its cultured, ironist despisers.[8]

On this reading, the crucial opposition in Orwell's thought is the standard metaphysical one between contrived appearance and naked reality. The latter is obscured by bad, untransparent prose and by bad, unnecessarily sophisticated theory. Once the dirt is rubbed off the windowpane, the truth about any moral or political situation will be clear. Only those who have allowed their own personality (and in particular their resentment, sadism, and hunger for power) to cloud their vision will fail to grasp the plain moral facts. One such plain moral fact is that it is better to be kind than to torture. Only such people will try to evade plain epistemological and metaphysical facts through sneaky philosophical manoeuvres. Among such facts are that truth is 'independent' of human minds and languages, and that gravitation is not 'relative' to any human mode of thought.

For reasons already given, I do not think there are any plain moral facts out there in the world, nor any truths independent of language, nor any neutral ground on which to stand and argue that either torture or kindness are preferable to the other. So I want to offer a different reading of Orwell. This is not a matter of wanting to have him on my side of a philosophical argument. He had no more taste for such arguments, or skill at constructing them, than did Nabokov.[9] Rather, it is a matter of insisting that the kind of thing Orwell and Nabokov both did – sensitising an audience to cases of cruelty and humiliation which they had not noticed – is not usefully thought of as a matter of stripping away appearance and revealing reality. It is better thought of as a redescription of what may happen or has been happening – to be compared, not with reality, but with alternative descriptions of the same events. In the case of the Communist oligarchs, what Orwell and Solzhenitsyn did was to give us an alternative context, an alternative perspective, from which we liberals, the people who think that cruelty is the worst thing we do, could describe the political history of our century.

Deciding between the descriptions which Sartre and Orwell were offering of that history in the late 1940s, like deciding between the descriptions which Fredric Jameson and Irving Howe now offer of our present political situation, is not a matter of confronting or re-fusing to confront hard, unpleasant facts. Nor is it a matter of being blinded, or not being blinded, by ideology. It is a matter of playing off scenarios against contrasting scenarios, projects against alterna-tive projects, descriptions against redescriptions.

Redescriptions which change our minds on political situations are not much like windowpanes. On the contrary, they are the sort of thing which only writers with very special talents, writing at just the right moment in just the right way, are able to bring off. In his better moments, Orwell himself dropped the rhetoric of trans-parency to plain fact, and recognised that he was doing the same *kind* of thing as his opponents, the apologists for Stalin, were doing. Consider, for example, the following passage:

'Imaginative' writing is as it were a flank attack upon positions that are impregnable from the front. A writer attempting anything that is not coldly 'intellectual' can do very little with words in their primary meanings. He gets his effect, if at all, by using words in a tricky roundabout way.

(*CEJL*, II, p. 19)

Orwell's tricky way, in *Animal Farm*, was to throw the incredibly complex and sophisticated character of leftist political discussion into high and absurd relief by retelling the political history of his century in terms suitable for children. The trick worked, because efforts to see an important difference between Stalin and Hitler, and to continue analysing recent political history with the help of terms like 'socialism', 'capitalism', and 'fascism', had become unwieldy and impracticable. In Kuhnian terms, so many anomalies had been piling up, requiring the addition of so many epicycles, that the overextended structure just needed a sharp kick at the right spot, the right kind of ridicule at the right moment. That was why *Animal Farm* was able to turn liberal opinion around. It was not its relation to reality, but its relation to the most popular alternative description of recent events, that gave it its power. It was a strategically placed lever, not a mirror.

To admirers like Trilling, Orwell provided a fresh glimpse of obvious moral realities. To his Marxist contemporaries, like Isaac Deutscher, and to present-day Marxists like Norris, he was, at best, simpleminded.[10] On my view, Orwell's mind was neither transparent nor simple. It was not *obvious* how to describe the post-World War II political situation, and it still is not. For useful political description is in a vocabulary which suggests answers to the question 'What is to be done?' just as useful scientific description is in a vocabulary which increases our ability to predict and control events. Orwell gave us no hints about how to answer Chernyshevsky's question. He merely told us how *not* to try to answer it, what vocabulary to *stop* using. He convinced us that our previous political vocabulary had little relevance to our current political situation, but he did not give us a new one. He sent us back to the drawing board, and we are still there. Nobody has come up with a large framework for relating our large and vague hopes for human equality to the actual distribution of power in the world. The capitalists remain as greedy and shortsighted, and the Communist oligarchs as cynical and corrupt, as Orwell said they were. No third force has emerged in the world, and neither the neoconservatives nor the post-Marxist left has come up with more than exercises in nostalgia. The possibility that we shall be able to look back on Orwell as blinkered and shortsighted remains, alas, purely theoretical. For nobody has come up with a plausible scenario for actualising what Orwell called the 'technical possibility of human equality'.

Such a scenario was what the pre-World War II liberals thought they had. There were times, in the 1930s, when Orwell himself thought he had such a scenario. But the recurrent disconfirmation of his own predictions, his realisation that his generation had been suckered by the use of 'Marxist theory' as an instrument of Russian politics, and his disgust with cynical prophecies like James Burnham's, led him to write *Animal Farm* and the first two-thirds of *1984*. These books achieved their purpose not by confronting us with moral realities but by making clear to us that we could no longer use our old political ideas, and that we now had none which were of much use for steering events toward liberal goals. All the accusations of 'masochistic despair' and 'cynical hopelessness' which are flung at Orwell will fall flat until somebody comes up with some new scenarios.

But Orwell did achieve something more than this negative, though necessary and useful, job of sending us back to the drawing board. He did this in the last third of *1984* – the part which is about O'Brien. There he sketched an alternative scenario, one which led in the *wrong* direction. He convinced us that there was a perfectly good chance that the same developments which had made human equality technically possible might make endless slavery possible. He did so by convincing us that nothing in the nature of truth, or man, or history was going to block that scenario, any more than it was going to underwrite the scenario which liberals had been using between the wars. He convinced us that all the intellectual and poetic gifts which had made Greek philosophy, modern science, and Romantic poetry possible might someday find employment in the Ministry of Truth.

In the view of *1984* I am offering, Orwell has no *answer* to O'Brien, and is not interested in giving one. Like Nietzsche, O'Brien regards the whole idea of being 'answered', of exchanging ideas, of reasoning together, as a symptom of weakness. Orwell did not invent O'Brien to serve as a dialectical foil, as a modern counterpart to Thrasymachus. He invented him to warn us against him, as one might warn against a typhoon or a rogue elephant. Orwell is not setting up a philosophical position but trying to make a concrete political possibility plausible by answering three questions: 'How will the intellectuals of a certain possible future describe themselves?' 'What will they do with themselves?' 'How will their talents be employed?' He does not view O'Brien as crazy, misguided, seduced by a mistaken theory, or blind to the moral facts. He simply views him as *dangerous* and as *possible*. Orwell's second great achievement, in addition to having made Soviet propaganda look absurd, was to convince the rest of us that O'Brien was, indeed, possible.

As evidence that this way of reading the last part of *1984* is not entirely factitious, I can cite a column which Orwell wrote in 1944. There he dissects what he calls 'a very dangerous fallacy, now very widespread in the countries where totalitarianism has not established itself':

> The fallacy is to believe that under a dictatorial government you can be free *inside*. ... The greatest mistake is to imagine that the human being is an autonomous individual. The secret freedom which you can supposedly enjoy under a despotic government is nonsense, because your thoughts are never entirely your own. Philosophers, writers, artists, even scientists, not only need encouragement and an audience, they need constant stimulation from other people. ... Take away freedom of speech, and the creative faculties dry up.
>
> (*CEJL*, III, p. 133)

How does this passage mesh with the passage from Winston's diary I quoted earlier, the one which concludes, 'Freedom is the freedom to say that two plus two equals four. If that is granted, all else follows'? I suggest that the two passages can both be seen as saying that it does not matter whether 'two plus two is four' is true, much less whether this truth is 'subjective' or 'corresponds to external reality'. All that matters is that if you do believe it, you can say it without getting hurt. In other words, what matters is your ability to talk to other people about what seems to you true, not what is in fact true. If we take care of freedom, truth can take care of itself. If we are ironic enough about our final vocabularies, and curious enough about everyone else's, we do not have to worry about whether we are in direct contact with moral reality, or whether we are blinded by ideology, or whether we are being weakly 'relativistic'.

I take Orwell's claim that there is no such thing as *inner* freedom, no such thing as an 'autonomous individual', to be the one made by historicist, including Marxist, critics of 'liberal individualism'. This is that there is nothing deep inside each of us, no common human nature, no built-in human solidarity, to use as a moral reference point.[11] There is nothing to people except what has been socialised into them – their ability to use language, and thereby to exchange beliefs and desires with other people. Orwell reiterated this point when he said, 'To abolish class distinctions means abolishing a part of yourself', and when he added that if he himself were to 'get outside the class racket' he would 'hardly be recognisable as the same person'. To be a person is to speak a *particular* language, one which enables us to discuss particular beliefs and desires with particular sorts of people. It is a historical contingency whether we are socialised by Neanderthals, ancient Chinese, Eton, Summerhill, or the Ministery of Truth. Simply by being human we do not have a common bond. For all we share with all other humans is the same thing we share with all other animals – the ability to feel pain.

One way to react to this last point is to say that our moral vocabulary should be extended to cover animals as well as people. A better way is to try to isolate something that distinguishes human from animal pain. Here is where O'Brien comes in. O'Brien reminds us that human beings who have been socialised – socialised in any language, any culture – do share a capacity which other animals lack. They can all be given a special kind of pain: They can all be humiliated by the forcible tearing down of the particular structures of language and belief in which they were socialised (or which they pride themselves on having formed for themselves). More specifically, they can be used, and animals cannot, to gratify O'Brien's wish to 'tear human minds to pieces and put them together again in new shapes of your own choosing'.

The point that sadism aims at humiliation rather than merely at pain in general has been developed in detail by Elaine Scarry in *The Body in Pain: The Making and Unmaking of the World*. It is a consequence of Scarry's argument that the worst thing you can do to somebody is not to make her scream in agony but to use that agony in such a way that even when the agony is over, she cannot reconstitute herself. The idea is to get her to do or say things – and, if possible, believe and desire things, think thoughts – which later she will be unable to cope with having done or thought. You can thereby, as Scarry puts it, 'unmake her world' by making it impossible for her to use language to describe what she has been.

Let me now apply this point to O'Brien's making Winston believe, briefly, that two and two equals five. Notice first that, unlike 'Rutherford conspired with the Eurasian General Staff', it is not something O'Brien himself believes. Nor does Winston himself believe it once he is broken and released. It is not, and could not be, Party doctrine. (The book O'Brien co-authored, *The Theory and Practice of Oligarchical Collectivism*, notes that when one is 'designing a gun or an airplane' two and two *have* to make four [*1984*, p. 858].) The *only* point in making Winston believe that two and two equals five is to break him. Getting somebody to deny a belief for no reason is a first step toward making her incapable of having a self because she becomes incapable of weaving a coherent web of belief and desire. It makes her irrational, in a quite precise sense: She is unable to give a reason for her belief that fits together with her other beliefs. She becomes irrational not in the sense that she has lost contact with reality but in the sense that she can no longer rationalise – no longer justify herself to herself.

Making Winston briefly, believe that two plus two equals five serves the same 'breaking' function as making him briefly desire that the rats chew through Julia's face rather than his own. But the latter episode differs from the former in being a final, irreversible unmaking. Winston might be able to include the belief that he had once, under odd conditions, believed that two and two equals five within a coherent story about his character and his life. Temporary irrationality is something around which one can weave a story. But the belief that he once wanted them to *do it to Julia* is not one he can weave a story around. That was why O'Brien saved the rats for the best part, the part in which Winston had to watch himself go to pieces and simultaneously know that he could never pick up those pieces again.

To return to my main point: the fact that two and two does not make five is not the essence of the matter. What matters is that Winston has picked it as symbolic, and that O'Brien knows that. If there were a *truth*, belief in which would break Winston, making him believe that *truth* would be just as good for O'Brien's purposes. Suppose it were the case that Julia had been (like the purported antique dealer, Mr Charrington) a longtime member of the Thought Police. Suppose she had been instructed by O'Brien to seduce Winston. Suppose that O'Brien told Winston this, giving him no evidence save his own obviously unreliable word. Suppose further that Winston's love for Julia was such that only the same torture which made him able to believe that two and two equals five could make him believe that Julia had been O'Brien's agent. The effect would be the same, and the effect is all that matters to O'Brien. Truth and falsity drop out.

O'Brien wants to cause Winston as much pain as possible, and for this purpose what matters is that Winston be forced to realise that he has become incoherent, realise that he is no longer able to use a language or be a self. Although we can say, 'I believ*ed* something false', nobody can say to himself, 'I am, right now, believing something false'. So nobody can be humiliated at the moment of believing a falsehood, or by the mere fact of having done so. But people can, their torturers hope, experience the ultimate humiliation of saying to themselves, in retrospect, 'Now that I have believed or desired *this*, I can never be what I hoped to be, what I thought I was. The story I have been telling myself about myself – my picture of myself as honest, or loyal, or devout – no longer makes sense. I no longer have a self to make sense of. There is no world in which I can picture myself as living, because there is no vocabulary in which I can tell a coherent story about myself.' For Winston the sentence he could not utter sincerely and still be able to put himself back together was 'Do it to Julia!' and the worst thing in the world happened to be rats. But presumably each of us stands in the same relations to some sentence, and to some thing.

If one can discover that key sentence and that key thing, then, as O'Brien says, one can tear a mind apart and put it together in new shapes of one's own choosing. But it is the sound of the tearing, not the result of the putting together, that is the object of the exercise. It is the breaking that matters. The putting together is just an extra fillip. When Winston comes to love Big Brother, for example, it is irrelevant that Big Brother is in fact unlovable. What matters is that there is no way of going back and forth between a Winston who loves Big Brother and the Winston who loved Julia, cherished the glass paperweight, and could remember the clipping which showed that Rutherford was innocent. The point of breaking Winston is not to bring Winston into line with the Party's ideas. The Inner Party is not torturing Winston because it is afraid of a revolution, or because it is offended by the thought that someone might not love Big Brother. It is torturing Winston for the sake of causing Winston pain, and thereby increasing the pleasure of its members, particularly O'Brien. The only object of O'Brien's intensive seven-year-long study of Winston was to make possible the rich, complicated, delicate, absorbing spectacle of mental pain which Winston would eventually provide. The only point in leaving the thing sitting in the Chestnut Tree Café alive for a while is that it can still feel pain when the telescreen plays 'Under the spreading chestnut tree / I sold you and you sold me.' Torture is not for the sake of getting people to obey, nor for the sake of getting them to believe falsehoods. As O'Brien says, 'The object of torture is torture.'

For a gifted and sensitive intellectual living in a post-totalitarian culture, this sentence is the analogue of 'Art for art's sake' or 'Truth for its own sake', for torture is now the only art form and the only intellectual discipline available to such a person. That sentence is the central sentence of *1984*. But it is also the one which has been hardest for commentators to handle. Many of them have agreed with John Strachey that

> ... from the moment when Winston and Julia are, inevitably, caught and their interrogation and torture begins, the book deteriorates. ... the subject of physical torture, though it was clearly another of his obsessions, was not one with which Orwell was equipped to deal. He had never been tortured, any more than most of the rest of us have been. And those who have no personal experience of this matter may be presumed to know nothing whatever about it.[12]

This last point of Strachey's is, I think, fairly easy to answer. What Strachey neglects is that the last third of *1984* is about O'Brien, not about Winston – about torturing, not about being tortured.

This neglect is the result of a natural desire to identify Orwell with Winston. If we yield to this desire, then passages like the one I quoted earlier, in which Winston insists on the importance of believing that two and two equals four, will be the centre of the novel. The last third of the novel will be merely a hysterical and unnecessary tailpiece. The passages I have been emphasising – the ones in which O'Brien tells about how things look from inside the Inner Party – will be read as reductiones ad absurdum of O'Brien's dialectical position, or else as Raymond Williams reads them. He reads 'The object of torture is torture. The object of power is power' as saying that (in a phrase which Orwell had used to describe James Burnham's position) 'power hunger ... is a natural instinct which does not have to be explained'.

Williams recognises that it is too easy just to identify Orwell with Winston, but he thinks that Orwell's identification with O'Brien was a last-minute self-betrayal. Williams comments:

> It is not necessary to deny the existence, even the frequent occurrence, of persecution and power and torture 'for their own sake' ... to go on resisting the cancellation of all links between power and policy. And this cancellation *must* be resisted, if only because it would then be pointless to try to distinguish between social systems, or to inquire, discriminatingly, where this or that system went good or bad.[13]

Williams thinks that if Burnham were right about power hunger's being a natural instinct, there would be no 'fact of the matter', no 'objective truth' about whether social democracy is better than fascism. He says that Burnham's position 'discredits all actual political beliefs and aspirations, since these are inevitably covers for naked power and the wish for it. ... There is also a cancellation of inquiry and argument, and therefore of the possibility of truth.' Williams takes Orwell to have succumbed, briefly and at the last moment, to the pernicious view that there *is* no such possibility. Like Strachey, Williams thinks that the novel goes off the rails at the end.

Quoting Orwell's stricture against Burnham – 'Power worship blurs political judgement because it leads, almost unavoidably, to the belief that present trends will continue' – Williams ends his book on Orwell as follows:

> Yet Orwell himself, always an opponent of privilege and power, committed himself, in the fiction, to just that submissive belief. The warning that the world could be going that way became, in the very absoluteness of the fiction, an imaginative submission to its inevitability. And then to rattle that chain again is to show little respect to those many men and women, including from the whole record Orwell himself, who have fought and are fighting the destructive and ignorant trends that are still so powerful, and who have kept the strength to imagine, as well as to work for, human dignity, freedom and peace.[14]

William's reference to 'the strength to imagine ... human dignity, freedom and peace' brings me back to my claim that we are still at the drawing board. I do not think that we liberals *can* now imagine a future of 'human dignity, freedom and peace'. That is, we cannot tell ourselves a story about how to get from the actual present to such a future. We can picture various socioeconomic setups which would be preferable to the present one. But we have no clear sense of how to get from the actual world to these theoretically possible worlds, and thus no clear idea of what to work for. We have to take as a starting point the world Orwell showed us in 1948: a globe divided into a rich, free, democratic, selfish, and greedy First World; an unchanging Second World run by an impregnable and ruthless Inner Party; and a starving, overpopulated, desperate Third World. We liberals have no plausible large-scale scenario for changing that world so as to realise the 'technical possibility of human equality'.

This inability to imagine how to get from here to there is a matter neither of loss of moral resolve nor of theoretical superficiality, self-deception, or self-betrayal. It is not something we can remedy by a firmer resolve, or more transparent prose, or better philosophical accounts of man, truth, or history. It is just the way things happen to have fallen out. Sometimes things prove to be just as bad as they first looked. Orwell helped us to formulate a pessimistic description of the political situation which forty years of further experience have only confirmed. This bad news remains the great intransigent fact of contemporary political speculation, the one that blocks all the liberal scenarios.[15]

In contrast to the Strachey–Williams view that the book might have done well to end sooner, I think that the fantasy of endless torture – the suggestion that the future is 'a boot stamping on a human face – forever' is essential to *1984*, and that the question about 'the possibility of truth' is a red herring. I can outline my own view by taking issue with Williams on three points.

First, I do not think that any large view of the form 'political beliefs are really …' or 'human nature is really …' or 'truth is really …' – any large philosophical claim – *could* discredit political beliefs and aspirations. I do not think it is psychologically possible to give up on political liberalism on the basis of a philosophical view about the nature of man or truth or history. Such views are ways of rounding out and becoming self-conscious about one's moral identity, not justifications of that identity or weapons which might destroy it. One would have to be very odd to change one's politics because one had become convinced, for example, that a coherence theory of truth was preferable to a correspondence theory. Second, no such view can (in Williams's phrase) 'cancel' inquiry, argument, and the quest for truth – any more than it can 'cancel' the search for food or for love. Only force can effect such cancellations, not philosophy. Third, one should not read O'Brien as if he were Burnham – a philosopher making large claims about what is 'natural'. O'Brien is not saying that everything else is a mask for the will to power. He is not saying that the nature of man or power or history ensures that that boot will grind down forever, but rather that it just *happens* that it will. He is saying that it just so happens that this is how things came out, and that it just so happens that the scenario can no longer be changed. As a matter of sheer contingent fact – as contingent as a comet or a virus – that is what the future is going to be.

This seems to me the only reading which accords with the fact that O'Brien's account of the future is the part we all remember best about *1984*, the really *scary* part. If we take O'Brien not as making large general claims but as making specific empirical predictions, he is a much more frightening figure. Somewhere we all know that philosophically sophisticated debate about whether human nature is innately benevolent or innately sadistic, or about the internal dialectic of European history, or about human rights, or objective truth, or the representational function of language, is pretty harmless stuff. O'Brien the theorist is about as likely to cause real honest-to-God belly-fear as Burnham or Nietzsche. But O'Brien, the well-informed, well-placed, well-adjusted, intelligent, sensitive, educated member of the Inner Party, is more than just alarming. He is as terrifying a character as we are likely to meet in a book. Orwell managed, by skilful reminders of, and extrapolations from, what happened to real people in real places – things that nowadays we know are still happening – to convince us that O'Brien is a plausible character-type of a possible future society, one in which the intellectuals had accepted the fact that liberal hopes had no chance of realisation.

Our initial defence against this suggestion is that O'Brien is a psychologically implausible figure. In this view, the only torturers are insensitive, banal people like Eichmann, Gradus, and Paduk. Anybody who has O'Brien's 'curiously civilised' way of settling his spectacles, just *couldn't* have the intentions O'Brien professes. O'Brien is a curious, perceptive intellectual – much like us. Our sort of people don't do that sort of thing.

Orwell showed us how to parry this initial defensive move when he said of H. G. Wells that he was 'too sane to understand the modern world'. In context, what Orwell meant was that Wells did not have what he called 'the Fascist streak' which, he said, Kipling and Jack London had had, and which was necessary to find fascism intelligible.[16] I think that Orwell was half-consciously priding himself on sharing this streak with Kipling. He was priding himself on having the imagination to see that history very well might not go the way he wanted it to go, the way Wells thought it was *bound* to go. But this does not mean that Orwell at any time, even when creating O'Brien, believed that it was *bound* to go that way. The anti-theoretical streak in Orwell, which he shared with Nabokov and which made them both unable to take Marxist theory seriously, made him quite certain that things could usually go either way, that the future was up for grabs.

One can see the point of saying that Wells was 'too sane' by imagining an optimistic Roman intellectual, living under the Antonines and occupied with charting the progress of humanity from the beginnings of rational thought in Athens to his own enlightened time. He happens to get hold of a copy of the recently collected and edited Christian Scriptures. He is appalled by the psychological implausibility and moral degradation of the figure called 'Jesus', for the same reasons that Nietzsche was later to be appalled. When told by an imaginative friend that efforts to emulate this figure may permeate empires larger than Rome's, and may be led by men 'who consider themselves enlightened and progressive', he is incredulous. As his friend remarks, he is too sane to grasp the possibility that the world may swerve.[17]

The point of my analogy is that the complex of ideas associated with Christianity – for example, the idea that reciprocal pity is a sufficient basis for political association, the idea that there is something importantly wrong with (to use Orwell's list) 'imprisonment without trial, the use of war prisoners as slaves, public executions, torture to extract confessions, the use of hostages, and the deportation of whole populations', the idea that distinctions of wealth, talent, strength, sex, and race are not relevant to public policy – these ideas were once fantasies as implausible as those associated with O'Brien's Oligarchical Collectivism. Once upon a time people like Wilberforce and the Mills would have seemed distasteful hysterical projections of a fantast's morbid imagination. Orwell helps us see that it *just happened* that rule in Europe passed into the hands of people who pitied the humiliated and dreamed of human equality, and that it may *just happen* that the world will wind up being ruled by people who lack any such sentiments or ideas. Socialisation, to repeat, goes all the way down, and who gets to do the socialising is often a matter of who manages to kill whom first. The triumph of Oligarchical Collectivism, if it comes, will not come because people are basically bad, or really are not brothers, or really have no natural rights, any more than Christianity and political liberalism have triumphed (to the extent they have) because people are basically good, or really are brothers, or really do have natural rights. History may create and empower people like O'Brien as a result of the same kind of accidents that have prevented those people from existing until recently – the same sort of accidents that created and empowered people like J. S. Mill and Orwell himself. That it might be thought importantly wrong to get amusement from watching people being torn apart by animals was once as much an implausible historical contingency as O'Brien's Oligarchical Collectivism. What Orwell helps us see is that it may have *just happened* that Europe began to prize benevolent sentiments and the idea of a common humanity, and that it may *just happen* that the world will wind up being ruled by people who lack any such sentiments and any such moralities.

On my reading, Orwell's denial that there is such a thing as the autonomous individual is part of a larger denial that there is something outside of time or more basic than chance which can be counted on to block, or eventually reverse, such accidental sequences. So I read the passage from Winston's diary about the need to insist that two and two equals four not as Orwell's view about how to keep the O'Briens at bay but, rather, as a description of how to keep ourselves going when things get tight. We do so by talking to other people – trying to get reconfirmation of our own identities by articulating these in the presence of others. We hope that these others will say something to help us keep our web of beliefs and desires coherent. Notice that when Winston wrote in his diary that 'everything follows' from the freedom to say that two and two equals four, he had 'the feeling that he was speaking to O'Brien'. He describes himself as 'writing the diary for O'Brien – *to* O'Brien; it was like an interminable letter which no one would ever read, but which was addressed to a particular person and took its colour from that fact' (*1984*, p. 79). Notice also that when he is arrested O'Brien tells him that he has 'always known' that O'Brien was not on his side, and Winston agrees (p. 880).

Because in an earlier passage Winston says he 'knew with more certainty than before, that O'Brien was on his side', this agreement is hard to understand. The best explanation we get of the contradiction comes in a later passage when, just after finally managing to get Winston briefly to believe that two and two equals five, O'Brien asks:

> Do you remember writing in your diary that it did not matter whether I was a friend or an enemy, since I was at least a person who understood you and could be talked to? You were right. I enjoy talking to you. Your mind appeals to me. It resembles my own mind except that you happen to be insane.
>
> (p. 892)

This passage echoes the first mention of O'Brien in the novel. There we were told that Winston

> ... felt deeply drawn to him, and not solely because he was intrigued by the contrast between O'Brien's urbane manner and his prize-fighter's physique. Much more it was because of a secretly held belief – or perhaps not even a belief, merely a hope – that O'Brien's political orthodoxy was not perfect. Something in his face suggested it irresistibly. And again, perhaps it was not even unorthodoxy that was written in his face, but simply intelligence.
>
> (*1984*, p. 748; see also p. 757)

We learn, in the end, that it *was* a hope rather than a belief, and that it *was* intelligence rather than unorthodoxy.

It is tempting to say that this passage, like Winston's abiding and constant love for O'Brien, merely exhibits Winston's masochism, the other side of his sadism.[18] But that would dismiss such love too easily. What the passage does is to remind us that the ironist – the person who has doubts about his own final vocabulary, his own moral identity, and perhaps his own sanity – desperately needs to *talk* to other people, needs this with the same urgency as people need to make love. He needs to do so because only conversation enables him to handle these doubts, to keep himself together, to keep his web of beliefs and desires coherent enough to enable him to act. He has these doubts and these needs because, for one reason or another, socialisation did not entirely take. Because his utterances detour through his brain – rather than, as in duckspeak, coming straight from the well-programmed larynx – he has Socratic doubts about the final vocabulary he inherited.[19] So, like Socrates and Proust, he is continually entering into erotic relationships with conversational interlocutors. Sometimes these relationships are masochistic, like Marcel's first relationship to Madame de Guermantes. Sometimes they are sadistic, like Charlus's hoped-for maieutic relationship to Marcel. But which they are is not as important as that these relationships be with people intelligent enough to understand what one is talking about – people who are capable of seeing how one might have these doubts because they know what such doubts are like, people who are themselves given to irony.

This is the function O'Brien serves for Winston. But can one call O'Brien an ironist? Orwell gives him all the standard traits of the British intellectual of Orwell's youth. Indeed, my (unverifiable) hunch is that O'Brien is partially modelled on George Bernard Shaw, an important Socratic figure for Orwell's generation. But unlike Shaw, who shared Nietzsche's taste for the historical sublime, O'Brien has come to terms with the fact that the future will exactly resemble the recent past – not as a matter of metaphysical necessity but because the Party has worked out the techniques necessary to prevent change. O'Brien has mastered doublethink, and is not troubled by doubts about himself or the Party.[20] So he is *not*, in my sense, an ironist. But he still has the *gifts* which, in a time when doublethink had not yet been invented, would have made him an ironist. He does the only possible thing he can with those gifts: He uses them to form the sort of relationship he has with Winston. Presumably Winston is only one of a long series of people, each with a mind like O'Brien's own, whom O'Brien has searched out, studied from afar, and eventually learned enough about to enjoy torturing. With each he has entered into a long, close, intensely felt relationship, in order at the end to feel the pleasure of twisting and breaking the special, hidden, tender parts of a mind with the same gifts as his own – those parts which only he, and perhaps a few of his Minitru colleagues, know how to discover and torment. In this qualified sense, we can think of O'Brien as the last ironist in Europe – someone who is employed in the only way in which the end of liberal hope permits irony to be employed.

I take Orwell to be telling us that whether our future rulers are more like O'Brien or more like J. S. Mill does not depend – as Burnham, Williams, and metaphysicians generally suggest it does – on deep facts about human nature. For, as O'Brien and Humbert

Humbert show, intellectual gifts – intelligence, judgement, curiosity, imagination, a taste for beauty – are as malleable as the sexual instinct. They are as capable of as many diverse employments as the human hand. The kinks in the brain which provide these gifts have no more connection with some central region of the self – a 'natural' self which prefers kindness to torture, or torture to kindness – than do muscular limbs or sensitive genitals. What our future rulers will be like will not be determined by any large necessary truths about human nature and its relation to truth and justice, but by a lot of small contingent facts.

From Richard Rorty, *Contingency, Irony, and Solidarity* (Cambridge, 1989), pp. 169–88.

NOTES

[In Richard Rorty's analysis, Orwell provides possible and highly ironic theoretical scenarios for intellectuals in potentially post-totalitarian cultures and future worlds; frightening and pessimistic scenarios. For Rorty, Orwell's *1984* in particular provides an insight into how the haphazard and the accidental inform the indeterminacies and contingencies of history. For Rorty the continued interest in Orwell depends upon a growing propensity to read him topically, in the light of historical contingencies that project beyond this century, and he considers Orwell's 'prospective' on the future via a 'rediscription' or 'alternative scenario' of Communist Russia in *Animal Farm* and particularly via the torturer O'Brien in *1984*. Rorty shows how Orwell's work cuts across boundaries of literary criticism, politics and philosophy, emphasising his impact across disciplines. Eds]

1. Howe continues: 'Such writers, it is possible, will not survive their time, for what makes them so valuable and so endearing to their contemporaries – that mixture of desperate topicality and desperate tenderness – is not likely to be a quality conducive to the greatest art. But it should not matter to us, this possibility that in the future Silone or Orwell will not seem as important as they do for many people in our time. We know what they do for us, and we know that no other writers, including far greater ones, can do it' ('*1984*: History as Nightmare', in Samuel Hynes [ed.], *Twentieth Century Interpretations of 1984* [Englewood Cliffs, NJ, 1971], p. 53).

2. *The Penguin Complete Novels of George Orwell* (Harmondsworth, 1983), p. 861. I shall refer to *1984* in this edition by parenthetical page numbers. Notice that these practices were common enough

outside Europe – in Africa and Asia, for instance – during the nineteenth century. But Orwell is talking about Europe. Orwell is being consciously provincial, writing about the particular kinds of people he knows and their moral situation. The provisional title of *1984* was *The Last Man in Europe*.

3. Howe says, 'It is extremely important to note that the world of *1984* is *not* totalitarianism as we know it, but totalitarianism after its world triumph. Strictly speaking, the society of Oceania might be called post-totalitarian' (p. 53).

4. 'Openly in England, more cautiously in America, there has arisen a desire among intellectuals to belittle Orwell's achievement, often in the guise of celebrating his humanity and his "goodness". They feel embarrassed before the apocalyptic desperation of the book, they begin to wonder whether it may not be just a little overdrawn and humourless, they even suspect it is tinged with the hysteria of the deathbed. Nor can it be denied that all of us would feel more comfortable if the book could be cast out' (p. 42).

5. Lionel Trilling, 'Orwell on the Future', in Hynes (ed.), *Twentieth Century Interpretations of 1984*, p. 24.

6. Sonia Orwell and Ian Angus (eds), *The Collected Essays, Journalism and Letters of George Orwell* (London, 1968), I, p. 7. Hereafter cited parenthetically as *CEJL*.

7. See, for example, *CEJL*, III, p. 119.

8. Samuel Hynes, for example, sums up the moral of *1984* by saying, 'Winston Smith's beliefs are as simple as two plus two equal four: the past is fixed, love is private, and the truth is beyond change. All have this in common: they set limits to men's power; they testify to the fact that some things cannot be changed. The point is beyond politics – it is a point of essential humanity' (p. 19).

9. On Orwell's failure to read philosophy, see Bernard Crick, *George Orwell: A Life* (Harmondsworth, 1980), pp. 25, 305, 343, 506. See also *CEJL*, III, p. 98.

10. For an example of the latter reaction, see Isaac Deutscher's discussion of Orwell in 'The Mysticism of Cruelty', in Hynes. For a later use of the 'renegade' label, and further doubts about whether Orwell knew enough philosophy, see Christopher Norris, 'Language, Truth and Ideology: Orwell and the Post-War Left', in Christopher Norris (ed.), *Inside the Myth* (London, 1984).

11. Or even, I would add, to use as a reference point for clear and distinct ideas about the equality of two twos with four. But this is a philosophical quarrel about the 'status' of mathematical truth which need not be pressed here.

12. John Strachey, 'The Strangled Cry', in Hynes, pp. 58–9. I think that
    Orwell implicitly answered Strachey when he wrote, 'The people who
    have shown the best understanding of Fascism are either those who
    have suffered under it or those who have a Fascist streak in them-
    selves' (*CEJL*, II, p. 172). His biographers have remarked upon
    Orwell's spurts of sadism. See especially Crick, *George Orwell, A Life*,
    p. 275n, and also pp. 504, 572. See also Daphne Patai, *The Orwell
    Mystique: A Study in Male Ideology* (Amherst, MA, 1984). Patai
    argues that sadism was pretty close to the centre of Orwell's character;
    I do not find her case convincing, but she certainly has lots of evidence
    to cite. Orwell also had a good eye for sadism in others; see his
    remarks on George Bernard Shaw's sadism at *CEJL*, III, p. 222. The
    choice of the name 'O'Brien', and the description of O'Brien's physical
    appearance (*1984*, p. 748), may have been a conscious or unconscious
    slap at Shaw.

13. Raymond Williams, *Orwell* (London, 1984), pp. 124–5.

14. Ibid., p. 126.

15. I think of the European and American left as having tried to evade this
    fact by taking refuge in theoretical sophistication – acting as if practi-
    cal scenarios were unnecessary, and as if the intellectuals could fulfil
    their political responsibilities simply by criticising obvious evils
    in terms of ever more 'radical' theoretical vocabularies. See my
    'Thugs and Theorists: A Reply to Bernstein', *Political Theory* (1987),
    pp. 564–80.

16. See *CEJL*, II, p. 172. Orwell's use of his own sadism to create the
    character of O'Brien seems to me a triumph of self-knowledge and
    self-overcoming.

17. Both Wells and my imaginary Roman were metaphysicians – people
    incapable of seeing their final vocabulary as contingent, and thus
    driven to believe that something in the nature of reality would preserve
    that vocabulary.

18. For Winston's sadism, see *1984*, p. 751.

19. For duckspeak, see *1984*, pp. 923, 775. See also the description of
    Winston in torment at p. 882.

20. I think of doublethink as a kind of deliberately induced schizophrenia,
    the dwelling of two systems of belief and desire within a single body.
    One of these systems is able to talk to Winston about his doubts; the
    other is not. O'Brien shifts back and forth between them in the uncon-
    scious way in which those with split personalities can switch into
    another personality as needed.

9

On the Political Sociology of Intellectuals: George Orwell and the London Left Intelligentsia

JOHN RODDEN

I

Contemporary social theorists have written extensively about the modern intellectual's class origins, political allegiances, and social function.[1] Yet, as Charles Kadushin notes, 'Despite (or perhaps because of) the many works on intellectuals, there is no adequate sociological theory of intellectuals or intellectual life. ... Theory-building in this field has been marred by an abundance of opinion and moralisation, a dearth of facts, and a plethora of parochial definitions.'[2] Much of the scholarship on the sociology of intellectuals is purely descriptive; and even worse, unlike the case in other subfields of the sociology of occupations, as Robert Brym notes, sociologists have tended to accept the self-descriptions (or 'professional ideologies') of intellectuals about their political outlooks at face value.[3] Brym calls for a moratorium on general theories about the correlation between social structure and intellectuals' patterns of mobility, and he instead urges careful study of the relation between partisan affiliation and the intellectual's career trajectory through the changing social structure.[4] Given the observations of Kadushin and Brym about the theoretical imprecision and 'intellectual backwardness' of the political sociology of intellectuals,[5] it may prove a modest contribution merely to broach the conceptual issues of the field through the single rich example of a particular intellectual and his intellectual milieu.[6]

George Orwell and the London intelligentsia of the 1930s and 1940s provide an instructive case. The special historical relation of Orwell to the British intellectuals of his day sheds light on the changing situation of the modern Western intellectual. 'When the history of intellectuals of the twentieth century is written', William Steinhoff has predicted, 'some part of it will be devoted to Orwell's analysis and criticism of his fellow intellectuals.'[7] The case of Orwell, however, possesses more than merely historical interest, for it represents not just one man's dispute with his fellow literary intellectuals. Rather, it signals the emergent position of the modern writer-intellectual in Britain, responding to two new, related historical developments in the 1930s: the birth of a radical intelligentsia and the rise in Europe of totalitarianism.

How did English writer-intellectuals react under such conditions? What factors contributed to the rise and decline of widespread intellectual dissidence? What accounts for political rebellion and adaptation occurring variously in political, religious, and aesthetic terms? How do the intellectual's class origins, education, and mature social experience shape his political orientation? Does the writer-intellectual have a special political function to fulfil in society?

These broad historical, conceptual, and normative questions cannot, of course, be addressed adequately in a single example. Moreover, to approach them via the filter of the vivid historical personalities and complicated social conditions of the 1930s and 1940s in Britain runs the risk of generalisation from skewed or impoverished data. Yet advantages emerge too. The sociologist's restricted case allows for a combination of observational detail and conceptual delimitation seldom found in cultural history, and the case of Orwell, an unusually rich and suggestive one, is particularly well-suited to a study of the political sociology of intellectuals. His appropriateness arises, perhaps paradoxically, from the adverse stance which he took toward his adopted 'class' of fellow intellectuals.

By the very fact of his distinctiveness, Orwell offers insight into the typicality of his intellectual generation. Because he was never directly affiliated with the left-wing writers of the 'Auden generation' – 'a generation he was in but never part of', in Stuart

Samuels' characterisation[8] – he could stand at once inside and outside the Left. He thereby could both participate in and give witness to his generation's experience, reflecting its larger dilemma between political detachment and commitment. 'To learn what the world then looked like to an English intellectual', wrote his friend and *Tribune* (London) colleague T. R. Fyvel in *Intellectuals Today* (1968), 'one can go to George Orwell, who wrote so explicitly and precisely about this, and one can also see how the issues of the time were reflected in his own career.' His diverse engagement with poverty, imperialism, fascism, and socialism established Orwell, in Fyvel's view, as 'the characteristic literary figure of the thirties', and Fyvel urged readers 'to consider Orwell's historical role as an intellectual of his day'.[9]

This essay takes this exhortation as a point of departure for addressing the theoretical issues framed by the foregoing questions. Periods of political crisis invariably raise such questions with special directness, whose responses often manifest themselves most clearly in the experience of one centrally involved in the struggle. As his intellectual generation's posthumously proclaimed 'conscience' and 'voice',[10] Orwell and his work constitute not only a sociological but also an ethical guide to the contemporary relation of the intellectual and politics.[11]

[...]

II

Orwell's indecision about his politics in the mid-1930s furnishes a clue to his lifelong 'outsider' stance toward the London intelligentsia. Superficially his career does possess a comparable shape and sequence to other 1930s intellectuals: public school, travel abroad, return to teach, occasional journalism, a 'new signature', contact with the British unemployed, embrace of socialism, and off to Spain. But that narrative abstract masks and bleaches the very different experience which Orwell actually had from most intellectuals of his generation, at least after public school, and which set him apart from them. Detailed attention to the trajectory of his career suggests both the fallacy of linking mechanically class origins with political affiliation and the necessity of injecting a dynamic, historical dimension into an inquiry on the conditions for intellectuals' political radicalisation.

How and why did Orwell differ from the members of the Auden group and the majority of other 1930s intellectuals? Three factors stand out, all of them reinforcing his antagonism toward English 'clubbishness' and shaping his evolving 'outsider' stance toward the London intelligentsia.

First, although Orwell was from the middle class, his family was poorer than most of those which produced public school boys, from whose ranks the leading intellectuals of his generation emerged. He evidently retained this acute consciousness of his relative poverty throughout his adult years, as the bitterness and anguish of 'Such, Such Were the Joys' suggests.[12]

Secondly, Orwell was slightly older than the decade's radicals. Although just a year senior to Day Lewis, he was four years older than Auden and MacNeice and fully six years older than Spender. This age difference may account in part for Orwell's much stronger attachment to pre-World War I England and Edwardian memories. If Cyril Connolly's recollections are accurate, Eric Blair had already read much of Butler, Wells, and Shaw by the time of his entry to Eton (1916), and seems to have possessed an extraordinarily mature (and fatalistic) outlook on the ultimate consequences of World War I for the Empire.[13] It is interesting too that in *Coming Up for Air* (1939) Orwell casts George Bowling, the most autobiographical of Orwell's heroes and a thinly-disguised mouthpiece for many of the author's own views, exactly one decade older than himself. For Eric Blair at 13 evidently had the political sophistication of Bowling at 23. (Orwell, according to Richard Rees, felt guilty throughout his adulthood for being too young to serve in the war – and appropriately enough, Bowling gets wounded in 1916 on a French battlefield.[14]) It may have been that Blair–Orwell was just over the generational divide which permitted a passionate identification with the 'eternal summer' of Edwardian England represented by Bowling's long lazy days at the Mill Farm fishing pond.

A third difference was the crucial one: Blair's Burma police service. His Burma years put him on a track which was to divide him permanently and irrevocably from his coevals, even after his return home. Virtually all of the leading intellectuals of the 1930s and 1940s had gone up to Oxford or Cambridge. Very few intellectuals did not go to some university. At the time that Oxford's literary 'Lads of the Earth' encircled Auden in 1928, Orwell was already back from five gruelling years in Burma – where, as John

Wain once remarked, five years would seem like fifteen in a young Etonian's development.[15] Indeed, Blair had missed the relatively prosperous 1920s and the dramatic political events that would give rise to 1930s radicalism: Lloyd George's fall from grace in 1922; the rise to power in 1923 of the first, short-lived Labour government and the May 1926 General Strike, prompted by proposed reductions in the miners' wages. Numerous upper- and middle-class families viewed the strike as a possible syndicalist revolution in the making. With their support – and that of hundreds of undergraduates – Stanley Baldwin's Conservative government put down the strike. The Auden group watched from a distance and treated the whole affair as springtime amusement. Quite probably Orwell met some of these same miners exactly a decade later at Wigan.

Blair had also missed the heyday of the literary revolution. By the early 1920s Eliot's *The Waste Land* (1922) and Joyce's *Ulysses* (1922), and also the doctrines of the publicists of modernism (e.g., Pound, Hulme, Ford Madox Ford) had begun to filter down to the Oxbridge undergraduates. When Blair returned from Paris at Christmas 1929, having spent little more than six months in England during the previous seven years, many of his peers were already well-established in literary London and the new Auden era of committed political art was dawning.[16]

This personal history may suggest that Orwell was always 'one step behind' his generation and therefore forever playing intellectual 'catch-up' in the 1930s. The political, and even the literary, evidence seems copious. For instance, by choice and circumstance, he never felt completely at home with the modernists and the 'committed' thirties' writers: the Victorian and Edwardian avant-garde of his boyhood (Dickens, Charles Reade, Butler, Gissing, Wells) remained his favourite novelists. Thus, he was still reading the advanced writers of two decades earlier, went to Paris to live like a bohemian when the 'poet-in-the-garret' vogue about Paris was ending, and saw lower-class life from the gutter up when the university youths were editing manifestos and publishing books.

Yet this way of explaining Orwell's development – as if he experienced a literary-political 'lag' *vis-à-vis* his generation as a result of having gone to Burma rather than university – frames a comparison which, once again, rests on a superficial appearance of mere belatedness to his contemporaries. But it is not just that his experience was *later*; his experience was *different* from theirs, and he learned different things from it. He did, it is true, come to fashions when they were no longer fashionable. For example, like some of his contemporaries, he reached political consciousness abroad, but whereas they arrived *en bloc* as a politicised coterie, he arrived alone, and his stance, unlike theirs, was never simply that of a spectator. Orwell *lived* with the tramps and miners; he *fought* at the Aragon front (significantly, with the POUM dissident Marxist militia rather than the Stalinist-controlled International Brigades), not merely visited it like Auden and Spender (or like the numerous British delegates to the 1937 International Conference of Writers Against War and Fascism in Valencia). Orwell engaged so deeply in the events of the decade that he could digest and reflect on them only somewhat later – approximately when the intellectual spectators, who had observed events at a distance, were no longer caught up in them. But this participant-witness stance, as an outsider able to feelingly describe what he has seen 'from the inside',[17] gave Orwell valuable psychological distance (and subsequently, high credibility and immense authority) which most intellectuals of his generation did not possess. When Orwell made a decision, as he did in 1936–37, to embrace democratic socialism, it was a firm and enduring one.

The fact is, as Samuels remarks in a passage already quoted, Orwell belonged to 'a generation he was in but never part of'; he stood outside 'a movement he toyed with but never joined'.[18] He could stand outside precisely because, in the most literal sense, he was never part of 'the Auden generation' – nor of any other. His Burma years had placed him among working-class men slightly older than himself, many of whom had served in World War I; and even after Burma and Paris in the mid-1930s in Hampstead, he associated not with his coevals but mainly with provincial university graduates and other bohemians (e.g., Rayner Heppenstall, Michael Sayers) eight to ten years younger than himself. Some of them looked upon 32-year-old Eric Blair, in Heppenstall's phrase, as 'a nice old thing, a kindly eccentric' – 'ill-read', middlebrow, without a university degree, and always going on insufferably about Butler, the *Magnet*, and comic postcards.[19] Thus Orwell found himself always 'between' and 'outside' generations, not just political groups.[20] That, too, is why his mature experience was so 'different' from that of the Auden group, and it is revealing that Hynes opens and closes *The Auden Generation* with quotations from Orwell's *oeuvre*.[21] Orwell possessed neither the generational consciousness of 'the Auden generation', which is acquired only by shared participation in psychologically decisive events, nor that of the younger and older generational groups in Hampstead and Burma with which he associated. Yet this separation from his contemporaries, especially in the case of his contact with the provincial graduates, probably helped form Orwell's quixotic, plain-speaking character: he could be less inhibited with such youthful, unthreatening, still-unestablished fellow bohemians, caring less that they disagreed with or mocked him. Generational discontinuity thus nourished Orwell's natural antinomianism, inadvertently furnishing him with a setting in which he could do his own thinking, draw on his own experience, and work out his own positions without the pressure to bend to the institutional and intellectual authority of his already-successful coevals. As Bernard Crick observes:

> His time-out in Burma had made him older than most of the young writers still leading this kind of 'floating life'; but it also gave him an emotional detachment from them and immunised him from fashion.
>
> (GO, pp. 177–8)

Indeed, the singularity of Orwell's early manhood, marked by police work in Burma rather than attendance at Oxbridge, further helps explain the specifics of the distinctive arc of his career in the late 1930s and early 1940s: his exceptional responses to the course of the Spanish Civil War, to the revelations about Stalin's crimes, and to the changing CPGB line. What may have seemed Orwell's non-university 'untrained mind', as Crick notes, turned out to be a fiercely independent radical's un*tamed* mind.[22]

Typically, Orwell arrived at the Spanish war late, after the fighting had been on for nearly a half year (December 1936) and just as some leading British Marxist intellectuals (e.g., Ralph Fox, David Guest) were killed in action. The Loyalists' prospects were already dimming by the time Orwell was defending Barcelona in May 1937, and most intellectuals in 1937–38 were quickly growing disillusioned with Stalinism and Left politics. Precisely at this moment, in the face of Franco's looming triumph and the Stalinists' suppression of POUM and other non-Communist militias, Orwell was wholeheartedly committing himself to socialism and penning his eloquent *Homage to Catalonia* (1938). 'I have seen wonderful things', he wrote Cyril Connolly from his Barcelona sickbed in June 1937, after having narrowly escaped death from a throat wound, '& at last really believe in Socialism, which I never did before' (*CEJL*, I, p. 269). Very few other returning leftists felt the same.

And for the intellectuals who stayed home, their skin-deep commitment to socialism was waning, largely as a result of an avalanche of evidence no longer deniable about Stalin's betrayal of the Revolution during the 1930s: the Kirov murder, the brutal extermination of the *kulaks*, the deliberate scheme of mass famine in the Ukraine, the labour camps, the wholesale purges of rival Party members, the mock show trials of fellow Old Bolsheviks, the ferocious repression of all dissent. Just at the time when most Left intellectuals were beginning to doubt the Marxist pieties, Orwell had met his Italian militiaman in Catalonia and found his communitarian vision.

For Orwell had never been attached to Marxism, Stalin, or Russia, unlike most 1930s radicals, and so he (unlike the Auden group, the Webbs, Kingsley Martin and the *New Statesman*, and thousands of other CPGB members and fellow-travellers) had nothing to lose by branding 'the Soviet myth' – 'the belief that Russia is a Socialist country' – for what it was. The USSR, he declared, embodied 'the corruption of the original idea of Socialism ...' (*CEJL*, III, pp. 404–5). While many British leftists became defensive about the transformation of Bolshevism into 'oligarchical collectivism', Orwell only became more confirmed in his negative judgement of Stalinism, which he claimed to have arrived at as early as 1931 – long before the purges and show trials, the Spanish war, and the 1939 Ribbentrop–Molotov pact. To CPGB members like Day Lewis and Spender, Russia was 'the god that failed'. Not for Orwell. For he had already experienced his period of disillusion, much earlier in Burma. He had seen 'the dirty work of Empire at close quarters' – and he had hated and finally rejected it (*CEJL*, I, p. 236). His attempts to expunge his guilt and his search for social reintegration followed in Paris, London, and Spain. By the time his fellow intellectuals were touting the organised efficiency of the Soviet state, Orwell's Burma years had confirmed and deepened 'my natural hatred of authority' (*CEJL*, I, p. 4). This early experience – his ordeal in Burma and his subsequent vocational and political crises in the 1920s and early 1930s – was probably no less traumatic than his contemporaries' agonised reappraisal of Stalin and communism a decade later. It did, however, act as an ideological vaccine: he became no Stalinist dupe. Thus, what Orwell once described as a waste of five years in a tropical swamp may have actually inoculated him against leader-worship and literary cliques, and thereby saved him from the more serious political errors of his

generation, particularly 'the stupid cult of Russia' (*RWP*, p. 216).
He had 'chucked' Burma; many of his contemporaries would not do
the same with Stalin and the CPGB until years later. In this respect
Orwell was not only 'behind' but also 'ahead' of his generation, as
well as 'between' and 'outside' it.

When his intellectual contemporaries finally did repudiate communism, as Orwell pointed out in 'Inside the Whale', the 'something to believe in' which they embraced was not a political party
line but rather a religious orthodoxy or aesthetic doctrine (*CEJL*, I,
p. 515). Many intellectuals in the 1930s and 1940s discovered the
Anglican or Catholic churches; others opted out of politics and
rededicated themselves to Art. Cyril Connolly's editorial policy in
the inaugural issue of *Horizon* (March 1940) ushered in the latter
aspect of the new mood of the 1940s: 'Our standards are aesthetic,
and our politics are in abeyance.' Or, as Connolly put it two years
later in *The Unquiet Grave*: 'The true function of a writer is to
produce a masterpiece ... no other task is of any importance.'[23]

The turn toward Art in 1940 was, however, sharply different from
the case of the 1920s: whereas the undergraduates of the 1920s re-
belled via Art, young and maturing intellectuals of the 1940s escaped
into it. Whereas political detachment was the posture of the 1920s
and commitment of the 1930s, disenchantment was the attitude of
the 1940s. One notes here that radicalism and conservatism can take
many forms. Religious or aesthetic radicalism may not only accom-
modate but also often entails political quietism. What determined the
outbreak of radicalism in a specifically political form in the 1930s
was in part British intellectuals' recent rejection of other possible
manifestations: God was already dead and Art had failed as
Hulmean 'spilt religion'. In the middle of a depression and with a
revolution eastward already succeeding, Marxism and Russia offered
intellectuals of the day a model and a plan of action.

By the decade's close, however, many leading London Left intellectuals were politically deradicalised. The advent of World War II
catalysed the process by giving them something productive to do *as
intellectuals* – in the BBC, the Ministry of Information, the War
Office selection boards, military intelligence – and thereby *reinte-
grating* them into society. 'Probably in no belligerent country
had the intelligentsia volunteered so wholeheartedly as in England
to serve the State at war', Fyvel later observed. 'The meaningful
social integration which had been talked about in the Thirties was
suddenly easier.'[24] The English tradition of intellectuals' cooperative

participation in government and official politics – or what one critic has termed the venerable British practice of 'massive cooptation of intellectuals by the State'[25] – had reasserted itself. It would continue largely undisturbed – through the war years, the Labour government under Attlee, and the consensus politics of 'Butskellism' – until the Suez crisis and the birth of the New Left in 1956–57.

However, because Orwell was so alienated from and malinte-grated within the London Left intelligentsia, he was never quite so well socially reintegrated as a BBC broadcaster in the early 1940s, either. The ideological moderation characteristic of most other wartime Left intellectuals began at a time when Orwell was at his most revolutionary and optimistic about the possibilities for an English socialist revolution (1939–1941). In *The Lion and the Unicorn* (1941), he argued that the war would transform Britain into a democratic socialist nation. It was not his hope alone, but few others held such a rosy view, and his own faith soon dimmed. Although he enjoyed much of the social contact of his BBC work, he formally reassumed his stance as intellectual 'outsider' and radical iconoclast in 1943, eagerly accepting the literary editorship of *Tribune*, Aneurin Bevin's still-struggling dissident Left paper (*GO*, pp. 318–24).

III

This brief sketch of the interrelations among the Left intelligentsia, British politics in the 1930s, and Orwell's development highlights important theoretical issues and inadequacies in the accepted socio-logy of intellectuals. For the intellectual is that difficult creature, neither worker nor owner. He is, as it were, ideologically ambidex-trous according to the literature of the sociology of occupations, which argues variously that the intellectual invariably serves the elite, allies with the workers, constitutes a separate class, and is essentially 'classless'.[26]

Thus, functionalists (S. N. Eisenstadt, Daniel Bell) have portrayed intellectuals as gradually becoming coopted into the service of the presiding bureaucracy and becoming what C. Wright Mills in *White Collar* (1951) termed 'Brains, INC'. They experience *embourgeoise-ment*. Classical Marxist sociology has also cast the intellectual with the middle class, as a *petit bourgeois*, a tag once much applied by Stalinist critics to Orwell and generating more heat than light.

Conversely, neo-Marxists (Bettina Aptheker, Alain Touraine), influenced by New Left social theory, have taken the opposing view that the intellectual's institutional incorporation effectively 'prole-tarianises' him, making him a wage earner. The necessity for 'teams' to pursue sophisticated scientific projects, the modern cor-poration's demand for the 'expertise' of a wide range of specialist consultants, and the existence of large bureaucratic research staffs alienate intellectuals from the fruits of their labour. They become radicalised 'Brain Workers'. Classical and recent elite theorists (Robert Michel, Alvin Gouldner) have held that intellectuals consti-tute a class in their own right, a 'New Class'. In developing coun-tries they often form the political elite; under advanced capitalism intellectuals become a credentialled professional class deriving income and status from their 'cultural capital' (technical and lan-guage skills). Finally, in his *Ideology and Utopia* (1929), the first influential discussion of intellectuals via the sociology of knowl-edge, Karl Mannheim characterised them famously as 'a relatively classless stratum which is not too firmly situated in the social order'. Mannheim held that intellectuals constitute a unique, so-cially 'rootless' class of their own whose spiritual preoccupations enable them to transcend ordinary, material class interests. Intellectuals emerge from various classes, and their education, rather than their class origin, decisively shapes their development and unites them in political outlook. Their education makes it pos-sible for them to place 'ideals before interests', in Martin Malia's phrase, to see political issues sensitively and with an open mind. Intellectuals thus *choose* their partisan affiliations; their class back-ground is a secondary influence.[27]

It requires no attempt to apply these categories mechanically to the case of Orwell and his contemporaries in order to glimpse how and where these theories fall short as heuristic tools for understanding the relationship between interwar politics and the British intellectual. The old Marxist notion of class origins as the lifelong determinant of political allegiance is obviously insufficient. Although Orwell had a similar middle-class birth and rearing to most thirties' intellectuals, his course in the educational system and his subsequent occupational experience led him to adopt an 'outsider' stance toward the intelligentsia at large – for example, his early anti-Stalinism and brief active member-ship in the anti-war Independent Labour Party (1938–39) (*GO*, pp. 245–57).

Nor are intellectuals necessarily 'embourgeoisified' – or radicalised – by government or official institutional employment. For many intellectuals in the 1930s who were formerly dislocated from English society, wartime service brought reintegration and a renewed feeling of usefulness, identity, and power. For Orwell, however, the war years first brightened and then clouded his socialist hopes, and he sought by 1943 to escape 'integration' and London for independent work and greater privacy (e.g., his purchase in 1944–45 of a home on Jura in the Scottish Hebrides (GO, pp. 353–70). The divergence of Orwell from the patterned responses of his generation makes it imperative to approach the multivalent relationships among class, education, occupation, and partisan affiliation in dynamic, concrete, and interpersonal terms, rather than simply according to theoretical paradigms: the conditions of political allegiances are not reducible to a single factor or invariable structural pattern.

Yet this does not mean that the intellectual constitutes a separate class or is socially unanchored, as the elite theorists and Mannheim have argued, respectively. Rather, as Brym notes, and as the case of Orwell's distinctive career exemplifies, it is to intellectuals' *shifting* patterns of *rootedness* that attention must be paid, to the dynamics of political affiliation and disaffiliation.[28] The case of Orwell points up, in the first place, the significance of how *evolving* intellectual attachments to *other* mass agents (the British worker, the British war machine) and how 'generational consciousness' condition partisan affiliation. The intellectual is not 'relatively classless' and 'rootless' but rather variously and complexly rooted in the spongy, ever-malleable soil of social and historical relations. His political behaviour can therefore only be understood by appreciating the institutional web and stages of his complicated mobility pattern within and among different classes and groups, that is, by scrutinising the course of his class origins, education, and employment and career experience. As Brym, following Gramsci, notes, partisan allegiance is not non-causal but radically contingent:

> ... intellectuals' partisan loyalties [are not] mere mechanical and static responses to their current class and other group locations. ... In order to explain intellectuals' partisan affiliations one must trace their paths of social mobility, from their origins to their social destinations, as these are shaped by the capacity of classes and other groups to expand the institutional milieu through which they pass in the course of their

careers. ... [T]he determination of intellectuals' ideological outlooks is really a problem of multivariate causation. That is to say, social origins, school, and economic and political opportunities are independent causes of political allegiance, and one variable may reinforce or, at the other extreme, cancel out the effects of another.[29]

Thus, unlike Orwell, British intellectuals in the 1930s were radicalised during or after their university years; their disenchantment with communism late in the decade and absorption into the literary Establishment and the war bureaucracy produced political moderates. On the other hand, Orwell's Burma service, his 'belated' bohemianism, and the Wigan Pier and Spain trips radicalised him and effectively 'cancelled out' the integrative potential of his BBC work. The political orientations and actions of intellectuals evolve according to their career mobility paths. No single general factor conditions or freezes their partisan affiliations.

Moreover, contrary to what Gouldner and Mannheim imply, the example of Orwell makes clear that '*the* intelligentsia' is not monolithic, nor does education lead to uniform intellectual-political outlooks, as the postwar decline of the Left's dominance of intellectual life and the rise of strong conservative and neoconservative intellectual movements throughout the West in the 1970s and 1980s demonstrates. Despite our casual use of the word 'intelligentsia' in the singular, intellectuals constitute a multiform, heterogeneous stratum whose members' diverse ideologies are linked to various mass institutional groups and classes (business, labour, working-class movements, etc.). Intellectuals do not constitute an ideological bloc, and even in the British Thirties the degree and intensity of their radicalism was by no means uniform.

Third and finally, what this case study suggests about the frenzied embrace of communism by European intellectuals throughout the West in the 1930s also problematises Mannheim's thesis that intellectuals grandly 'choose' their political allegiances, dispassionately and with reasoned calculation, as if immune to the historical pressures acting upon lesser men. Intellectuals do *in part* choose their loyalties, as do other historical actors, but their choices are enabled and constrained by their historical situation. The personal and group histories of intellectuals are bound up in social history, just the same as that of other individuals and groups. Hence the need to enrich the political sociology of intellectuals with the empirical concreteness of intellectual history: one must approach the study of their political allegiances in historical and social context, for intellectuals' ideas are developed in an engagement with events and thus can only be understood via an attempt to recover that engagement.[30]

IV

Orwell's independent stance toward the Left intelligentsia of his generation furnishes one man's answer by word and deed to a normative issue in the sociology of intellectuals with an even longer history of controversy than the previous historical and conceptual ones, that is: Does the intellectual have a 'proper' social function? What should be his special role, if any, in the modern age of ubiquitous ideology and totalitarian politics? The adversaries alternately define these questions in terms of personal integrity (Julien Benda, Ortega y Gasset, Allen Tate) and social responsibility (Trotsky, Sartre).[31]

The *locus classicus* of the traditionalist position advocating intellectual disengagement from politics is Benda's *La Trahison des Clercs* (1927). Writing in the aftermath of World War I, Benda saw the danger of the intellectual's Hegelian tendency to spiritualise history and political leaders, to 'deny God and then shift Him to man and his political work'.[32] Instead, Benda argued that the intellectual, the rightful heir of the medieval clerk, betrayed his vocation and legacy if he abandoned the universal and attached himself to the particular and practical. Again Benda's view has been the Marxist-existentialist 'responsible artist' position. Radicals and existentialists have argued that the rise of totalitarianism has ushered in a new age of pervasive ideology, in which all cultural activity is politicised and therefore precludes the luxury of detachment. The intellectual 'objectively' supports injustice and tyranny by political disengagement. He must be willing to 'change' the world, not just 'interpret' it, to risk getting 'dirty hands', per the title of one of Sartre's plays.

Orwell stands firmly in the latter tradition, but in a characteristically unorthodox way. His pragmatic stance signals a reluctant commitment that is spiritual in its defiant insistence on a higher, objective, this-worldly truth. In 'Writers and Leviathan' (1948) he gave his ambivalent answer to the intellectual's 'proper' social function. Acknowledging the 'invasion of literature by politics',

Orwell insisted on 'the need to take sides politically' in 'an age of State control'.[33] The totalitarian leviathan had to be confronted and resisted. 'Keeping out of politics' was not possible, Orwell said. One possibility presented itself: the split self. Orwell urged *engagement*, but only on the condition that the writer-citizen divide himself in two – and that the 'literary' self remained untainted:

> ... we should draw a sharper distinction than we do at present between our political and literary loyalties, and should recognise that a willingness to do certain distasteful but necessary things does not carry with it any obligation to swallow the beliefs that usually go with them. When a writer engages in politics, he should do so as a citizen, as a human being, but not as a writer. I do not think that he has the right, merely on the score of his sensibilities, to shirk the ordinary dirty work of politics. Just as much as anyone else, he should be prepared to deliver lectures in draughty halls, to chalk pavements, to canvass voters, to distribute leaflets, even to fight in civil wars if it seems necessary. But whatever else he does in the service of his party, he should never write for it. He should make it clear that his writing is a thing apart.
>
> (*CEJL*, IV, p. 412)

To get one's hands dirty yet keep one's spirit clean: this was Orwell's pained compromise. He recognised that his stance amounted to an 'orthodoxy' like any other, insofar as it entailed 'unresolved contradictions' (*CEJL*, IV, p. 411). He was not blind to the tensions in his position:

> To suggest that a creative writer, in a time of conflict, must split himself into two compartments, may seem defeatist or frivolous: yet in practice I do not see what else he can do. To lock yourself up in an ivory tower is impossible and undesirable. To yield subjectively, not merely to a party machine, but even to a group ideology, is to destroy yourself as a writer.
>
> (*CEJL*, IV, p. 413)

Caught between the ivory tower and the party machine, 'between the priest and the commissar', as Orwell put in a 1936 poem, one had to reject both (*CEJL*, I, p. 5). Politics was merely another aspect of the supreme dilemma which he had first identified at St Cyprian's: 'The good and the possible never seemed to coincide' (*CEJL*, IV, p. 360). Politics was always a choice of lesser evils, 'and there are some situations from which one can only escape by acting like a devil or a lunatic' (*CEJL*, IV, p. 413). These escape routes, which he associated with the aestheticism of a Dali and the derangement of a Pound, respectively, Orwell himself would never take. The quandary of commitment versus detachment was *the* torturous predicament of the modern intellectual as citizen-artist, and it could be neither evaded nor reconciled. Orwell rightly saw that the writer faced the general problem in a particularly acute way:

> If you have to take part ... and I think you do ... then you also have to keep a part of yourself inviolate. For most people the problem does not arise in the same form, because their lives are split already. They are truly alive only in their leisure hours, and there is no emotional connection between their work and their political activities. Nor are they generally asked, in the name of political loyalty, to debase themselves as workers. The artist, and especially the writer, is asked just that – in fact, it is the only thing that politicians ever ask of him.
>
> (*CEJL*, IV, pp. 413–14)

Orwell finally, in effect, argued that the writer's spiritual self, the noble Don Quixote inside him, could and must act independently of the fat little Sancho Panza within:

> If [the intellectual] refuses [to compromise himself], that does not mean that he is condemned to inactivity. One half of him, which in a sense is the whole of him, can act as resolutely, even as violently if need be, as anyone else. But his writings, in so far as they have any value, will always be the product of the saner self that stands aside, records the things that are done and admits their necessity, but refuses to be deceived as to their true nature.[34]

To love truth more than power: that was Orwell's injunction to his fellow intellectuals. The special function of the intellectual in a totalitarian age was to bear witness to historical and political Truth – the 'record' as objective reality and social fact. Orwell's allegiance to 'truth' was the screeching brake on his political commitment: beyond or outside it he would not go.

However satisfactory Orwell's attempt to negotiate between the Scylla and Charybdis of commitment and detachment, contemporary advocates of both traditional positions – the intellectual as activist and as *clerc* – have hailed Orwell for his *praxis*, if not his theory. To Noam Chomsky, Orwell is no dispassionate critic but the model of 'the responsible intellectual', whose documentary 'honesty, decency, and concern with the facts' in *Homage to Catalonia* signified his exemplary commitment to democratic socialism.[35] To John Wain, Orwell the truth-teller was the intelligentsia's relentless critic, whose role was to 'keep their consciences alive': 'As for his relevance, who can feel that the situation that faces free men has changed much from what it was in the '30s and '40s. The thing to be feared is still a *trahison des clercs*: freedom still needs to be defended against those whom Nature most favours, whom she showers with advantages.'[36]

As Wain notes, to argue, as some New Left critics have done, that Orwell, given his pragmatic ethos and distaste for theory, was no intellectual whatsoever, is to misconceive the nature of his intellectuality and of his dispute with his fellow radical intellectuals. For Orwell indicated precisely their cowardly flight into Abstraction, their 'pea-and-thimble trick with those mysterious entities, thesis, antithesis, and synthesis ...' (*RWP*, p. 177). He was indeed their harshest critic; he held them to the same ruthlessly severe standards that he set for himself.[37] As the intelligentsia's scourge, particularly toward his own side, he may thereby seem 'the supreme example of the intellectual who hated intellectuals'.[38] But this elides the point; in fact, he hated not intellectuals but rather their readiness to do dirt on the intellect and betray their spiritual vocation: the defence of truth, liberty, *and* social justice. Orwell was no intellectual-baiter. He mercilessly criticised the intelligentsia's literary cliques 'just because I do take the function of the intelligentsia seriously'. To keep Civilisation's conscience alive, thought Orwell, was the intelligentsia's function, and his own self-appointed task did indeed become to keep the consciences of the intellectuals themselves alive. He castigated their equivocations about Stalinist Russia and their prolix jargon 'not because they are intellectuals but because they [are] not ... true intellectuals ...' True intellectuals thought and spoke clearly, independently, courageously. Clique members took their ideas and language prefabricated.[39]

By this standard, Orwell was indeed a 'true' intellectual. Furthermore, his criticism was almost always directed at social*ists*, not social*ism*: he railed at socialists because he wanted socialist intellectuals to be worthy of socialism. A 'conscience of the Left' *does* criticise from within; and though Orwell may sometimes have been the guilty or excessively scrupulous 'wintry conscience of his generation', he flayed the Left intelligentsia in order to fortify it, not to weaken or abandon it.[40] In this respect his distinctive career not only illumines the complex conditions underlying the formation and fluctuations of intellectual rebellion, adaptation, and radicalisation. It also serves, as so many admirers of George Orwell have testified, as a radiant example of how to live the intellectual life.

From *The Revised Orwell*, ed. Jonathan Rose (East Lansing, MI, 1991), pp. 207–9, 214–33.

NOTES

[John Rodden locates Orwell within an intellectual milieu but determines that Orwell was an 'outsider' from the 'Auden group' of the 1930s intellectuals and intelligentsia. Rodden's analysis relies on a mapping of Orwell's personal as well as his political history in order to understand Orwell's independent stance and his views on the social function of a writer-intellectual. Eds]

1. See, for example, Bennett Berger, 'Sociology and the Intellectuals: An Analysis of a Stereotype', *Antioch Review*, 17 (September 1957), 12–17; Lewis Coser, *Men of Ideas: A Sociologist's View* (New York, 1965); A. Gella (ed.), 'An Introduction to the Sociology of the Intelligentsia' in *The Intelligentsia and the Intellectuals: Theory, Method and Case Study* (Beverly Hills, CA, 1976), pp. 9–34.

2. Charles Kadushin, *The American Intellectual Elite*, quoted in Robert J. Brym, 'The Political Sociology of Intellectuals: A Critique and a Proposal', in Alain G. Gagnon (ed.), *Intellectuals in Liberal Democracies: Political Influence and Social Involvement* (New York, 1987), p. 208. I am much indebted to this article and Brym's *oeuvre* throughout this essay.

3. Brym, 'Political Sociology of Intellectuals', p. 199.

4. Ibid., p. 206–8. See also Robert J. Brym, *Intellectuals and Politics* (London, 1980), pp. 70–3.

5. Brym, 'Political Sociology of Intellectuals', p. 208.

6. No attempt is made here to define the term 'intellectual' precisely. The word first entered the French lexicon in the 1890s as a description of a group of prominent defenders of Alfred Dreyfus. It should be taken in this essay as a general characterisation of those who are producers, rather than merely consumers, of ideas, especially through the medium of writing.

7. William Steinhoff, *George Orwell and the Origins of 1984* (Ann Arbor, MI, 1976), p. 57.

8. Stuart Samuels, 'English Intellectuals and Politics in the 1930s', in Philip Rieff (ed.), *On Intellectuals* (New York, 1969), p. 247.

9. T. R. Fyvel, *Intellectuals Today* (London, 1968), p. 44.

10. See, for example, V. S. Pritchett, 'George Orwell', *New Statesman and Nation*, 39 (28 January 1950), p. 96; and George Woodcock, 'Orwell's Conscience', *World Review*, 14 (April 1950), 28–33.

11. On this relation, see G. E. Hanson, 'Intellect and Power: Some Notes on the Intellectual as a Political Type', *Journal of Politics*, 31 (1969), pp. 28–31; and Martin Malia, 'The Intellectuals: Adversaries or Clerisy?' in S. N. Eisenstadt and S. Graubard (eds), *Intellectuals and Tradition* (New York, 1973), pp. 206–16.

12. Cf. 'Such, Such Were the Joys', in Sonia Orwell and Ian Angus (eds), *The Collected Essays, Journalism and Letters of George Orwell*, (London, 1968), IV, pp. 330–69. One old colleague of Orwell's at the BBC, Henry Swanzy, has also recalled a conversation around 1942 with Orwell about being 'the poorest boy in the school' at Eton. See Bernard Crick, *George Orwell: A Life* (Boston, 1980), p. 281. See also George Orwell, *The Road to Wigan Pier* (New York, 1958). These books will hereafter be cited as *CEJL*, *GO* and *RWP*, parenthetically in the text.

13. Cyril Connolly, *Enemies of Promise* (New York, 1948), p. 164.

14. Richard Rees, *George Orwell: Fugitive from the Camp of Victory* (Carbondale, IL, 1961), pp. 123–4.

15. John Wain, 'Here Lies Lower Binfield', *Encounter*, 17 (October 1961), 75.

16. On the influence of Eliot and Joyce and his circle, see Samuel Hynes, *The Auden Generation* (London, 1976), pp. 27–37. On Orwell during the period 1922–29, see Crick, *George Orwell*, pp. 76–104.

17. This 'outsider' stance of a man who had once been 'inside' was first identified by Q. D. Leavis in her influential *Scrutiny* essay-review on Orwell in September 1940. She noted that Orwell belonged, 'by birth and education', to 'the right Left people', a leftist 'nucleus of the literary world who christian-name each other and are in honour bound to advance each other's literary career'. But she noted that Orwell was 'in' yet not 'of' his generation: 'He differs from them in having grown up. He sees them accordingly from outside, having emancipated himself, at any rate in part, by the force of a remarkable character.' Quoted in Jeffrey Meyers (ed.), *George Orwell: The Critical Heritage* (London, 1975), p. 187.

18. Samuels, 'English Intellectuals', p. 247.

19. Rayner Heppenstall, *Four Absentees* (London, 1960), p. 59.

20. On Orwell's 'outsider' stance toward all political groups, see John Rodden, 'The Separate Worlds of George Orwell', *Four Quarters* (Summer 1988).

21. On the generational consciousness of the 'Auden generation', see Hynes, *The Auden Generation*, pp. 17–37.

22. Crick, *George Orwell*, p. xx.

23. 'Comment', *Horizon*, 1 (1940), 5; Cyril Connolly, *The Unquiet Grave*, (London, 1942), p. 1.

24. Fyvel, *Intellectuals Today*, p. 49.

25. Alan Swingewood, 'Intellectuals and the Construction of Consensus in Postwar England', in Alain G. Gagnon (ed.), *Intellectuals in Liberal Democracies: Political Influence and Social Involvement* (New York, 1987), p. 94.

26. For an overview of these positions, see Gagnon (ed.), *Intellectuals in Liberal Democracies*, pp. 6–10.

27. Karl Mannheim, *Ideology and Utopia* (New York, 1936), pp. 137–8. For this summary I have relied chiefly on Gagnon's overview and Brym's analysis in *Intellectuals and Politics* and 'The Political Sociology of Intellectuals'. Malia is quoted on p. 200 of the latter.

28. Brym, *Intellectuals and Politics*, p. 13.

29. Brym, 'Political Sociology of Intellectuals', pp. 206, 208.

30. Neglecting the historical dimension of political sociology not only blurs the process whereby radical movements form and fragment. It can also impose a false set of polarised categories on the past, which, if they persist, skew analyses of subsequent political configurations. And, as George Watson argues, the dissident politics of the 1930s has bred precisely such distortions. That single, aberrant decade of British radicalism has drawn a false line of demarcation between supporters of the 'Left' and 'Right' which stretches into the 1990s. The very language of 'spectrum' politics is historically inappropriate to the liberal, British political heritage. Indeed, the entry of the terminology of 'Left' and 'Right' into the English political lexicon around 1930 invited the 'reclassification' of figures from the Victorian age – who had not thought in terms of the sharply dichotomous, near-monolithic, party ideological taxonomies of Left and Right. Thus Dickens, Cobbett, and others soon became 'writer[s] well worth stealing' by Marxists and Tories alike. The irony is that Orwell's reputation, subject to repeated grave-robbing by intellectuals of all political stripes, has fallen victim

since his death in 1950 to the very same oversimplifications from the 1930s which he so clearly saw through. See George Watson, *Politics and Literature in Modern Britain* (Totowa, NJ, 1977), pp. 85–97.

31. For an overview of these two traditions and their exponents, see G. de Huszan (ed.), *The Intellectuals: A Controversial Portrait* (Glencoe, IL, 1960).

32. Julian Benda, *The Betrayal of the Intellectuals* (Boston, 1955), p. 32.

33. *CEJL*, IV, pp. 410–11, 407–8. I have inverted the order of the last quotation.

34. Ibid., pp. 413–14.

35. Noam Chomsky, *American Power and the New Mandarins* (New York, 1967), pp. 95–102, 144–8. The second quotation is from Chomsky's interview on Melvyn Bragg's BBC programme, 'The Road to the Left' broadcast 10 March 1971. See also Chomsky's distinction between 'responsible' and 'combative' intellectuals in *Intellectuals and the State* (Amsterdam, 1978), pp. 12–13.

36. John Wain, 'Orwell and the Intelligentsia', *Encounter*, 21 (December 1968), pp. 76–7.

37. On Orwell's excruciating integrity, see Arthur Koestler, 'A Rebel's Progress to George Orwell's Death', in *The Trail of the Dinosaur* (New York, 1955), pp. 102–5.

38. Watson, *Politics and Literature*, p. 45.

39. *CEJL*, II, p. 229.

40. Crick, *George Orwell*, p. 237; Pritchett, 'George Orwell', p. 96.

10

George Orwell's England

MICHAEL WALZER

I

'George Orwell' is a pseudonym; 'Orwell' was Orwell's free choice and not a choice that is easy to understand. Why did he need a pseudonym at all? Perhaps we don't have to answer this question in order to come to grips with the man and his work – indeed, I incline to this philistine and distinctly Orwellian opinion. But there is a sharply critical view of Orwell that makes much of his pseudonym, almost as if names were ontologies. He chose his new name in the early 1930s, on this view, when he became a new man and a radical critic of English society. But the name corresponded to no stable moral reality, and he could not sustain the critical stance to which it committed him. Imitating the heroes of his own novels, so Raymond Williams has argued in the most powerful version of this critique, Orwell breaks with the 'orthodox routines' of his class and culture, fails to realise the hopes that motivate the break, and then, disillusioned, returns. He begins as Eric Blair and, without acknowledging what has happened, ends as Blair again; begins as an imperial policeman and ends as a cold war ideologist.[1]

It comes as no surprise, of course, that Orwell's last books, *Animal Farm* and *1984*, made many people on the left uneasy; but so did *The Road to Wigan Pier* and *Homage to Catalonia* much earlier. There seems to have been a roughly determinate group of people, leftists of a particular sort, who winced every time Orwell took up his pen (this gave him great pleasure), and such people must see his last books prefigured in his earliest political writings. Raymond Williams isn't quite a leftist of that sort; he tells a more sophisticated story. *Homage to Catalonia* is for him an unqualified success, the grand moment of Orwell's political career – the first pages, the celebration of Barcelona as 'a town where the working class was in the saddle', the grandest moment. In fact, Orwell's celebration is characteristically restrained: 'There was much in [the life of the city] that I did not understand, in some ways I did not even like it, but I recognised it immediately as a state of affairs worth fighting for.'[2] It is Orwell's roughly similar judgement of England in 1940, based on much greater understanding, that Williams takes as the sign of his disillusion and return. The crucial text is *The Lion and the Unicorn*, published in February 1941, in which Orwell succumbs to a disease called 'social patriotism', rejoins the family of 'sensible, moderate, and decent' Englishmen, and ceases to be a radical critic.

Williams isn't entirely unsympathetic – or wasn't unsympathetic when he wrote his study of Orwell in 1970; seven years later in an interview with the editors of *New Left Review*, bullied a bit by the editors, he took a harder line. Class identity is his central theme, and given his view of class, social patriotism looks very much like an inherited disease.[3] Orwell's political difficulties and his final defeat, as Williams describes them, are the (predetermined?) outcome of his heroic effort to make himself over as 'Orwell' – cool, dispassionate, relentlessly honest, freed above all from the conventional respectability of his class. So he left the police, went down and out in Paris and London, descended again into the mines of the North Country, fought and was wounded in Spain. But he never became, could not become, an organic intellectual of the working class. He tore up his roots and then found himself rootless, without a clear social identity. This is the ideal position for the radical critic – so goes the standard argument, elegantly expounded by Julien Benda, about the prerequisites of criticism itself. But Williams's argument is different, more overtly sociological, perhaps, or more committed to his own (Welsh working-class) roots. Rootlessness for him is a condition of loss, from which even an Orwell, who chose his condition much as he chose his name, must eventually seek an escape. Hence Orwell's return to England and English patriotism, 'an act not so much of membership as of conscious affiliation'. Standing nowhere, he can't keep up the struggle that criticism requires. He is trying in his 'patriotic' pieces to prove that he really belongs to the extended English family: 'The emotions are understandable, and honourable', says Williams, 'but ... they are too easy, too settling, too sweet.'[4]

Ironically, this criticism of Orwell coincides in part with Orwell's criticism of the left intellectuals of the popular front – though Orwell is rather more savage. Middle-class intellectuals, alienated at home, become communists or fellow travellers through an act of the will, he argues, and then their wilfulness knows no bounds; it is matched only by their ignorance of the world they have entered. They become wilful proletarians, party stalwarts, apologists for the Soviet Union. The popular front, Orwell says in a phrase that Williams might have applied to Orwell's own politics, is the 'patriotism of the deracinated'.[5] Orwell has an intense dislike for deracination, and his mockery of the men and women who display its symptoms like badges of honour is often very cruel. There isn't much excuse for his reiterated lists of the cranks and eccentrics, the marginal, graceless people who are drawn to socialism and then to communism because of some dim hope for kinship and discipline: 'all that dreary tribe of high-minded women and sandal-wearers and bearded fruit-juice drinkers' and so on. Clearly, Orwell did not want to be associated with *them*, though it is too quick a piece of psychologising to suggest that he feared he might himself be one of the tribe. Sometimes, in any case, his mockery is more perceptive, as in his brief comment on W. H. Auden's line (which Orwell immortalised) about 'the necessary murder'. The time will come, Auden writes, for poetry readings, walks by the lake, and 'perfect communion'. But today something else is required:

> Today the deliberate increase in the
>   chances of death,
> The conscious acceptance of guilt in
>   the necessary murder;
>   Today the expending of powers
> On the flat ephemeral pamphlet and
>   the boring meeting.[6]

These lines sketch, says Orwell, a day in the life of a 'good party man'. 'In the morning a couple of political murders, a ten-minutes' interlude to stifle "bourgeois" remorse, and then a hurried luncheon and a busy afternoon and evening chalking walls and distributing leaflets.'[7] Auden is striking a political pose, and the pose is wholly inauthentic, therefore available for caricature. The 'conscious acceptance of guilt' is all too easy when one has no experience of crime. This sort of thing is considerably worse than wearing sandals or drinking fruit juice, and Orwell's critique is serious, a crucial indication of his political commitment. It suggests that he had a view of his own radicalism very different from the one that Williams provides. Despite his new name, he did not think of himself as a deracinated intellectual, a socialist-by-virtue-of-will-alone. What was he, then, this man who 'became' George Orwell?

At bottom, he was always Eric Blair, the 'lower upper-middle class' Englishman who went to school at Eton and who joined, and left, the Burmese police. One can easily enough describe Orwell's life as if it were a parade of selves, himself a one-man cast of characters – though the description requires more than Williams's trio of Blair, Orwell, and Orwell betrayed. It is at least as important, however, to notice a broad continuity not only of moral character but also of social identity. He gave up the authority of his class and its claims to wealth and prestige (his own family had never known either); he changed his mind – more than once – and his political positions too. But there were no radical conversions and no 'emergency exits'. He avoided the Communist party, never worshipped the god that failed, was only distantly a Trotskyite. He was not easily a comrade, never a proletarian. One can find in *Wigan Pier* and *Homage to Catalonia* idealised portraits of individual workers, but the authorial voice in the two books is consistently that of a middle-class (lower, upper) reporter. Interviewed in 1940 on the subject of 'The Proletarian Writer', he said what he would have said at any point in the previous decade: 'I believe that [the proletariat's] literature is and must be bourgeois literature with a slightly different slant.'[8] *Wigan Pier*, written in 1936, ends with a political argument that points directly to his World War II politics. If you bully me about my 'bourgeois ideology', he told the members of the Left Book Club,

> if you give me to understand that in some subtle way I am an inferior person because I have never worked with my hands, you will only succeed in antagonising me. For you are telling me either that I am inherently useless or that I ought to alter myself in some way that is beyond my power. I cannot proletarianise my accent or certain of my tastes and beliefs, and I would not if I could. Why should I?[9]

Orwell was faithful to what he was, as if following the moral injunction that Albert Camus later made the maxim of his own politics during the Algerian war. He did resign from the Burmese police, and he did become a socialist, but he did both these things without renouncing his 'tastes and beliefs'. He moved left and remained whole. One can see something of the inner process earlier on in the controversial second part of *Wigan Pier* when he describes the dawning sense of British imperialism as an 'oppressive system'. He resigned from its service, he says, 'with an immense weight of guilt', with the memory vivid in his mind 'of subordinates I had bullied and aged peasants I had snubbed, of servants and coolies I had hit with my fists in moments of rage'. Out of this experience he constructed 'the simple theory that the oppressed are always right and the oppressors are always wrong: a mistaken theory, but the natural result of being one of the oppressors yourself'.[10] The comment is important, 'a mistaken theory', and it is equally important that Orwell sensed the mistake almost from the beginning; the simple theory is hardly in evidence, for example, in his first published novel, *Burmese Days*, which turns a critical eye on English and Burmese alike.

Guilt is a bad guide to politics, and cant about guilt a worse guide; the two together probably account for much of the self-abnegating wilfulness of middle-class intellectuals in the 1930s, dressed up for the occasion as workers and revolutionaries. When he went down and out, Orwell dressed up too: 'I wanted to submerge myself, to get right down among the oppressed, to be one of them and on their side against their tyrants.'[11] But he learned that he could not be one of them, and he always came back and changed back into his own clothes. It was possible to be 'on their side' without pretending to an unfamiliar identity. Williams seems bound to deny this last point, even if he also denies that the pretence can ever be the basis of a lasting socialist commitment. But Orwell managed to connect his old self and his new politics. Bourgeois ideology, after all, had fuelled the commitment of many generations of English radicals.

Coming back is one of Orwell's central themes, though the return is always more wary than Williams suggests. The last paragraph of *Homage to Catalonia* is a nice example. Orwell describes his homeward voyage from Spain to England, the seasickness of his Channel crossing, and the dawning sense of his country's deep and dangerous sleep, 'from which I sometimes fear we shall never wake till we are jerked out of it by the roar of bombs'.[12] That return, at least, isn't 'too easy, too settling, too sweet'. Orwell doesn't end his books in places like Wigan or Barcelona or even Lower Binfield but typically brings himself or his hero home, to a place he knows, though always uneasily, as his own. He doesn't return like a prodigal son, however, and after the publication of *Animal Farm*, when conservative cold warriors gave him a prodigal son's welcome, he did not like it. To what, then, was he faithful? The standard answer is, to some construction of 'ordinary decency'. That's not wrong, but it isn't specific enough; it doesn't help to explain his resistance to crucial, and by no means indecent, aspects of leftist ideology (collectivism and Marxist internationalism, for example); nor does it suggest the critical force of his writings about England. The resistance and the criticism are closely connected, but I will take them up separately, beginning with Orwell's anti-ideological socialism. For Williams, that last phrase must be an oxymoron, and perhaps that is why he describes Orwell, after the war, as an ex-socialist. But Orwell comes back to 'England, Your England' without giving up his opposition to the men and women who tyrannised over the working class. His success has something to do with his ability, on all his journeys, physical and intellectual, to take himself along. He travels light, says Williams.[13] I don't think so.

II

One of the most persistent themes of left-wing thought in the twentieth century is the critique of 'consumerism'. Marx had described the 'fetishism of commodities' as a feature of capitalist production: the things the worker makes take on an existence independent of his own productive work, out of his control. But fetishism is present also in capitalist consumption, so post-Marxist critics like Herbert Marcuse have argued, where the commodity is the be-all and end-all of everyday life. The desire for goods, for possessions and conveniences, turns into a social force distinct from the men and women whose desire it is; and the more that desire is met, the more inexorable it becomes. Modern belongings are things to which people belong, a form of domination, like work itself. The endless stream of shoddy and replaceable goods is a sign simultaneously of capitalist success and popular corruption. All this is fairly standard among leftist writers and it has a right-wing counterpart, a generalised dislike of commerce, industry, urban life, the mass market, and the mass media. One can find traces of this sort of thing in Orwell; indeed, one can find both its left- and right-wing varieties. He was never at ease in the world of modern conveniences, and he was capable of a remarkably sustained and almost lyrical nostalgia, as in his last thirties novel, *Coming Up for Air*. But he never expressed an ideological aversion for things themselves, the physical objects that men and women long to possess; his critique of English capitalism does not extend to the 'fetishism of commodities'. On the contrary, he seems to sense, in *1984* especially, that everyday fetishism has a kind of saving grace.

It is never a good idea for the left to set itself in stark opposition to the values of ordinary people. The attack on consumer goods is the work of social critics at the farthest reach of their wilfulness. For men and women deprived of things are not liberated for radical politics any more than starving artists are liberated for art. Deprivation is deprivation; one can't escape from the world of getting and spending by not getting and not spending. Ordinary life makes its own demands, not only for what is absolutely necessary but also for what is merely desirable. Orwell was from the beginning sensitive to these demands. Or, better, almost from the beginning: there was a time, he says in *Wigan Pier*, when 'failure seemed to me the only virtue'.[14] A mistake, again, and Orwell's *Keep the Aspidistra Flying* is a novelistic working out of the mistake. When he wrote the book, Orwell was not yet politically engaged; its terms are set by the traditions of bohemia, not those of radical militancy. Its hero, Gordon Comstock, the author of a slim but 'promising' volume of poetry, has dropped out of bourgeois life and declared war on the 'money world'. The war is intensely private, fought mostly by self-imposed suffering and internal diatribe. Gordon's denunciations of the power of money, though they have no political resonance, could have come out of the pages of the young Marx. But his is a losing war, partly because of his own absolutism, his rejection of any compromise with bourgeois respectability. He brings himself too low, can't write, can't find friends, can't live with Rosemary whom he loves, can't find any degree of contentment or joy. Orwell's novel is about the failure of 'failure'. It ends with Gordon's return: back from bohemia to the lower middle class. The last pages celebrate the apartment that Gordon and Rosemary have found and furnished. 'It seemed to them a tremendous advantage to have this place of their own. Neither of them had ever owned furniture before ... And it was all their own, every bit was their own – at least, so long as they didn't get behind with the instalments!'[15]

Strange sentences from a writer who was only a few months away from declaring himself a socialist. Lionel Trilling finds in them 'a dim, elegiac echo of Defoe and of the early days of middle-class ascendency as Orwell's sad young man learns to cherish the small personal gear of life, his own bed and chairs and saucepans – his own aspidistra, the ugly, stubborn, organic emblem of survival.'[16] Not quite 'his own', in fact, his and Rosemary's, and the point is worth making for Rosemary is almost the only sympathetic and strong woman in all of Orwell's writing. Gordon is not alone at the end of the novel. But the novel is, at the end, a celebration of private life and private ownership, and so it does recall the earlier triumphs of the middle class. But it also points to Orwell's later conviction that socialism cannot, should not, any more than art or literature, require the reversal of those triumphs.

This is a conviction often evident in Orwell's work, but it finds its most remarkable expression in *1984* where, also remarkably, it has gone largely unnoticed. It's not only sexual love that symbolises opposition to the regimented life of party members on Airstrip One but also the love of things: the notebook in which Winston Smith writes his dairy, 'a peculiarly beautiful book [with] smooth creamy paper'; the coral paperweight, smashed later on by the thought-police, 'a beautiful thing'; the bed in the furnished room where he and Julia make love, 'a beautiful mahogany bed'. For Winston and Julia, the room is as much an adventure as the apartment is for Gordon and Rosemary – and its joys are not only those of sex but also those of privacy and possession. It inspires fantasies of ordinary life: 'He wished that he were walking through the streets with her ... openly and without fear, talking of trivialities and buying odds and ends for the household.'[17]

Is this the wish of an oppositional figure, a social critic? Only, it might be said, in the world of *1984*, while in Orwell's own world, it represents a reconciliation with bourgeois society, a surrender of critical weapons. That seems to me exactly wrong. The recognition that things have their place and value, that 'the very stupidity of things', as Trilling says, 'has something human about it, something meliorative, something even liberating', sharpens the critique of inequality and oppression.[18] It repudiates, indeed, an ascetic or puritanical socialism but not a socialism that aims to make 'the small personal gear of life' equally available to everyone – and if available, why not beautiful? Orwell's socialism is conditioned and concrete; hence his interest in material possessions. He is an advocate of collective control of the means of production but not of collectivism as an abstract ideal. His is a socialism suited to himself and defended with a firm sense that this self, at least as it aspired to beds, chairs, and saucepans, and even as it aspired to beautiful books and paperweights, was sufficiently ordinary. With 'small-scale ownership', he wrote in *The Lion and the Unicorn*, describing his political programme, the state should not interfere.[19]

Socialism with a bourgeois face? Orwell might better have said that it was socialism with an English face. As he was attached to things, so he was attached to place and culture; and once again he thought the attachment ordinary. 'Above all', he told what he must have assumed were sceptical readers, 'it is *your* civilisation, it is *you*. However much you hate it or laugh at it, you will never be happy away from it for any length of time. The suet puddings and the red pillar-boxes have entered into your soul.'[20] Any knowledge-able leftist would indeed be sceptical. From the time of *The Communist Manifesto* onward, he would have been taught that the workers had no country; they were a class radically dispossessed, first of things, then of places, and the love of these two was an inau-thentic love, concealing social reality. Preached by the ruling class, consumerism and patriotism were ideological mystifications; the task of the social critic was to demystify commodities and countries alike. I suppose that Raymond Williams marks out *The Lion and the Unicorn* as Orwell's turning point, the beginning of his backsliding, because it is in this text that he most explicitly adopts a patriotic stance: 'I believe in England'; Orwell does try, however, to appropriate patriotism for the left. That's why he isn't merely a patriot, but a 'social patriot'.

Patriotism, Orwell writes,

> has nothing to do with Conservatism. It is actually the opposite of Conservatism, since it is a devotion to something that is always changing and yet is felt to be mystically the same. It is the bridge between the future and the past. No real revolutionary has ever been an internationalist.[21]

That last sentence is probably wrong, unless the word 'real' conceals some further qualification. But it is not difficult to see what Orwell means. Revolutionary politics requires the mobilisation of the people; the people can be mobilised only by appealing to their sentiments and values as well as to their interests; and those sentiments and values are historically formed, culturally specific. The workers he knew or knew about, Orwell thought, 'have a great deal to lose besides their chains'. In 1941, one of the things they had to lose was their country. For it was theirs, even though they were not in control of its social arrangements or governmental policies. Put them in control and England would become more English: 'By revolution we become more ourselves, not less.'[22] That sentence, I think, is not wrong. Every genuinely popular revolution (perhaps that is the meaning of Orwell's 'real') has intensified the particularity, the political or religious specificity, of the society in which it takes place. Old and established elites, aristocracies especially, are always more cosmopolitan than the men and women they rule. So, indeed, are Marxist vanguards; internationalism is a vanguard ideology. Orwell himself, of course, was acting on internationalist principles when he fought in Spain (he tried several times to join the International Brigade). But he did not believe that these principles could ever be a source of authority in Spanish or in English politics. They determined the allegiance of individuals, not the substantive creed of revolutionary movements. Local struggles were sustained by local values.

At the same time, Orwell despised nationalism, to which he gave a very broad meaning: it included every sort of collective self-aggrandisement, every claim to group advantage or superiority. English nationalists wanted to rule India; English patriots wanted only to defend England against the Nazis.[23] It is a morally neat distinction, but it avoids the hard question: why do patriotic feelings so often take on nationalist political forms? Orwell seems to believe that the success of right-wing nationalism has a lot to do with the unwillingness of left-wing intellectuals to value and work with patriotism. That may well be part of the story, but it can hardly be the whole of it. Here, and elsewhere too, Orwell exaggerates the importance of left-wing intellectuals. He may still have been right, however, to criticise the intellectuals for 'their severance from the common culture of the country'. (One can be both disconnected and ineffective.) The disconnection did not make it any less likely that many intellectuals would become nationalists in Orwell's extended sense of the term; they merely defended the aggrandisement of foreign collectivities, Stalin's Russia above all. Orwell's internationalism, by contrast, required the critique of every form of aggrandising politics, the defence of local and particular arrangements; one might think of it as the reiteration of patriotism.

III

'A family with the wrong members in control – that, perhaps, is as near as one can come to describing England in a phrase.' Thus wrote Orwell in 1941.[24] Williams concedes that many people on the left felt that way during the war: the blitz made England whole, even if it didn't reconcile leftists to the rule of the Tory upper class.

But Orwell, writing at this critical moment, gave the myth of wholeness lasting life, and for this Williams cannot forgive him:

> If I had to say which [of Orwell's] writings have done the most damage, it would be ... the dreadful stuff from the beginning of the war about England as a family with the wrong members in charge, the shuffling old aunts and uncles whom we could fairly painlessly get rid of. Many of the political arguments of the kind of labourism ... usually associated with the tradition of Durbin or Gaitskell can be traced to those essays.[25]

Not quite fair, for Orwell in *The Lion and the Unicorn* warns of a 'bitter political struggle' and thinks that 'at some point or other it may be necessary to use violence': 'The bankers and the larger businessmen, the landowners and dividend-drawers, the officials with their prehensile bottoms, will obstruct for all they are worth. ... It is no use imagining that one can make fundamental changes without causing a split in the nation.'[26] What he doubted was not the ability of the ruling class to defend itself but its ability to defend the country, to mobilise the people and win the war. He thought that revolution, 'a fundamental shift of power', was the prerequisite of victory. Here Orwell turned out to be wrong. England won the war without dislodging the 'prehensile bottoms' of the old elite. There was indeed a shift of power; the war initiated, and the first postwar election confirmed, the triumph of English social democracy. But this was not the fundamental shift that Orwell anticipated. It did not make London (or Manchester or Liverpool or Glasgow) into a second Barcelona, with the workers 'in the saddle'. It did not create that matey egalitarianism that Orwell had relished so much in Spain and that had made socialism come alive for him.

But it would only repeat Orwell's exaggeration of the importance of intellectuals to blame *The Lion and the Unicorn* for the emergence and remarkable stability of 'labourist' politics. The family image as Orwell develops it does indeed suggest the absence of revolutionary fervour. Images, however, do not cause absences; they only evoke and record them. Orwell points, honestly enough, toward a popular culture that isn't wholly estranged from the hegemonic culture of English capitalism. Williams's charge is that he missed, or perhaps that he deliberately repressed, the systematic character of capitalist hegemony and so misled his readers about the necessary harshness and inevitable difficulties of the coming struggle. In fact, Orwell seems to have recognised that even politics-in-the-family can get pretty rough. What he did not recognise was the possibility, even the likelihood, of compromises along the way and stopping points short of victory. Nor did he acknowledge that patriotic feelings like his own made compromise more likely, not less. For reasons available in his text, but not fully articulated there, England achieved only a welfarist socialism. Was this a defeat? Perhaps; but one might also say that this was (at least the beginning of) the socialism 'native to England' that Orwell had always called for. It's that thought that Williams rejects, clinging to the hope of a socialism at once native and far more radical. And then he is driven to argue that the divisions in English society go much deeper than Orwell admits. It is not a family at all, or it is more like Freud's primordial family, with the sons plotting to overthrow and kill the father.

Thus far, however, the plot has not been successful; it has, in fact, hardly engaged the energies of the people whom Williams would call its subjects. Nor has it produced a critique of English society more powerful than Orwell's – though it has certainly produced critiques harsher, more violent, nastier in tone. Orwell's power derives from his intimate grasp of the society he is criticising and his admiration for many of its cultural and material artifacts: English gentleness, respect for the law, tolerance of eccentricity; English pubs, music hall songs, even English cooking; cricket, comic postcards, country gardens, flowers, Stilton cheese, suet pudding, warm beer, and 'a nice cup of tea'.[27] Orwell appropriate all this for an egalitarian socialism, much as he appropriates 'the small personal gear of life' in the same cause. It's not surprising that revolutionary ferocity is lost along the way. Of course, the appropriation is meant to be provocative. Though Orwell was the most European of twentieth-century English writers (a point I will come back to later on), he disliked intensely what might be called the continentalising tendencies of well-placed or upwardly mobile Englishmen. He loved to offend high-minded intellectuals and the culturally ambitious middle class. But this was more a hobby than a serious politics, and it would be wrong to see in Orwell's critical work only an easy, if occasionally perverse, sentimentality about the life of the common people. His opposition is directed against the class system itself. Hatred of hierarchy is the animating passion of his social criticism.[28] Domination and arrogance on the one hand, subordination, deference, and fear on the other – these are the features of English life that he sets himself against. The real purpose of cricket, flowers, and the nice cup of tea is to establish his own connection to the life he is criticising. I think of it as a kind of home remedy for intellectual pride and vanguard presumption.

But this very connectedness, Richard Wollheim has argued, presses Orwell toward a view of society that is deeply conformist in character. Socialism for him meant the realisation of a 'determinate way of life'. Men and women would be free, of course, to lead whatever individual lives they chose, but Orwell anticipated a particular set of choices, defined by English decency and working-class self-respect. 'It would be no great parody of Orwell to say that for him a free society was [nothing more than] a society in which no man touched his cap to another.' He rejected servility, but then he also rejected crankiness, affectation, and perversity – whatever might seem (in England) indecent. He would not have suppressed such things, writes Wollheim, but he also would not have thought it any great breach of liberty to crowd them out. 'And there I am sure he was wrong.'[29] Wollheim captures something of Orwell's tone here, but he misses the extent of his commitment to democracy – not the sovereign people only but also the political process: the rough and tumble of debate and the mutual tolerance that keeps the rough and tumble from getting too rough. Orwell railed unfairly against crankiness on the left, but he admired the larger society that tolerated leftist cranks.

Orwell is less a radical egalitarian than he is a simple democrat. His goal was the transfer of power to ordinary men and women and the creation of a lively, open, frank, and plain-spoken politics. This would require only an 'approximate' equality of income: the highest income should not exceed the lowest, he argued in *The Lion and the Unicorn*, by more than ten to one. It would also require, and this was at least equally important, a democratic reform of the schools – a demand frequently repeated on the labour left after the war. In his autobiographical essay, 'Such, Such Were the Joys', Orwell took the prep school he attended as a child as a prime example of an unjust society and explored the connections between class snobbery and political tyranny. It is an oblique but savage piece of social criticism; no ferocity is lost here. Where other 'labourist' radicals held back, he straightforwardly advocated a state takeover of public (i.e., private) schools like his own Eton. Finally, and most important, the transfer of power, he argued, required a more direct and continuous control by the people over their government. What institutional arrangements might make this possible, Orwell didn't say; he would no more have abolished Parliament than he would have shut down the local pub. He meant only to bring the two into some closer contact.

His democratic commitments are best revealed by his literary and cultural interests. Consider, for example, his enthusiasm for the pamphlet (he was a collector and anthologist as well as an occasional author), which Alex Zwerdling nicely contrasts with Auden's reluctant readiness to 'expend his powers' (but did he ever actually make the expenditure?) on 'the flat ephemeral pamphlet'.[30] This is the more common attitude among literary intellectuals whose true ambition, I suppose, is never to write anything ephemeral. But the ephemeral pamphlet, Orwell believed, is the concession one makes to a lively politics and a mass audience. A pamphleteering intelligentsia, writing in a plain English and aiming to reach that audience, would be connected to the people in a way that Orwell thought exemplary. Here is another 'dim, elegaic echo of Defoe and the early years of middle-class ascendency'. Such connections had once existed in England; a successful socialism would restore and enlarge them.

But Orwell was always alert to the dangers of an unsuccessful socialism – more alert, his leftist critics might say, than to the dangers of an established capitalism. He has, in fact, little to say about capitalism. Though he recognised its political strength, he assumed its failure as a productive system, and his programme for an economic succession was the standard left programme of his time: 'nationalisation of land, mines, railways, banks, and major industries' (this is from *The Lion and the Unicorn*).[31] He was more concerned, however, to argue that nationalisation would only bring new forms of oligarchy and privilege unless it was accompanied by 'a fundamental shift in power'. Not a shift from capitalists to state bureaucrats: that would not be fundamental, since the same people or the same sort of people, educated in the same schools, would fill both categories. For Orwell, a fundamental shift required a democratic revolution. Much of his critical writing was aimed at the two groups that he thought might obstruct or usurp such a revolution once the capitalists had been defeated – the political and technical intelligentsias, the masters of ideological truth and scientific knowledge. He is a student of James Burnham in this regard, but his argument is very much his own.[32] His social criticism follows his literary criticism; in both he aims at breaking through the barriers of elite culture. Hence his interest in the appeal of good writers like Charles

Dickens and of 'good bad' writers like Rudyard Kipling across the lines of class and schooling. 'The fact that good bad poetry can exist', he says in his essay on Kipling, 'is a sign of the emotional overlap between the intellectual and the ordinary man.'[33] There is a mental overlap too, and so vanguard ideologies not only should be, but can be, opposed. It's because opposition is possible that the degradation of the proles in *1984* represents such a terrible defeat.

Orwell's hatred of hierarchy, shared in principle by other leftists, also expressed itself as a fear, hardly shared at all, that one set of inegalitarian arrangements would merely be replaced by another – and this in the name of socialism. And so he was a critic of oppositional as well as of established elites, more savage, perhaps, in his criticism of the first than of the second, not only because the opposition was nearer to hand but also because he thought it was going to win. What separates him from other 'labourist' radicals is his intense uneasiness about that victory and his constant irritation with advanced ideas that served only, he thought, to feed the pride of the few. He was, says Zwerdling, 'an internal critic of socialism'.[34] Writers like Williams deny the internality and see in the criticism only Orwell's obsession with totalitarian politics – as if this wasn't an obvious and necessary socialist obsession in the age of Stalin. Anyway, that is only part of the story, not the whole of it. Orwell's internal critique begins before his obsession; it begins at the beginning, in his first socialist book, *The Road to Wigan Pier.* He worried even then that socialism might reproduce the old hierarchy in a new form, that it might mean nothing more than 'a set of reforms which "we", the clever ones, are going to impose upon "them", the Lower Orders'.[35] The clever ones are the products of the old regime, not of Ingsoc but of bourgeois society. Orwell knew them well, and when he attacked them, he evoked their own putative commitment to the central values of the bourgeois revolution: freedom and equality.

These were also the values of the English working class. They had penetrated, he wrote in his essay on Dickens, 'to all ranks of society'.[36] That's why Orwell could be a patriot and still, in his own fashion, a revolutionary. And that's why his criticism of the hegemonic culture is never so wholesale as to satisfy Raymond Williams – and why, again, his criticism of popular culture and working-class 'common sense' entirely lacks Gramsci's ideological edge. Orwell was, nonetheless, the very model of a 'national-popular' intellectual; perhaps for that reason he sensed that a democratic politics was more readily available, more immanent in English life, than any Marxist analysis could allow. At the same time, he worried that the defeat of democratic politics might open the way for a hegemony far worse than anything the bourgeoisie had ever achieved.

IV

Orwell's essays on Dickens and Kipling, on patriotism and radical politics, on pubs, postcards, and popular culture, belong to his daylight hours. They are sometimes clouded but never dark. Totalitarianism is his nightmare. By day, Orwell is an Englishman; at night, he is a European, fully responsive to a range of experience from which England had been shielded. In an essay on Arthur Koestler, written in 1944, he argued that the twentieth-century English were virtually incapable of serious political writing; they had produced no equivalent of Ignazio Silone, André Malraux, Gaetano Salvemini, Franz Borkenau, Victor Serge, or even Arthur Koestler (to whom they gave refuge but did not really understand). They suffered from their own good fortune: 'There is almost no English writer to whom it has happened to see totalitarianism from the inside ... England is lacking, therefore, in what one might call concentration camp literature. The special world created by secret police forces, censorship of opinion, torture, and frame-up trials is, of course, known about and to some extent disapproved of, but it has made very little emotional impact.'[37] Almost no English writer: Orwell himself is the exception, partly because of his months in Spain, partly because of a remarkable imaginative effort sustained over a number of years, which turned out to be his last years. He made himself into a European writer and produced the first, virtually the only, English examples of the political *roman noir*.

Raymond Williams's judgement of these dark novels, as if by perverse design, bears out Orwell's claim about the failure of English political writing. 'As for *1984*', Williams told the editors of *New Left Review*, 'its projections of ugliness and hatred ... onto the difficulties of revolution or political change, seem to introduce a period of really decadent bourgeois writing in which the whole status of human beings is reduced.'[38] 'The difficulties of revolution' invites comparison to Auden's 'the necessary murder' – a line that could never have been written, Orwell rightly said, by anyone who had ever seen a man murdered. So Williams's line could never have been written by anyone who had actually experienced those 'difficulties'. It represents a refusal to respond, intellectually or emotionally, to the central events of the twentieth century.

What is the political meaning of Orwell's response? Not, surely, to close off all hope of democratic or socialist success: nightmares threaten to do that but don't finally do it; one wakes up sweating and goes on with daytime life. But Orwell did want to make English socialists sweat. The description of totalitarian politics has often had a conservative intention; its purpose is to turn the minds of one's fellow citizens toward horrors far away, so that local faults look like mere blemishes and efforts to deal with them seem overly zealous. The horrific description is curiously comforting. It is hard, indeed, not to produce effects like that whatever one's purpose, but that was not what Orwell had in mind. He thought that Western socialism could not succeed unless its defenders recognised *and learned to worry about* what was happening in the East. *Animal Farm* and *1984* were part of his 'internal critique'.

It is an interesting question whether one can be a social critic of someone else's society. By now, Orwell has become an honorary East European, and his books have been incorporated into the literature of resistance. But he himself aimed only at local effects: 'Even if I had the power, I would not wish to interfere in Soviet domestic affairs. ... But on the other hand it was of the utmost importance to me that people in western Europe should see the Soviet regime for what it really was ... for the past ten years I have been convinced that the destruction of the Soviet myth was essential if we wanted a revival of the socialist movement.' This is from the preface to the Ukrainian edition of *Animal Farm*.[39] Among Orwell's Ukrainian readers the destruction of the Soviet myth had been accomplished long before; they would put the book to other uses, and Orwell has nothing to say about what those uses might be. As he wrote on an earlier occasion: 'What I am concerned with is the attitude of the British intelligentsia. ...'[40]

I don't think that Orwell feared – not in his daylight hours anyway – the internal transformation of English socialism into Ingsoc. Bureaucratic aggrandisement and elite presumption might generate new inequalities, but nothing quite so drastic as the inequality of proles and party members. English culture as he himself described it had strong built-in defences against that sort of thing. The overt argument of *1984*, nonetheless, is that *it can happen here*: immunity is an illusion. Totalitarian politics had an international logic; it invited, perhaps even compelled, imitation. And so the experience of total war and then of ideological cold war could, over time, produce repression at home, against the grain of English decency. That's why Orwell was so radically unwilling to leave socialism in the hands of men and women who talked too quickly about 'necessary' murders. Nor would he have been willing to leave it in the hands of men and women who thought of Stalinist crimes as 'difficulties' encountered in the course of the revolutionary process. He insisted that English intellectuals face those crimes, name them, imaginatively experience them. The 'neo-gothic torture scenes in Room 101', sometimes taken as a sign of Orwell's final illness, a loss of literary control, have instead a firm political intention.[41] They enlist the fears and fantasies of the reader in an act of recognition: this is what politics in the twentieth century can come to, has come to in countries that are not, after all, so far away.

One senses in *1984* a barely contained fury at the complacency of English leftists, still sleeping England's deep sleep. Even the bombs had not awakened them, for those were Nazi bombs, right-wing bombs, as it were, and required no confrontation with the crimes of the left. It was still possible, in England, 'to be anti-fascist without being anti-totalitarian' – the 'sin' of leftist intellectuals since the early thirties.[42] Given the sin, *1984* is the punishment. To make sure the punishment hurt, Orwell named the totalitarian regime of Airstrip One 'Ingsoc', though he must have known to what uses the name would be put. It is not so much that he wanted English socialists to have minds free of sin (their hands were free enough: they had not actually committed any 'necessary' murders). He wanted them to have comprehending minds; he wanted them to understand, even if the politics he described defied complete understanding. 'I can understand HOW', says Winston Smith, 'I do not understand WHY.'[43]

But the novel seems to reject the idea that understanding might open the way to an alternative politics. That, according to Williams, is Orwell's final betrayal. The vision is too grim, denying any hope of resistance; there are no positive heroes. Indeed, there aren't; both *Animal Farm* and *1984* are fables, not tracts or programmes. What they describe is the nightmare of the boot pressing down on the human face ... forever. Nightmares would not be what they are if they marched toward some upbeat ending. They inspire fear, not hope. *1984* particularly is a novel of absolute bleakness, not so much a reduction of humankind as a refusal of political comfort, an unremitting portrait of totalitarianism in its own terms. And yet, Orwell's purpose in writing the book was surely to inspire opposition: disgust with the apologists, hatred for the dictators. He tells the story of Winston Smith, 'the last man in Europe', to other men and women in whose power it is to deny that finality. The positive hero of the book is its author – and, possibly, its reader.

'The book appals us', writes Irving Howe, 'because its terror, far from being inherent in the "human condition", is particular to our century; what haunts us is the sickening awareness that in *1984* Orwell has seized upon those elements of our public life that, given courage and intelligence, were avoidable.'[44] Are avoidable: since 'England, Your England' is not yet Airstrip One. Orwell's England has only a dim presence in *1984*, symbolised by the old jingle, which Winston Smith can't quite remember, about the bells of St Clement's. But we remember, we know intimately, the life and values that Ingsoc obliterates and to which Orwell consistently appeals. Writing *1984* was not an act of closure. Orwell undoubtedly felt the pressure of his illness, and that may have added to the urgency with which he wrote. But he was not dead yet; nor had he withdrawn from the world in order to pronounce a final judgement upon it. He meant to write again. The story of the last man was not intended to be his last word on politics. Nor need it be ours, so long as we speak with the terrifying awareness that was his gift.

From Michael Walzer, *The Company of Critics: Social Criticism and Political Commitment in the Twentieth Century* (London, 1989), pp. 117–35.

NOTES

[Michael Walzer examines Orwell's political views in a number of contexts creating a politico-historical trajectory across Orwell's writing whilst also engaging with and critiquing Raymond Williams's study of Orwell. He considers the literature as a working through in the formal and aesthetic qualities of the novel of Orwell's seemingly contradictory political trajectory and he takes on Williams's claims and judgements together with Orwell's own, in order to approach an appreciation of Orwell's version of English Socialism. Eds]

1. Raymond Williams, *George Orwell* (New York, 1981). Reading Williams on Orwell, I have been helped by Paul Thomas's lively and

perceptive essay, 'Mixed Feelings: Raymond Williams and George Orwell', *Theory and Society*, 14: 4 (July 1985), 419–44.

2. George Orwell, *Homage to Catalonia*, intro. Lionel Trilling (Boston, 1955), p. 5.

3. Raymond Williams, *Politics and Letters: Interviews with New Left Review* (London, 1981), pp. 384–92. The phrase 'social patriotism' is first used in the interview by the *NLR* editor, but it is adopted by Williams (see p. 386).

4. Williams, *George Orwell*, pp. 12, 24.

5. George Orwell, 'Inside the Whale', in Sonia Orwell and Ian Angus, (eds), *The Collected Essays, Journalism and Letters of George Orwell* (New York, 1968), I, p. 515. Hereafter referred to as *CEJL*.

6. I have quoted the poem as Orwell quotes it in 'Inside the Whale'. Auden revised the poem sometime in 1939, dropping the line about 'necessary murder'. For the revised version, see Edward Mendelson (ed.), *The English Auden: Poems, Essays and Dramatic Writings: 1927–1939* (New York, 1977); the changes are described by Mendelson on pp. 424–5.

7. *CEJL*, I, p. 516.

8. *CEJL*, II, p. 38.

9. George Orwell, *The Road to Wigan Pier* (New York, 1958), p. 261.

10. Ibid., pp. 179–80.

11. Ibid., p. 180.

12. Orwell, *Homage to Catalonia*, p. 232.

13. Williams, *George Orwell*, p. 91.

14. Orwell, *The Road to Wigan Pier*, p. 180.

15. George Orwell, *Keep the Aspidistra Flying* (New York, 1957), p. 219.

16. Trilling 'Introduction', in *Homage to Catalonia*, p. xv.

17. George Orwell, *1984* (New York, 1982), p. 114.

18. Trilling, 'Introduction', in *Homage to Catalonia*, p. xvi.

19. *CEJL*, II, p. 97.

20. *CEJL*, II, p. 57.

21. *CEJL*, I, p. 539; repeated in *CEJL*, II, p. 103.

22. *CEJL*, II, p. 109.

23. *CEJL*, III, p. 362.

24. *CEJL*, II, p. 68.

25. Williams, *Politics and Letters*, p. 391.

26. *CEJL*, II, p. 95.

27. Williams, *George Orwell*, p. 87.

28. Alex Zwerdling, *Orwell and the Left* (New Haven, CT, 1974), p. 16.

29. Richard Wollheim, 'Orwell Reconsidered', *Partisan Review*, 27: 1 (Winter 1960), pp. 95–6.

30. Zwerdling, *Orwell and the Left*, pp. 9–10. See also George Orwell and Reginald Reynolds (eds), *British Pamphleteers* (London, 1948).

31. *CEJL*, II, p. 96.

32. See *CEJL*, IV, pp. 160–81.

33. *CEJL*, II, p. 195.

34. Zwerdling, *Orwell and the Left*, p. 13.

35. Orwell, *The Road to Wigan Pier*, p. 212.

36. *CEJL*, I, p. 459.

37. *CEJL*, III, p. 235.

38. Williams, *Politics and Letters*, pp. 391–2.

39. *CEJL*, III, pp. 404–5.

40. *CEJL*, III, p. 226.

41. See the useful reading in George Woodcock, *The Crystal Spirit: A Study of George Orwell* (New York, 1984), pp. 217–19.

42. *CEJL*, III, p. 236.

43. Orwell, *1984*, p. 62.

44. Irving Howe, *Politics and the Novel* (New York, 1957), p. 236.

11

'The journalists do the shouting': Orwell and Propaganda

SIMON DENTITH

I

Since the very name George Orwell has become a byword for honesty and authenticity, and since these are so often juxtaposed to rhetoric, there is initially something sacrilegious about associating Orwell with rhetoric. But it is of course an association that Orwell would have been keen to repudiate, to judge by his own admittedly casual uses of the word. Thus in various contexts he can contrast 'high-flown rhetoric' to 'brutal coarseness' as the two extremes of the tonal range of English, can refer disparagingly to a 'rhetorical trick', and suggest an equivalence between 'magnificent rhetorical verse' and 'pieces of resounding nonsense'.[1] The final example is the most significant, since it forms part of a persistent set of categorical oppositions that dominate Orwell's writing about writing – between ornate, 'art-for-art's-sake', formally interesting *art*, and plain-style, dogged, pamphleteering prose. In general, however, these uses of the word are not important as indicative of his attitude towards the practice of rhetoric – he has other words for that, as we shall see – and of course in no way suggest that Orwell is not a motivated or committed writer. What they rather suggest is how, in this as in other things, Orwell repeats, with his own distinctive emphases, some classic Enlightenment positions with respect to the relationships between truth, writing and political power.

The Enlightenment commonplaces have become for Orwell a sardonic reminder of how far contemporary society has moved away from the Enlightenment ideals of freedom, truth and justice. One has only to think of the Ministry of Truth in *Nineteen Eighty-Four* and the centrality of *deception* in Orwell's various dystopic visions. This is as true of the pre-war writing as it is of the full-blown pessimism of the last novel. Thus in a review of Bertrand Russell in January 1939 he wrote:

> It is quite easy to imagine a state in which the ruling caste deceive their followers without deceiving themselves. Dare anyone be sure that something of the kind is not coming into existence already? One has only to think of the sinister possibilities of the radio, state-controlled education and so forth, to realise that 'the truth is great and will prevail' is a prayer rather than an axiom.[2]

This is a useful reminder that it was not only the dramatic cases of Fascism and Stalinism that suggested to Orwell the dark possibilities of the defeat of truth. But in addition, in his anxiety about whether 'the truth is great and will prevail' (a more familiar version of Godwin's central assumption), we can see both Orwell's commitment to a recognisable Enlightenment paradigm and his use of it as the measure of contemporary danger. This commitment can be seen in other contexts also. Thus in *Tribune* in 1945 he argued that the advantages of a lie, even in the progressive interest, are short-lived: 'So often it seems a positive duty to suppress or colour the facts! And yet genuine progress can only happen through increasing enlightenment, which means the continuous destruction of myths.'[3] And in another echo of the eighteenth century he can aver that the ruling class in a totalitarian society only clings to power 'by force or fraud'.[4] It is not surprising, given these affiliations, that Orwell should promote an ethic of objectivity and veracity in writing, or that he should follow Godwin also in his notion of its transparency; his famous dictum, 'good prose is like a window-pane', repeats Godwin's prescription for writing not because Orwell had read *The Enquirer* but because the two writers share the same understanding of epistemology and its implications for state power. It is this complex network of relations, linking, in Orwell's writing, questions of realism, 'good writing' and its relation to 'content' or 'political purpose', propaganda and language, that I hope to unravel in this chapter, before going on to examine Orwell's own rhetorical practice.

That Orwell was a committed or interested writer is not of course in doubt. What is important here is his own understanding of that commitment and its relationship to what he thought of as 'good writing' or the aesthetic element in writing. In perhaps the most interesting chapter in his book on Orwell, Raymond Williams has argued that behind the apparently straightforward categorical distinctions with which Orwell works – form versus content, or 'art-for-arts-sake' versus writing which is *about* something – lies a whole social history, in which, in response to the 'practicality' of the commercial middle class, writers repeatedly, and with growing typicality from the 1880s and 1890s onwards, offered their writing as representing a value outside and above the 'practical' commodity system.[5] In Williams's account, this social history, and the categorical confusions it engendered, remained to nag at Orwell throughout his writing career, leading him to downgrade his own writing as mere journalism or pamphleteering, yet leading him also to harbour a residual respect for writing that he simultaneously thought of as 'higher' and useless.

The categorical difficulty here leads to varying emphases in the course of his writing, allowing him at one time to praise good writing as an independent value, and at other times to suggest that he sees it as no more than a frill tacked on to the real business of getting the meaning across. An example of the first emphasis is his attitude to Joyce, especially *Ulysses*; his response to the novel included the notion that '*good writing* ... can exist almost as it were in vacuo and independent of subject'.[6] By contrast, consider his attitude to Conrad, about whom Orwell expressed impatience that he was unable to 'tell a story straightforwardly in the third person'.[7] Such contradictoriness is doubtless unimportant in itself – other than to those recently described by Christopher Hitchens, in connection with Orwell, as 'textual sectarians' – but it does point to a crucial aspect of Orwell's understanding of literary value, which feeds directly into his polemics against the dishonesty of reviewing, from both left and right. 'Literary value' is typically defended by Orwell as a value quite independent of the immediate political colouring of a book, as in the following article in *Tribune* on 'Literature and the Left':

> To dislike a writer's politics is one thing. To dislike him because he forces you to think is another, not necessarily incompatible with the first. But as soon as you start talking about 'good' and 'bad' writers

you are tacitly appealing to literary tradition and thus dragging in a
totally different set of values. For what is a 'good' writer? Was
Shakespeare 'good'? Most people agree that he was.[8]

The difficulty here with this apparently commonsensical attitude is
that the categorical baggage with which Orwell is lumbered ('good
writing can exist almost as it were in vacuo') disables him from
giving any substance to the values appealed to by the tacit reference
to the literary tradition. Indeed he admits as much in another
context, also with regard to his canonical example of Shakespeare:
'in reality there is no kind of evidence or argument by which one
can show that Shakespeare, or any other writer, is "good". Nor is
there any way of definitely proving that – for instance – Warwick
Deeping is "bad".'[9] So that one can applaud the attack on the kind
of reviewing which tacitly substitutes political for literary values –
though I, for one, would not like to be the kind of reader who
could easily make the negotiations required when they conflict –
while recognising that none of the potentially contradictory emphases offered by Orwell himself promise an ultimately satisfactory
resolution to the problems he addressed.

So if I find Bernard Crick's 'resolution' of this set of problems
unsatisfactory, I do so not from any desire to score points – I
greatly admire the *Life* – but because he unduly tidies up an interesting and intractable knot. Crick writes:

> he was defending, in a truculent way, an essentially 'centrist' or mod-
> erate position in the Art and Society debate of the 1930s. The
> importance of the subject-matter or the sincerity of the writer can
> never excuse bad writing, but equally good writing is unlikely to
> come from someone with nothing to say about morality and society
> or who cultivates a delicate morality.[10]

The problem here is that it leaves the notions of 'good' and 'bad'
writing quite empty, just as Orwell himself does. In practice, Orwell
gets the best perspective on these issues when he steps outside his
habitual categorical boundaries, as he does when he discusses the
case of Swift in 'Politics vs Literature'. The problem is put simply
enough: 'what is the relationship between agreement with a writer's
opinions, and enjoyment of his work?'.[11] On this occasion Orwell,
while acknowledging the contribution made by 'good writing'
in a technical and instrumental way to the success of *Gulliver's
Travels*, nevertheless concedes that this is not enough on its own to

overcome the 'anti-human' slant of the book. The solution he proposes – that Swift's misanthropic physical disgust expresses a partial truth about humanity 'which we all know about while shrinking from mentioning it' – may in itself be only part of an answer, but it does at least remain within the realm of meanings, recognises the negotiations between writer and reader in which meaning is established, and makes the recourse to 'good writing' an instrumental and not a categorical one.

In general, however, Orwell is not as genial on these matters as the relatively safe topic of Swift allows him to be. As at least some of my other examples will have suggested, this whole area of discussion is overdetermined for Orwell by the question of propaganda, for he is nothing if not an insistently political writer. Once again, Crick's tidying up of the complex range of positions to be found in Orwell's writing serves as an unreliable guide to the issues here. A better starting point is Orwell's own belligerent assertion that 'Few people have the guts to say outright that art and propaganda are the same thing'.[12] The belligerence here, on examination, proves to be a kind of shadow-boxing. Do few people have the necessary guts because there are so few, like Orwell, who are prepared to cut through the waffle and proclaim the actual identity of art and propaganda? Or are there so few because none of those who switch from one criterion to the other are prepared to admit that they are actually judging art on political grounds? As it stands the statement will lend itself to either reading, and support for both can be found throughout Orwell's writing. There is a persistent strain in his writing which does indeed wish to insist on the identity of art and propaganda, as when he asserts that 'most books are propaganda, direct or indirect', or that 'I have always maintained that every artist is a propagandist'.[13] But equally one can find passages which assert the opposite, as when Orwell attempts to answer a correspondent to *Tribune* who had complained at the review space devoted to books: 'we also assume that books are not to be regarded simply as propaganda, that literature exists in its own right – as a form of recreation, to put it no higher'.[14] Crick is of course right to point out that Orwell is fighting on two fronts, and that this explains some of the inconsistencies here. On the one hand, the insistence on the identity of art and propaganda is a useful debunking position to take, directed against the high priests of 'art-for-art's sake'. On the other hand, the assumption of a separate sphere for literature is part of a different campaign, evident in his exchange with the *Tribune* correspondent, to retain a space for the *different* interests of literature ('to put it no higher') among the pressing political exigencies of the period. As always, matters of definition and category have a rhetorical aspect, though that does not mean that the attempt to find order and coherence can be simply abandoned.

Matters are further complicated by Orwell's belief that his contemporary period is peculiarly likely to make a politically disinterested literature impossible. 'All writing nowadays is propaganda', he wrote in 1941; but this proposition can take very different emphases. In its immediate context, an attack on pacifism provoked by reviewing a book by Alex Comfort, Orwell argues that it is the peculiar property of the present period to make 'any sort of joy in writing ... impossible'.[15] But as we have seen, Orwell is also capable of arguing that all writing is propaganda, quite irrespective of the 'nowadays'. Thus in reviewing the first three of *The Four Quartets*, he writes:

> It is fashionable to say that in verse only the words count and the 'meaning' is irrelevant, but in fact every poem contains a prose meaning, and when the poem is any good it is a meaning which the poet urgently wishes to express. All art is to some extent propaganda.[16]

Once again, the point is not to note the inconsistency but to note the particular alignment of categories. Williams is clearly right to consider that Orwell's categorical inheritance in this area was a negative one; even people unsympathetic to Williams's account might find reason to balk at the equivalence here between 'prose meaning' and 'propaganda'. But the problem here is with the inevitably adverse connotations of the word propaganda, connotations which affect Orwell's use of the word every bit as much as those who more evidently disdain it. If you try to imagine the word not as categorically opposed to, and on a lower level than, 'literature', but as alluding to the interested and agonistic aspect of writing, whether 'literary' or not, then Orwell emerges as an astute and demystificatory critic, acutely alert to the rhetorical interests of writing and to the rhetorical situation into which it is directed.

A further element of Orwell's sophisticated understanding of rhetoric – routed, as it is, through his various discussions of propaganda – is his commitment to the notion of objective truth. The image of The Ministry of Truth busy consigning the objective truths of history to the dustbin is sufficiently familiar to make Orwell's opinions on this matter apparently evident. The possibility of re-course to objective truth is an indispensable bulwark against the en-croachments of totalitarianism, so much so that the denial of the existence of objective truth is an infallible symptom, in Orwell's writing, of intellectual power-worship and dishonesty. In these matters, as elsewhere, Orwell's Enlightenment inheritance is clear and explicit, so that when, in a classic essay of 1946 like 'The Prevention of Literature', Orwell sees it as one of the chief symp-toms of the contemporary *malaise* that intellectuals are not pre-pared to face facts, this in itself is also a denial of the whole Enlightenment inheritance. 'Prose literature as we know it is the product of rationalism, of the Protestant centuries, of the au-tonomous individual.'[17] This is what is at stake in the demand that the writer be free to report on the truth. The enemies to this freedom are not simply the intellectual straitjackets imposed by rus-sophilia – though this is certainly the principal target of this essay – but also, and more immediately for British writers in 1946, 'the press lords, the film magnates, and the bureaucrats'.[18]

Whatever the epistemological difficulties with the concept of ob-jective truth – and I do not believe that all those in the academy who have attacked it in recent years are in headlong flight to total-itarianism – this seems to me to be an emphasis that is wholly worth retaining. But it is not the whole story of Orwell's notion of objective truth, for he also articulates it with the force of writing. This connection is repeatedly made throughout his career; the ethical or political reasons we have just seen expressed – truthful-ness and objectivity are values in themselves and ought to be pre-served – are habitually accompanied by the more prudential reason of the greater persuasiveness of telling the truth. Thus in an early review of Henry Miller's *Black Spring* he takes exception to the book's surrealism because it loses the reader's interest: 'The truth is that the written word loses its power if it departs too far, or rather if it stays away too long, from the ordinary world where two and two make four'.[19] This passing assertion (part of Orwell's complex negotiation with Henry Miller's writing which will culminate with *Inside the Whale*) receives a more definitive formulation in 'The Prevention of Literature', even, one might say, a more banal formu-lation: 'But after all, how is it that books ever come to be written? Above a quite low level, literature is an attempt to influence the viewpoint of one's contemporaries by recording experience.'[20] The flatness of the phrasing should not conceal the distinctiveness of this position; perhaps it is Orwell's insistently political preoccupations, or more simply his journalistic ones, that lead him to include a rhetorical element ('an attempt to influence the viewpoint of one's contemporaries') at the heart of a definition of literature. In fact the journalistic context is more likely to produce a formulation of this kind; M. H. Abrams, in *The Mirror and the Lamp*, has demonstrated how untypical this is of post-Romantic criticism of a more exclusively 'literary' kind. Indeed, Orwell's formulation is mappable on the Abrams diagram, though the result is a rather exiguous view of writing. The rhetorical function of literature (Abrams calls it 'pragmatic') is dependent for its force on the referential function. This account leaves out both the expressive function and the intrinsic character of writing, though the phrase 'recording experience' perhaps retains traces of both in vestigial and very subordinate ways. At all events, at the heart of Orwell's notions about writing (in 'The Prevention of Literature' he is careful to insist that the same considerations apply to both 'a mere journalist and the most "unpolitical" imaginative writer'[21]) is the dependence of rhetoric upon objective truth.

This obviously will not do as it stands, not even if it is read, as I believe all such definitions should be, as normative rather than neutrally categorical. Clearly, there is never such a perfect fit between rhetorical and referential functions, for neither can exhaust the function of the other. Painstakingly recorded truth will always be available for more than one appropriation, even the writer's own – to make a Bakhtinian point, no utterance is ever completed, but always carries with it further possibilities that can be realised in some other context or at some time in the future. Equally, there must be some activity in writing which transforms the truth and gives it force. This can be seen at least negatively; the propagandist charge of an utterance is not determined by the truth-value of its references. Orwell acknowledges this wittily; talking about the reality of fascist outrages, he writes that 'They happened even though Lord Halifax said they happened'.[22] More sharply, he writes in his verse controversy with Alex Comfort that

> All propaganda's lying, yours or mine;
> It's lying even when its facts are true.[23]

As always, Orwell is at his most acute in polemic, making the most of his categories and forcing them into interesting and paradoxical formulations. In both these instances, his practical understanding of the actualities of polemic and propaganda – his recognition, for example, of the importance of such matters as the source and context of an utterance in determining its force – make him produce formulations a long way from the flat literalness of his attempts at definition. But whatever the deficiencies of these definitions, Orwell is insistent, and rightly so, that the force of writing is dependent upon its truth, and that to abandon truth is ultimately to ensure the failure of that writing (though his faith in the historical actuality of that 'ultimately' obviously wavered).

Closely dependent upon Orwell's epistemology are his views upon language. Here, as elsewhere, we can trace the pressures of two contradictory impulses. Springing straight from his realist epistemology comes the famous injunction to 'Let the meaning choose the word and not the other way about'.[24] At times this can become very prescriptive; in one of his 'As I Please' pieces in *Tribune* he attacks the dead metaphors with which English is littered, seeing their continued use (especially in misspelt forms which show that their users do not know their origin) as evidence that 'people who are capable of this kind of thing evidently don't attach any definite meaning to the words they use'.[25] Coupled with this mistrust of metaphor is a similar mistrust of high-faluting language and, surprisingly perhaps for the satirist of Newspeak, considerable sympathetic interest in Basic English. The following paragraph from an '*As I Please*' piece of 1944 gives a good idea of the nature of his interest:

> One argument for Basic English is that existing side by side with Standard English it can act as a sort of corrective to the oratory of statesmen and publicists. High-sounding phrases, when translated into Basic, are often deflated in a surprising way. For example, I presented to a Basic expert the sentence, 'He little knew the fate that lay in store for him' – to be told that in Basic this would become 'He was far from certain what was going to happen'. It sounds decidedly less impressive, but it means the same. In Basic, I am told, you cannot make a meaningless statement without its being apparent that it is meaningless – which is quite enough to explain why so many schoolmasters, editors, politicians and literary critics object to it.[26]

I do object to this, even though he said I would. The notion of a language so transparently following the contours of the world that it makes meaninglessness self-evident is an empiricist fantasy old enough to have been satirised by Jonathan Swift in *Gulliver's Travels*, during Gulliver's stay in Laputa. Even Orwell's own example fails to make his case. 'He little knew the fate that lay in store for him' does not mean the same as 'He was far from certain what was going to happen'. Quite apart from the fact that 'to him' needs to be added to the second sentence in order to make it all equivalent, the 'translation' ignores all considerations of emphasis and irony, ineradicable elements of meaning in actual use of these sentences. It might be objected, on Orwell's behalf, that this is to ignore the principal reason he provides for his interest in Basic English, namely its capacity to deflate and demystify the high-sounding and obscurantist language of politicians and advertisers. I immediately concede. However, other demystificatory strategies can be devised which do not entail the same reductive and prescriptive attitudes as Orwell displays here. Paragraphs such as these are one terminus of his empiricist notions about language.

Yet it is not hard to find that other impulse in Orwell, which delights in the vigour of poetic and demotic speech. At much the same time as that paragraph from *Tribune* he was writing *The English People*, which includes a substantial section on the English language in praise of its potential range of meaning and tone. Quite properly, Orwell shows himself very aware of the class factors which both produce and deform the language. 'Language ought to be the joint creation of poets and manual workers, and in modern England it is difficult for these two classes to meet', he writes. This follows a happy list of the demotic alternatives to the objectionable Americanism *sez you*. The list includes '*not half, I don't think, come off it, less of it, and then you wake up*, or simply *garn*', noting that you would not expect to find any of these expressions in a *Times* leader because of their vulgarity.[27]

But his interest in demotic speech was not simply an aesthetic one; his ever-present consciousness of the rhetorical dimension meant that he was especially interested in the gap between the language of politics and the language of the 'average man' as a barrier to propagandist effect. 'Propaganda and Demotic Speech' is devoted to just this problem. In this essay Orwell attacks the language of 'official' politics, government information, newspaper editorials and left-wing political parties for their common remoteness from the language of ordinary spoken English. Noting again how the questions raised here are involved with class ('It seems certain that in modern England the "educated", upper-class accent is deadly to any speaker who is aiming at a large audience'), Orwell concludes by arguing the importance of these issues to a democratic politics:

> But some day we may have a genuinely democratic government, a government which will want to tell people what is happening, and what must be done next, and what sacrifices are necessary, and why. It will need the mechanisms for doing so, of which the first are the right words, the right tone of voice.[28]

This is a passage that Brian Vickers might have quoted in arguing, in *In Defence of Rhetoric*, for a link between the study of rhetoric and democratic politics. It is certainly a positive emphasis that one can elicit from Orwell's insistent grounding of questions of language in the political domain.

I earlier referred to the discomfort which might be provoked by associating Orwell with rhetoric. Orwell's own much harder word, propaganda – though clearly not precisely congruous with rhetoric – provokes commensurately greater discomfort; to associate Orwell with propaganda is to do no more than he invited ('all writing nowadays is propaganda'), but is to raise the stakes of the discussion perhaps unnecessarily high. It would disable us, for instance, from distinguishing between *Animal Farm* and the work that Orwell performed for the BBC Eastern Service between 1941 and 1943. Here, while it may be true that 'None of this work involved any "black" propaganda. The Indian Section and the BBC generally were seen by Orwell as essentially truthful',[29] he nevertheless was engaged in propaganda and did not always tell the absolute truth (a different matter, I dare say, from the 'essential' truth). His own understanding of his position was explicit on these points. Referring to the possibility of broadcasting to India as 'George Orwell', he recognised that the propagandist value of that name lay in his reputation as an anti-imperialist writer: 'clearly we should defeat our own object in these broadcasts if I could not preserve my position as an independent and more or less "agin the government" commentator'.[30] Orwell lays out here the beginnings of what might be called a pragmatics of propaganda, and he certainly admitted that 'one rapidly becomes propaganda minded'. It was in this context that he gave an example of his willingness to tamper with the truth: 'I am regularly alleging in all my news-letters that the Japanese are plotting to attack Russia. I don't believe this to be so.'[31] All this is certainly propaganda, even the 'university of the air' reproduced in *Orwell: The War Broadcasts*, one function of which was to provide legitimacy for the more overtly propagandist material broadcast elsewhere by the Indian Section.

But in seeking to distinguish between this work and, for instance, *Animal Farm*, it is evidently not the case that any categorical distinction can be drawn on the strength of the latter's greater disinterestedness. Nor will it do to argue the case on the grounds of the formal differences between the work – to say, for example, that *Animal Farm* is art because it is an animal fable while the BBC work is propaganda because it deals 'directly' with current affairs. These formal differences are important, not least for the rhetorical force of the writing; but they do not capture the attempted difference of a distinction between art and propaganda. In the spirit of Orwell's own occasional notion of a simply instrumental criterion for 'good writing', we might better capture the distinction by recognising the occasions which provoke this diversity of writing; the value of *Animal Farm* is not exhausted in a day or even a month, unlike the value of a news summary. This is not to say, of course, that the value of the novel, not being for an age, is for all time – let us hope indeed for a time when a satire of Stalinism is of only antiquarian interest! But it is to recognise that to preserve more than a passing interest the novel has to identify more permanent concerns with its particular, timely, provocations.

It is easy to find, in the range of Orwell's writing, a range of inconsistent and even contradictory positions on these matters to match his well-known contradictions on political matters. Like those political contradictions, these widely varying emphases can be traced to the extraordinarily diverse and powerful pressures of the world historical crises through which he lived, and the modalities of class and gender through which he lived them.[32] The particular belligerence with which he expressed himself, moreover, is traceable to his reading of the rhetorical situation in which his writing took on its force, where the stakes seemed, and indeed were, extremely high. In trying to trace these contradictions, and to register this belligerence, I have not been ticking off Orwell; criteria of academic coherence simply do not apply to the range of Orwell's novels, journalism and reportage, and I applaud the vehemence of his writing even when I find it misdirected. In a world in which Orwell is so insistently 'claimed' from all directions it is worth stressing what a complex and contradictory figure he is; nevertheless, in assessing the 'case' of Orwell, and in trying to describe the social and hence rhetorical ground of his writing, one is not simply engaged in an act of historical placement. The questions of truth and propaganda through which he addressed what I have discussed under the heading of 'rhetoric' remain real and pressing; despite his occasional reductiveness, his brutal dismissals, and his contradictions, there are emphases which it is well worth retaining. We now need to turn to his actual rhetorical practice to see, not only whether the positive positions that can be found in criticism and journalism are borne out in his other writing, but also to see how this writing is inserted into its particular rhetorical situation. For various reasons, not least the exemplary status conferred on it after it had lost its more pressing urgency, I have chosen to pursue this discussion with respect to *Homage to Catalonia*.

II

Let us retain Orwell's own vocabulary for a moment and ask, is *Homage to Catalonia* propaganda? He himself, in the body of the text, claims that it is not: 'I am not writing a book of propaganda',[33] and indeed the book is in no small part a polemic against the propaganda which surrounded the Spanish Civil War. 'One of the most horrible features of war', he writes, 'is that all the war-propaganda, all the screaming and lies and hatred, comes invariably from people who are not fighting' (p. 64); shortly after he adds:

> The people who write that kind of stuff never fight; possibly they believe it is a substitute for fighting. It is the same in all wars; the soldiers do the fighting, the journalists do the shouting, and no true patriot ever gets near a front-line trench, except on the briefest of propaganda tours.
>
> (p. 65)

In fact, the book is in part about propaganda, and the repudiation of propagandist intent is of course a central element in its own rhetorical stance. It is not unreasonable to quote Orwell against himself here: 'a propagandist does not declare himself as a propagandist'.[34] As we have just seen, Orwell was acutely aware that the truthfulness of a piece of writing does not absolve it of propagandist effect; no more do his own repudiation of propaganda and repeated invitations to the reader to discount his own bias absolve this text of its 'propagandist' implications. Orwell was quite explicit about his intentions in writing the book, though he considered that only about half the book was controversial.[35] Those sections of the book which are a defence of the POUM are clearly what he has in mind; these he is prepared to describe concessively to Stephen Spender as 'Trotskyist propaganda'. But the other sections of the book, the first-hand account of Orwell's experiences as a militia-man, are equally propagandist even by Orwell's own admittedly wide interpretation of the word at times – recall how he wanted to make 'propaganda' equivalent to 'prose-meaning'. Perhaps after all it is safer to revert to the language of rhetoric and conclude that the authority of the text is grounded on its repudiation of the large claims of propaganda and the consequent authenticity of the narrative in being grounded in personal experience. This is in fact the characteristic Orwellian stance, which asks you to disbelieve all the big claims made by others, to recognise the worst that can be said, to believe no more than can be vouched for, and yet which still manages to produce a minimal or bottom-line commitment which requires your assent.

There is nothing the matter with this stance, and nothing to be said against it as long as it is recognised that it has limitations as well as strengths. This is precisely what some of the claims made on Orwell's behalf have not recognised. The paradigmatic instance is Lionel Trilling, whose influential review of the 1952 American publication of *Homage to Catalonia* established the terms of much subsequent discussion of both the book and Orwell himself. 'In saying the least it says the most', Trilling declares, registering the modesty of Orwell's rhetorical stance. But there is nothing modest about his expansion of this position:

> He liberates us. He tells us that we can understand our political and social life merely by looking around us, he frees us from the need for inside dope. He implies that our job is not to be intellectual, certainly not to be intellectual in this fashion or that, but merely to be intelligent according to our lights.[36]

This is a classic cold war end-of-ideology position. While there is undoubtedly plenty in *Homage to Catalonia* to justify Trilling's distrust of being intellectual, this wholesale empiricism is really too large an extrapolation from the book. It is instructive to contrast it with Robert Stradling's critique of the book as a piece of history-writing. Stradling finds the following to be an assumption that underlies the text: 'it will be apparent that Orwell's chief concern was with the concrete, atomic "facts" of history, which, preserved and guarded against interference, will inevitably yield a harvest of literal and universal truth'.[37] Stradling is clearly right to be sceptical of this assumption. Yet in fact both Trilling and Stradling are addressing the same aspect of Orwell's writing from opposite perspectives. Both are concerned with the absence of any analytical or theoretical perspective which might order or make more general sense of the empirical information which the text contains. For Trilling this is a matter for congratulation, for Stradling a matter for regret. Is it the case, however, that the concrete and atomic facts of history are thought to yield a *universal* truth for Orwell? Rather these facts, particularly of the May 1937 street-fighting, are ordered in a particular, if rather confusing, narrative, and are explained, if at all, by the malign operations of the Communist Party and its allies. In other words, the absence of any more general or analytical account does not yield *no* explanation: that absence is filled by a combination of the cock-up theory and the conspiracy theory. Both these 'theories' of historical explanation – neither of them, surely, simply wrong – are congruous with Orwell's rhetorical stance throughout the book, that is, with his stance of the plain man, with his own biases duly allowed for, trying to make sense of the events that happen across his path. Needless to say, in agreeing with Stradling about the insufficiency of atomic facts as a basis for historical explanation I do not say that it is possible to do without them or that it is acceptable for anybody to tamper with them.

As ever, there is no rhetoric without an epistemology and no epistemology without a rhetoric. We need to examine Orwell's rhetorical stance more closely, which, as I have suggested, is as important a feature of the sections of the book dealing with Orwell's first-hand experiences as a militiaman as it is of the more obviously controversial sections. Indeed there is a close link between the two parts of the book, since the authority established in the accounts of the front-line fighting is crucial to the success of the accounts of the May events in Barcelona. Here is a characteristic example:

> The position stank abominably, and outside the little enclosure of the barricade there was excrement everywhere. Some of the militia-men habitually defecated in the trench, a disgusting thing when one had to walk round it in darkness. But the dirt never worried me. Dirt is a thing people make too much fuss about. It is astonishing how quickly you get used to doing without a handkerchief and to eating out of the tin pannikin in which you also wash.
>
> (p. 33)

There is a lot of excrement in *Homage to Catolonia*, functioning generally as a mark of authenticity – if Orwell is prepared to mention *that*, we are invited to think, then there is nothing that is being omitted. In this instance, however, having established himself by breaking this minor taboo, Orwell then belittles its importance; quickly establishing his own exceptional immunity to dirt-consciousness compared to 'people', and drawing intertextually perhaps on the 'George Orwell' of *Down and Out in Paris and London*, he concludes this little section by suggesting the reordered set of priorities that govern life at the front. The rhetorical stance in this instance, then, is of the man who is prepared to face and come to terms with the worst.

If George Orwell's own earlier writing provides one significant element of the intertext of passages such as these, however, still more significant is the general understanding of war in the 1930s. In *Homage to Catalonia* Orwell takes up one of the main themes of post Great War writing – a general insistence on the squalor and degradation of war – and redirects it away from the pacifist meanings with which it had, not unnaturally, become identified. This is how Orwell himself describes this element of the rhetorical situation surrounding the book in 'Looking Back on the Spanish Civil War':

> If there was one thing that the British intelligentsia were committed to, it was the debunking version of war, the theory that war is all corpses and latrines and never leads to any good result. Well, the same people who in 1933 sniggered pityingly if you said that in certain circumstances you would fight for your country, in 1937 were denouncing you as a Trotsky–Fascist if you suggested that the stories in *New Masses* about freshly wounded men clamouring to get back into the fighting might be exaggerated.[38]

One does not have to subscribe to Orwell's wholesale contempt for the Left intelligentsia to recognise that this was certainly how he perceived the situation, and that this perception profoundly affected his understanding of the rhetorical situation into which he was writing. The dirt in *Homage to Catalonia* – both Orwell's insistence on it and his capacity to deal with it – contributes crucially to his standing in the text and only takes on its full significance in the context of struggles over the meaning of war in the 1930s.

One simple way of describing Orwell's attitude here would be to see it, straightforwardly, as anti-heroic. Certainly that will go a long way to characterise that cool, debunking tone of voice, always assessing matters at their worst estimate, only, finally, to admit the base-line commitment: 'despite all this, ... nevertheless ...'. Even in his handling of conventionally heroic material Orwell works by understatement. Take this example, from his account of the original resistance to the military coup which precipitated the Civil War (Orwell is arguing that popular resistance was revolutionary):

> Men and women armed only with sticks of dynamite rushed across the open squares and stormed stone buildings held by trained soldiers with machine-guns. Machine-gun nests that the Fascists had placed at strategic spots were smashed by rushing taxis at them at sixty miles an hour ... it would be hard to believe that the Anarchists and Socialists who were the backbone of the resistance were doing this kind of thing for the preservation of capitalist democracy.
>
> (p. 49)

The sardonic understatement here ('this kind of thing') is a useful resource for admitting the heroism without resort to a more conventional and therefore more vulnerable heroic language. But this is evidently not the whole story, for even conventionally heroic language as often works by understatement as by inflation ('He works his work, I mine'). In fact that cool, understated, unruffled voice is not far from a stiff upper lip:

> Now that we had finished wrestling with those beastly sand-bags it was not bad fun in a way; the noise, the darkness, the flashes approaching, our own men blazing back at the flashes. One even had time to think a little. I remember wondering whether I was frightened, and deciding that I was not. Outside, where I was probably in less danger, I had been half sick with fright.
>
> (p. 94)

This is clearly not *The Boy's Own Paper*; that cool self-appraisal offers the surprising fact that he is not frightened as just one more piece of interesting information to be reckoned in with the rest. This tone reaches its apogee when Orwell is wounded: 'The whole experience of being hit by a bullet is very interesting and I think it is worth describing in detail' (p. 177). He proceeds to do so. Nevertheless, the fact of Orwell's physical courage, and the cool and non-committal way in which he records it, are essential elements of his rhetorical stance.

One can get a line on Orwell's rhetoric here by comparing it, as his frequent attacks do no more than invite us to, with that of Claud Cockburn, who wrote under the name of 'Frank Pitcairn' in *The Daily Worker*. Orwell specifically attacks him over his accounts of the May days in Barcelona; he is presumably one of those journalists who 'do the shouting', though it is not the case that he did all his shouting from a position of comfortable safety. Interestingly enough, Cockburn makes exactly the same rhetorical disclaimers that mark Orwell's text, disdaining 'fine phrases' and 'high-falutin rhetoric', and prefacing one particularly dramatic account with the assertion that 'in these articles I am telling you simply what I saw. The conclusions you can draw for yourself.'[39] But here the resemblance ends. Orwell could never have written this:

> Problems which would have disconcerted and even appalled men of lesser character and ability or men fighting for a lesser cause, were described and dealt with in a spirit of cool objectivity and with a calm grasp of the whole situation – local, national and international – which frequently gave one an impression of being present at a meeting of leaders from some almost fabulous or legendary race of persons endowed with more than human qualities.[40]

Or this:

> We have often said that from the blood of our murdered comrades new men, new champions would spring.
> Perhaps there were people who thought that was just a phrase we used: a way of saying things not meaning anything concrete or real.
> Today they know that when the people claims it will send new men to fill the places of every man that falls, the people means what it says.
> The new champions are really there. They are there in that roaring semi-circle of shell fire, bursting bombs, gas, machine-gun bullets and mud, around the city of Madrid, the men of the International Brigade.[41]

Orwell has already warned us, in that passage from 'Looking Back on the Spanish Civil War', about sniggering at fine phrases, and I certainly have no desire to say anything to belittle the courage of the International Brigades. The problem here is rather with the slighty mechanical, if not slightly cynical, manner in which 'Frank Pitcairn' draws on these heroic figures of speech. But whether unknowingly or not, this is prose which is untroubled by the gap between historic events and an appropriately heroic language to fit them. And it is just this characteristically modern consciousness of disjunction between an event and its significance that is at the heart of *Homage to Catalonia* and which, it can be said, the various rhetorical strategies of the book seek to overcome.

Here is a typical instance:

> I went back to my post on the roof with a feeling of concentrated disgust and fury. When you are taking part in events like these you are, I suppose, in a small way, making history, and you ought by rights to feel like a historical character. But you never do, because at such times the physical details always outweigh everything else. Throughout the fighting I never made the correct 'analysis' of the situation that was so glibly made by journalists hundreds of miles away. What I was chiefly thinking about was not the rights and wrongs of this miserable internecine scrap, but simply the discomfort and boredom of sitting day and night on that intolerable roof, and the hunger which was growing worse and worse.
>
> (p. 134)

The announcement that Orwell knows, retrospectively, that he is participating in historic events has to be prefaced by a couple of qualifying disclaimers ('I suppose, in a small way'). But even this chastened sense of the historic escapes Orwell as he actually takes part in the events he records. Only subsequently, in retrospect and as he pieces together a fuller account of the events and learns to see their full significance both for himself and politically, does he manage to capture the sense of their historic importance. *Homage to Catalonia* is a book, after all, and not a series of articles – only over the whole span of the book can this crucial sense be established. And here is a more secure way of distinguishing between Orwell's rhetoric and Cockburn's. The latter is writing a series of newspaper articles, where no gap between event and its significance can be tolerated. This instrumental consideration is more important than the question of taste – though taste in these matters is not arbitrary! There is a history behind my scepticism of 'some almost fabulous or legendary race of persons endowed with more than human qualities'. Moreover, a reader's scepticism is to be avoided for instrumental reasons too. We can thus in part account for the differences between the two styles by noticing their contrasting occasions. Cockburn was writing a series of articles for *The Daily Worker* with immediate propagandist intention, in particular to expose the arms starvation of the republican forces because of the policy of Non-intervention. Orwell wrote *Homage to Catalonia* from no less of a partisan position, but he is writing a book of retrospection and celebration (*Homage* to Catalonia), in which he has more space to establish and develop his sense of the historic significance of what he has witnessed.

The contrast between Cockburn's writing and Orwell's is not confined to their differing forms and their differing politics. These contrasts also expressed themselves especially clearly in their contrasting modes of publication and publishers. *The Daily Worker* was of course the Communist Party paper. *Homage to Catalonia* was published by Secker and Warburg who, according to Orwell, 'are coming to be known, rather inaccurately, as "the Trotskyist publishers"'.[42] It marked a break from Gollancz, who had previously published all of Orwell's books, issuing *Road to Wigan Pier* as a Left Book Club edition (though with a preface effectively disowning its second half). *Homage* was savaged by Communist Party reviewers, and by reviewers who were sympathetic to the Party; it only received good reviews in Independent Labour Party papers or in papers for which Orwell wrote himself. All this was to be expected in a political atmosphere in which the POUM was widely accepted as not only 'objectively' pro-fascist but actually in Franco's pay and part of his Fifth Column. In short, the rhetorical situation into which the book was issued was so fiercely partisan as to overwhelm the particularities of Orwell's rhetoric that I have been trying to elucidate, and to exhaust its meaning in its defence of the POUM. It did not even sell particularly well, some of the original print-run of fifteen hundred still being unsold in 1951.[43] The first American edition, as we have seen, was in 1952, attracting the attention of Lionel Trilling. In this very different climate, Orwell's anti-communism was now generally congenial, though the fact that he mounts his critique of communist policy from the left – 'objectively' pro-Trotskyist, we might say – is now forgotten. It was not issued as a Penguin until the 1960s. Altogether, this publishing and reception history indicates very clearly – doubtless because of the especially clear political issues of the book – the extent to which meanings are established in historically determinate but changing rhetorical situations.

The partisan nature of the original reviews obscures how, in the main, its style was a characteristic one of the period. The 1930s after all, was a decade of documentary writing, inevitably yielding a left meaning – or so it was thought: 'Descriptive reporting has a particularly revolutionary impact. (We have even invented a jargon name for it, *reportage*.) Certainly to describe things as they are is a revolutionary act in itself.' Thus Montagu Slater in *Left Review*.[44] Orwell's empiricism was thus a widespread assumption, and the accompanying style can be thought of as one of the formal elements of the rhetorical situation, whose mastery might have predisposed a left public towards the book – if not necessarily towards complete agreement, of course. But as Crick observes, 'critics are slow to recognise any literary merit in political writing', and though this is to reproduce the ultimately false abstraction of the 'literary' that Orwell himself makes, it does nevertheless indicate how the nature of the writing can be overwhelmed by the politics. In the Burkean terms of the 'scene/act ratio', the scene has flattened the act. What writing does is not always sufficient to overcome the conditions into which the writing is issued.

Let us conclude this look at *Homage to Catalonia* by recalling Orwell's famous account of Barcelona when he first encountered it:

> And it was the aspect of the crowds that was the queerest thing of all. In outward appearance it was a town in which the wealthy classes had practically ceased to exist. Except for a small number of women and foreigners there were no 'well-dressed' people at all. Practically everyone wore rough working-class clothes, or blue overalls, or some variant of the militia uniform. All this was queer and moving. There was much in it that I did not understand, in some ways I did not even like it, but I recognised it immediately as a state of affairs worth fighting for.
>
> (p. 9)

I read this as the paradigmatic instance of Orwell's rhetorical stance in the book, which I have described as a bottom-line commitment: 'despite everything ... nevertheless ...'. In my account of the book I have emphasised the 'everything' – all the negative aspects, the dirt, the confusion, the adverse politics – which Orwell had to overcome before he could make that final commitment. Indeed, I see the movement towards that final commitment as the fundamental structure of the book, a movement of reintegration of event and significance. But perhaps I have overemphasised these adverse elements, and not made enough of those positive moments of solidarity, across the barriers of nationality and class, which are also a striking feature of the book. The meeting with the Italian militiaman with which the book begins is the most fully developed of these. 'All this was queer and moving.' Perhaps, after all, Orwell was not so far removed from that 'pious Sodomite' Edward Carpenter, who also made a moment of individual contact the measure of a social system.

Ever since his death, people have been trying to 'claim' Orwell. Some such claims are simply grotesque; the *Sun* newspaper editorialised on 2 January 1984 thus:

> As 1984 opens, we have been spared the Orwell nightmare. We have liberty under Margaret Thatcher. We have hope of a better tomorrow.
>   Yet all these things are not automatic.
>   *We have to deserve them. We have to earn them.*
>   *We must be vigilant every day in 1984 and beyond to preserve them from any assault.*[45]

And according to Norman Podhoretz:

> [Orwell] was a forerunner of neoconservatism in having been one of the first in a long line of originally left-wing intellectuals who have come to discover more saving political and moral wisdom in the instincts and mores of 'ordinary people' than in the ideas and attitudes of the intelligentsia.[46]

That last *bonne bouche* was found by Christopher Hitchens, who in a fine piece on Orwell concludes that 'He is a founder and member of a modern rebel tradition that, in political writing, comprises Victor Serge and Dwight Macdonald, Albert Camus and Milan Kundera'.[47] This too constitutes a claim, one which better registers the dissidence, the belligerence, the downright awkwardness of Orwell than the tidied up and sanitised version of Crick's *Life* – though as a matter of intellectual history Crick's insistence on Orwell's commitment to democratic socialism is in danger of being lost in Hitchens's version. But I do not complain that people have tried to claim him, for that is the very process in which significance is established. Orwell's salience makes his writing a central site over which critical, literary and political battles are constantly being fought, in the course of which the various 'Orwells' emerge.[48] That is not to say, of course, that all these various 'Orwells' are equally valid – just as the ultimate reliance of rhetoric upon epistemology means that not *anything* can be persuasive, so not every construction of Orwell is as valid as the next. I have no intention of retracting that *grotesque*. This inevitable, this ordinary, process of interested exposition and contestation is complicated, or rather made easier, by the exceptional contradictoriness of Orwell's writing, partly as a result of its often fugitive and journalistic nature, partly as a result of the violent and dramatic political upheavals through which he lived. But it will not do to rest in that contradictoriness as Williams finally does – to see him as a 'case' who can finally be placed by the historical significance of his contradictions. That is true abstractly; but, as I have argued throughout this book, an epistemology implies a rhetoric, and an abstract truth – abstracted from any possible social ground – is a dead truth. There is no escaping the struggle over Orwell, and amid all the contradictions, aggressive denunciations and simple prejudices there are still many positions worth saving and promoting. 'All writing nowadays is propaganda.' Agreed. But not all propaganda, by definition, is on the same side.

From Simon Dentith, *A Rhetoric of the Real* (Hemel Hempstead, 1990), pp. 148–73.

NOTES

[Like Lynette Hunter, Simon Dentith explores the association between Orwell's plain-speaking politics and his practice of rhetoric. Dentith reads Orwell in relation to a range of difficult and somewhat critically elusive issues; questions of what is 'good writing' or 'commitment', 'political purpose' or 'writing as propaganda'. He argues that Orwell's work is a sophisticated formulation of a rhetorical and epistemological writing practice that he outlines with particular reference to *Homage to Catalonia* and through a comparison between Orwell and Claud Cockburn ('Frank Pitcairn'), writer for *the Daily Worker*. Eds]

1. Sonia Orwell and Ian Angus (eds), *The Collected Essays, Journalism and Letters of George Orwell* (Harmondsworth, 1970), III, p. 41; III, p. 262; and IV, p. 346. Hereafter this collection will be referred to as *CEJL*.

2. *CEJL*, I, p. 414.

3. *CEJL*, IV, p. 56.

4. *CEJL*, II, p. 89.

5. Raymond Williams, *George Orwell* (London, 1984), pp. 29–40.

6. *CEJL*, I, p. 150.

7. *CEJL*, III, p. 439.

8. *CEJL*, II, p. 335.

9. *CEJL*, IV, pp. 334–5.

10. Bernard Crick, *George Orwell: A Life* (London, 1987), p. 362.

11. *CEJL*, IV, p. 257.

12. *CEJL*, I, p. 290.

13. *CEJL*, I, p. 379 and *CEJL*, II, p. 57.

14. *CEJL*, III, p. 356.

15. *CEJL*, II, p. 195.

16. *CEJL*, II, p. 276.

17. *CEJL*, IV, p. 92.

18. *CEJL*, IV, p. 87.

19. *CEJL*, I, p. 261.

20. *CEJL*, IV, p. 87.

21. *CEJL*, IV, p. 88.

22. *CEJL*, II, p. 291.

23. *CEJL*, II, p. 345.

24. *CEJL*, IV, p. 168.

25. *CEJL*, III, p. 378.

26. *CEJL*, III, p. 244.

27. *CEJL*, III, p. 46.

28. *CEJL*, III, p. 168.

29. W. J. West (ed.), *Orwell: The War Broadcasts* (London, 1985), p. 13.

30. *CEJL*, II, p. 281.

31. *CEJL*, II, p. 465.

32. For the importance of *gender* in Orwell's writing, see Daphne Patai, *The Orwell Mystique: A Study in Male Ideology* (Amherst, MA, 1984).

33. George Orwell, *Homage to Catalonia* (London, 1982), p. 15. This edition retains the text published in Orwell's lifetime but does not

follow his instructions, sent to Secker & Warburg a few months before his death, to remove Chapters V and XI from the narrative. These changes, and other corrections (especially over the correct names for the various Guards with whom Orwell was engaged in Barcelona) are followed in the *Complete Works* (London, 1986) and the 1989 Penguin edition. The deleted chapters are precisely those described to Spender as 'Trotskyist propaganda'. The ideological divisions over writing and 'propaganda' which I describe in this chapter have now therefore reproduced themselves in the most directly material, textual form. All page numbers hereafter follow the quotation in brackets in the body of the text.

34. *CEJL*, IV, p. 227.

35. *CEJL*, I, p. 345.

36. Lionel Trilling, 'George Orwell and the Politics of Truth', in Harold Bloom (ed.), *George Orwell* (New York, 1987), pp. 33–4. The essay was first published in 1952.

37. Robert Stradling, 'Orwell and the Spanish Civil War: a Historical Critique', in Christopher Norris (ed.), *Inside the Myth* (London, 1984), p. 110.

38. Orwell, 'Looking Back on the Spanish Civil War' published with *Homage to Catalonia*, p. 227.

39. James Pettifer (ed.), *Cockburn in Spain: Despatches from the Spanish Civil War* (London, 1986), p. 106 and p. 77.

40. Ibid., p. 69.

41. Ibid., pp. 131–2.

42. *CEJL*, I, p. 331.

43. See Crick, *George Orwell: A Life*, p. 363.

44. Quoted in Valentine Cunningham, *British Writers of the Thirties* (Oxford, 1988), p. 318.

45. Quoted in Malcolm Evans, 'Text, Theory, Criticism: twenty things you never knew about George Orwell', in Norris (ed.), *Inside the Myth*, p. 16.

46. Quoted in Christopher Hitchens, 'Comrade Orwell' in *Prepared for the Worst: Selected Essays and Minority Reports* (London, 1989), p. 84.

47. Ibid., p. 90.

48. See John Rodden, *The Politics of Literary Reputation: The Making and Claiming of 'St George' Orwell* (Oxford, 1989).

12

The Anti-Imperialism of George Orwell

STEPHEN INGLE

The focus of this chapter is on George Orwell's attempt to define the nature of a perennial political concern – the proper relationship between the rulers and the ruled – by metaphor, by telling stories. I propose to analyse some of the stories he tells, in order to decipher what I take to be his central themes, and to indicate what Orwell, through imaginative literature, has added to our understanding of the ruler-ruled relationship. But first I should put some cards on the table. Whilst each reading of a work of imaginative literature, bound as it has to be in what Eagleton calls a 'socially structured way of perceiving the world',[1] constitutes what might be termed a deconstruction, texts can nevertheless be said to impose certain restraints on the reader; we are not free agents in this matter. I do not subscribe to the view that 'there are no poets only poems' (which can be interpreted as the reader pleases). This view implies trampling on 'the claim of literary texts in general – to be taken as a social act';[2] that is to say, a communication referring to the world as we know it, with a structure and meaning designed by human intelligence and accessible to human intelligence. I would argue that: 'In every sentence of a novel or poem, if we know how to read it, we feel the speaking voice of the writer',[3] what George Steiner referred to as the writer's real presence. In short, the writer's personality and experience will shape our understanding of a novel. We are not free to read, or deconstruct Orwell or anybody else as we please. Whilst there may be no absolutely right way to read him, there are very clearly wrong ways. We know enough about Orwell's experiences in Burma and about his own attitudes towards those experiences to have a very clear idea of what he felt about his function as an imperial policeman, and why he wrote so dismissively about the imperial mission. There can be little doubt that in his writings on Burma Orwell sought to use these experiences as a kind of metaphor for the whole imperial experience and later to construct from the same metaphor a critical model of relations in capitalist society which reflected the same 'imperial' nexus quite unambiguously.

I wish to pursue two objectives in this chapter. First, to tease out the constituent themes of Orwell's imperialist model from its origins in Burma to its development in the capitalist West and to see whether their interrelationship sheds any light on liberal views of the proper relationship between leaders and led, a relationship which exercises political thinkers as much today[4] as ever it did. Second, and much more briefly, I wish to make some comments upon what it is that Orwell contributes to this debate as an imaginative writer which a political 'scientist', philosopher or historian, for example, would not. First, and more substantively, the model.

Orwell's interest in the British Empire was in the blood. He was, after all, born in Bengal, the son of an administrator in the Indian Civil Service. R. W. Blair had devoted his life to an undistinguished and rather obscure branch of the service, the opium department. It was the task of this department to oversee the production, collection and distribution of Indian opium to China. What Orwell thought of his father's calling is not recorded, but a certain ambivalence might be assumed. With the benefit of historical perspective Michael Shelden refers to the opium trade as 'one of the worst evils of the British Colonial system'[5] and as he grew up in the privileged and sheltered atmosphere of Eton, even Orwell must surely have had some doubts concerning the nature of the specific paternal contribution to the great imperial enterprise. Yet his ambition when leaving Eton was to join the Service. A close friend at Eton spoke of a long-cherished notion of returning to the East. 'He used to talk about the East a great deal, and I always had the impression he was longing to go back there. I mean it was a sort of romantic idea ...'[6] No doubt the expectations of both his parents, who regarded a career in the Imperial Civil Service as highly prestigious, would have helped to reinforce the romantic notions of the young

Orwell and, following his success in the entry examinations for the Imperial Police, Orwell duly left for Burma in 1922, still only 19 years old.

To put it mildly, Burma and the Police did not live up to his expectations. Within a year, despite a congenial posting (by Imperial Police standards) he appears to have become entirely disenchanted with Burma and with his role as a policeman. He felt himself isolated from fellow expatriates (despite the proximity of his maternal grandmother), from the local Burmese (though he spoke their language) and above all from the values of imperialism. Etonian friend Christopher Hollis met Orwell in Burma whilst on his way to Australia and noted later that Orwell seemed to be a man divided between the conventional Imperial policeman and the radical critic of imperialism. Little doubt, all in all, that well before the end of his first term of duty Orwell heartily disliked Burma and his role in its governance. When he returned home at the end of his first term 'one sniff of English air' persuaded him to resign. He never went back.

Burmese Days,[7] Orwell's first published novel, tells the story of a small outpost in upper Burma, Kyauktada, of a middle-aged timber merchant John Flory, and of his relations with the expatriate community. Flory is an archetypal Orwellian hero, an outsider whose status as such is indicated by a disfiguring birthmark on one side of his face – a physical manifestation of his alienation from society, as one critic called it. His friendship with an Indian doctor in the community earns him not only the contempt of the ex-pats at the local pub but also enmeshes him, unknowingly, in the machinations of a ruthlessly ambitious Burmese magistrate, U Po Kyin. The club at Kyauktada has been advised to give membership to an Asian, as part of government policy, and U Po Kyin has set his sights on being that member. Veraswami, the doctor befriended by Flory, is his only competitor and the magistrate sets about discrediting Veraswami, and in the end Flory, in order to achieve his objective. As a sub-plot, Flory, too, has an objective: to marry Elizabeth, the niece of the Lackersteens, an attractive but small-minded young woman who takes Flory seriously only after the departure from Kyauktada of an arrogantly patrician military policeman who possesses all the social graces and martial virtues that Flory so palpably lacks. Flory's marital prospects are suddenly enhanced by his having proved instrumental in putting down a minor revolt which actually threatened the club and its members. His equally sudden humiliation and disgrace is engineered by U Po Kyin. Elizabeth spurns him and Flory takes his own life. Without the support of his white friend, Veraswami is undermined by the magistrate and U Po Kyin achieves his objective of membership of the club and indeed all his ambitions. This is a story without heroes, a story of mendacity, treachery and hypocrisy, of racial and social repression and hatred.

The story provides the author with the opportunity to expose the imperial elite to ruthless analysis. Amongst the ex-pats is Ellis, an intelligent and able timber executive who felt for all Asians 'a bitter, restless loathing as of something evil and unclean ... any hint of friendly feeling towards an Oriental seemed to him a horrible perversity'.[8] Ellis's feelings were roused to a fury by the government's policy of encouraging the admittance of non-Europeans to clubs. Orwell makes it clear that Ellis's attitude may be paranoid but it is not without some imperialist rationale: 'Here we are, supposed to be governing a set of damned black swine who've been slaves since the beginning of history, and instead of ruling them in the only way they understand, we go and treat them as equals.'[9]

Only the Lackersteens amongst the expats are as fully drawn as Ellis. Mrs Lackersteen's views on race relations in Burma signal that Orwell was already making connections between overseas and domestic 'imperialism': '"Really I think the laziness of these servants is getting too shocking", she complained. "We seem to have no authority over the natives nowadays, with all those dreadful reforms and the insolence they learn from the newspapers. In some ways they are getting almost as bad as the lower classes at home."'[10] As for Lackersteen himself, he is shown to be a drunkard and a lecher, part of an empire described by Flory as cemented together by booze (not his aptest metaphor).

Flory declares his own position to be not so much anti-empire as anti-humbug. He, too, wants to make money but not to the extent of participating in the 'slimy white man's burden humbug'. Let's not pretend, he argues, that the white man is in Burma to uplift the Burmese; he is there to rob them. Living the imperial pretence 'corrupts us ... There's an everlasting sense of being a sneak and a liar that torments us and drives us to justify ourselves night and day'.[11] The whole business of empire, Flory concludes, may be summed up as follows: 'The official holds the Burman down while the businessman goes through his pockets'.[12] This, says Flory, is the Pox Britannica.

Flory deludes himself for at base the humbug he attacks is the lubricant of the imperial machine, allowing both enthusiastic and reluctant imperialists to convince themselves that they are involved in a mighty enterprise for the good of all. As Arthur Koestler pointed out and Orwell himself acknowledged, that humbug constituted the difference between the British Empire in the East and the Japanese. Veraswami too argues that in building up the infrastructure of the subject nations in terms of transport and communications, irrigation, health, education and the legal system, the imperialists had contributed to the well-being of those they governed. But this did nothing to alter the nature of the underlying relationship of exploiter and exploited and indeed could be seen largely as a long-term investment which would facilitate exploitation over a far longer period.

At root Orwell is bitterly critical of a system in which louts fresh from school (where the school song would be something like Flory's own, 'The Scrum of Life'), could kick grey-haired servants, a system in which not only the natives have no liberty but also the masters. Free speech is impossible when every white man is a cog in the wheels of despotism. The only freedoms that existed for the masters were the freedoms to drink and to fornicate. All other actions and thoughts were dictated by the code of the *sahiblog*. Unlike Winston Smith, who finds a revolutionary soul-mate in Airstrip One, Flory discovers that 'in the end the secrecy of your revolt poisons you like a secret disease'.[13] Small wonder that Orwell, whose real-life experiences and perceptions shaped this remorselessly bitter novel, decided to get out of the imperial racket.

'Shooting an Elephant'[14] concerns an elephant on the rampage, an event reported to Orwell, the young Imperial policeman, by the local Burmese, so that this representative of law and order might go and kill the offending animal and minimise the damage it was causing – it had already killed one Indian coolie. Orwell followed the trail of destruction to discover the animal in a paddy field looking no more dangerous than a cow. He knew then that the elephant had not gone wild but had been subject to 'must', an intermittent sexual frenzy, which had since worn off. And he also knew that to shoot the elephant in such circumstances was not only unnecessary but quite immoral. But though master, he was not a free agent; he was part of the imperial system. He was hated by the local Burmese and in return he hated them. But his chief hatred he reserved for his job – 'I hated it more bitterly than I can perhaps make clear'. And here he was, confronting a docile animal, but willed forward by the crowd, willed to kill: he the man with the rifle, with the authority, they the unarmed and apparently power-less group of natives. But in reality, he goes on, 'I was only an absurd puppet pushed to and fro by the will of those yellow faces behind. I perceived in this moment that when the white man turns tyrant it is his own freedom that he destroys.'[15]

'A Hanging'[16] is a less overtly didactic essay which deals with the execution of a prisoner in Burma. We are not told of what the man is guilty, neither is any inference drawn overtly from the events which are described. What Orwell does, however, is to draw the reader up sharp by his reflections on the fact that the condemned man, walking to the gallows, actually steps aside to avoid a puddle.

> It is curious, but till that moment I had never realised what it means to destroy a healthy conscious man. When I saw the prisoner step aside to avoid the puddle I saw the mystery, the unsupportable wrongness, of cutting a life short when it is in full tide ... He and we were a party of men walking together, seeing, hearing, feeling, under-standing the same world; and in two minutes, with a sudden snap, one of us would be gone – one mind less, one world less.

For the reader, the important, untold part of the story is that 'justice' is the prerogative of the imperial power, the exploiter, and the recipient of justice is of the exploited nation. Justice is carried out, moreover, by a disillusioned young British officer and a group of Indians unenthusiastic for their task but anxious to win the favours of the British officer. The whole exercise, in short, was a sordid example of the exploiter/exploited relationship that charac-terised imperialism.

Supporters of imperialism had always acknowledged that the white man's burden was a heavy one, entailing in Kipling's words merely 'the blame of those ye better, the hate of those ye guard'. Yet the assumption had always been that, in the long run, the rela-tionship was of mutual benefit, bringing to the subject races all the advantages of modernisation and Christianity, and to the imperial race not merely clear economic advantages but also the opportu-nity of serving the great cause of civilisation. Orwell's view may be summarised as accepting the Marxist analysis of the economics of imperialism and as rejecting totally any notion of moral or cultural gains for either side: imperialism debased both sides utterly. Both sides were obliged to adopt policies and attitudes which they privately found distasteful. It is the very condition of the imperialist's role, says Orwell, that 'he shall spend his life in trying to impress the "natives", and so in every case he has got to do what the "natives" expect of him. He wears a mask and his face grows to fit it.'[17] So the nature of the imperialist relationship is an intensely alienating one; both sides are alienated from each other and from their roles (i.e., from themselves).

When Orwell returned to this country he may originally have believed that he was exchanging the tyranny of imperialism for liberty but he apparently did not believe this for long; perhaps he did not entirely believe it even at the beginning. Soon enough he was beginning to use imperialism as a metaphor not merely for the relationship between the classes in Britain but also for any relationship between those with and without power. Every such relationship was based implicitly or explicitly upon exploitation and he devoted the rest of his life to exploring the nature of that relationship, bringing to bear a sharpness of focus and an intimidating directness.

A good example of the use of the imperial metaphor is his account of his school days at St Cyprian's, with the ironic Blakean title 'Such, Such Were the Joys'.[18] Orwell portrays himself – Eric Blair – as the victim of an imperialist system. Although St Cyprian's was a fee-paying boarding school, Eric was on reduced fees (as a potential scholarship boy), a fact of enormous economic and political consequences. If the Head behaved with forbearance to the sons of the wealthy he was almost brutal with the poorer boys. The relationship was purely an economic one, the boys' abilities representing a long-term investment (though in the short term they could be underfed) and its governing principle was not love but fear. From the comfort and security of their families young boys were dropped into a world of power relations, dishonesty and hypocrisy, 'out of a goldfish bowl and into a tank full of pike'. The determining element of the imperialist model was that it was quite impossible, whatever their achievements, for the exploited ever fully to join the exploiters. 'If you climbed to the highest niche that was open to you, you could only be an underling, a hanger-on of the people who really counted.' That, indeed, had been the summit of U Po Kyin's ambition. The decisive factor, says Orwell, is class and the cornerstone of class is inherited wealth. Money, he continues, is synonymous with goodness, with moral virtue. The rich and the strong – the same thing really – always won, and since morality was their agent, they always *deserved* to win.

If the recreation of his school days represented one attempt to apply the imperialist model it was certainly not the chief one: that was to be the nature of class relations in Britain, and it was the one to which, following his return from Burma, Orwell devoted his life and sacrificed his health. It was his visit to the North of England, which bore fruit in the publication of the seminal *Road to Wigan Pier*,[19] that was to transform both his politics and his writing. Orwell understood (or so he thought) the values of the oppressed as he had never been able to do in Burma. By and large, he believed, the stable working class (i.e., those in full-time employment) lived in a 'warm, decent, deeply human atmosphere which is not easy to find elsewhere'.[20] This atmosphere was sustained by a deep sense of equality. Working-class life, he believed, was not dominated by social or financial considerations, was not uprooted by the social and geographical mobility which so often put middle-class family life at risk, rather it was integrated into a community where the values of togetherness – or equality – dominated. In a phrase, he believed he had discovered The Good Life.

This was a new development of the imperialist model. Orwell was now arguing, not merely that the relationship of exploiter and exploited was mutually destructive but that the oppressed actually possessed a moral superiority based primarily upon their espousal of equality. Was this very different to an orthodox definition of socialism? He thought so: the aim of many socialists, after all, to abolish poverty *from above*, actually entailed abolishing the working class. It was precisely because the working class realised that orthodox socialism would destroy its lifestyle and values, said Orwell, that ordinary working men showed such scant enthusiasm for it. In fact it was the values of ordinary workers which represented true socialism. Only they held firmly to the 'underlying ideals of socialism: justice and liberty'[21] and in doing so they rejected the 'socialism' of mechanisation and progress, of thesis, antithesis and synthesis, the 'socialism' of the planner, the sandal-wearing pacifist. The socialist movement, he concluded, should be not 'a league of dialectical materialists but a league of the oppressed against the oppressors'.[22] In the 'imperial' model, orthodox socialists, especially scientific socialists, might well be considered amongst the exploiters and not the exploited.

Orwell's experiences in the North of England were reinforced by those he gained when fighting in the Spanish Civil War. In *Homage to Catalonia*[23] he wrote of Barcelona, which he visited in December 1936, as the first town he had seen where the working class was 'in the saddle', a state of affairs worth fighting for because 'human beings were trying to behave like human beings and not as cogs in the capitalist machine'.[24] Those who define Orwell's socialism as quintessentially English overlook his unambiguous admiration for the Spanish working class whose defining characteristics are identified as decency and a 'real largeness of spirit which I have met with again and again in the most unpromising circumstances.'[25] When he declared that such a state of affairs was worth fighting for, that is exactly what he meant. For Orwell the Spanish Civil War was originally a war between working-class socialism (one might say Orwellian socialism) and fascism; that it manifestly became something other than this saddened him greatly. In many respects fascism (especially of the totalitarian variety) represented, for Orwell, the essential ideology of 'imperialism'; he had already identified working-class 'socialism' as its true opponent and Spain confirmed his earlier fears that the centralised, efficient state with which the communists wished to fight fascism, was another version of 'imperialism'.

Until about the middle of the Second World War Orwell appeared to believe that violent revolution was the obvious method by which the working class could end its exploitation; parliamentary methods, the 'rules of the game', were simply part of the mechanics of exploitation. Orwell wished for and expected a popular revolution which would overthrow the British imperial ruling class so that the Axis could be defeated. But the tumbrels of revolution steadfastly refused to rumble and when the government actually armed the potential revolutionaries (in the form of the Home Guard which Orwell himself joined), he must have realised that imminent revolution was beyond the bounds of credulity. Towards the end of the world war Orwell, reflecting on events in Spain and the USSR, came to the view that the betrayal of the working class would be an almost inevitable consequence of revolution. *Animal Farm*[26] was certainly written as a critique of the Soviet revolution and its consequences but it can also be read as a work which exposes the inevitable dominance, in the turmoil of revolution, of an intellectual class whose aim would be to capture and retain power. That power would not be used to further the causes of the revolution but to bolster the capacity of the intellectual class to exploit the workers. The model of revolutionary power, then, corresponds not to an egalitarian power model but to the imperialist one.

Much has been made of Orwell's patriotic writing during the war[27] by those who seek to emphasise his essential Englishness, and thus, by extension, his limitation as a thinker. Paradoxically in situating his final work, *Nineteen Eighty-Four*,[28] in the United Kingdom, Orwell gives the lie to any change of parochialism for he clearly intends it to be understood that any society, even the allegedly liberal and tolerant British, has a potential to develop into what he came to recognise as the most extreme model of imperialism/fascism, namely, totalitarianism. Moreover, Orwell identifies totalitarianism (and thus 'imperialism') not merely as a particularly pernicious ideology but as a personality trait. In *Nineteen Eighty-Four* power is measured by the capacity to inflict pain; this is the 'imperial' model finally stripped to its essentials, the strong triumphing over the weak, the exploiters over the exploited. A suitable logo for the 'imperial' relationship is to be found in an image taken from a book which Orwell quotes: that of the hero stamping on somebody's face and then grinding his heel round and round. The model recognises no value beyond the equation of might with right. As Gollo Mann summarised, Orwell's argument is that the 'totalitarian danger lies within ourselves and in all the political systems of our time'.[29] Yet Orwell goes further than this and associates this desire for power as he defined it *specifically* with socialist intellectuals in whom the 'imperialistic' concepts of the worship of success, totalitarianism and sadism interconnect. Intellectuals were 'imperialists', and socialist intellectuals such as Shaw and Wells were amongst the worst. No wonder Bellow's young 1960s radical in *Mr Sammler's Planet* describes Orwell as a 'sick counter-revolutionary fink'. Even as perceptive a critic as Raymond Williams was unable to forgive Orwell for attacking totalitarianism (imperialism) through the example of socialism.[30] Orwell's ruling elite in Oceania represents a perversion of Platonism for the sole reward for leadership was not virtue but power. This constitutes a theory of power as psychosis: those who seek power do so principally to inflict suffering on others in as direct a way as possible. George Kateb, amongst others, feels that Orwell's linking of power to sadism is unsound and diminishes the strength of his message.[31] Orwell is surely on firmer ground, however, when he links power to ideology and, like Popper, sees the latter as an instrument of power and not vice versa.

The alleged moral superiority of the poor is, in direct contrast, associated with their powerlessness. In an essay analysing the success of Charlie Chaplin, Orwell ascribed it to Chaplin's infallible ability to characterise 'the ineradicable belief in decency that exists in the hearts of ordinary people'.[32] He explored this decency in greater depth in another essay, 'The Art of Donald McGill'.[33] McGill's holiday postcards, like the antics of Chaplin, depict the world and the values of the oppressed, to whom those with incomes much above or below £5 per week were ridiculous. It was a world in which people actually wanted to be good – 'but not too good and not quite all the time'. It was a world which, though staunchly patriotic, guyed patriotism and mocked all pretensions pitilessly. Orwell declared that he could never hear solemn proclamations by Great Men without also hearing, in the background, 'a chorus of raspberries from all the millions of common men'. All over Britain '... there are men by scores of thousands whose attitude to life, if only they could express it ... would change the whole consciousness of our race'.[34]

To summarise the argument, I have suggested that Orwell's political perspective was shaped by his Burmese experiences which provided him with a framework of analysis of contemporary capitalist society. It must be borne in mind that he had gone to Burma with two conflicting sets of values concerning imperialism. The first was the product of his upbringing. It esteemed the traditional imperialist virtues as a modern adaptation of the classical concept of *virtu*. The second was the product of his intellectual nourishment at Eton and was iconoclastic, dismissive, Shavian. As we have seen, those who met him in Burma, such as old Etonian Christopher Hollis, described him as torn between these two visions of the imperial project. If he was intellectually able to will the *ends* of imperialism (or some of them), his experiences rendered him increasingly incapable of willing the *means*. Imperialism might or might not be justified as a concept; but it involved so much inhumanity as to be unjustifiable in reality. Like Arthur Koestler he was unimpressed by the 'necessity of breaking eggs to make an omelette' argument: he said that those who justify their actions in these terms never finish with an omelette.[35] Indeed, Orwell's position on this issue shows him to have been primarily concerned not so much with political thought as moral thought and to have focused on and made judgements about human conduct rather than political conflict. It was his intention to reduce political problems to their fundamentals and imperialism was reduced to the exploiter/exploited nexus. He was not concerned to unravel the ambiguities and complexities of imperialist political relationships so much as to lay bare what he took to be its essential moral constituents. The resulting 'imperialist' model needed to be simple; it had to expose actions as either morally right or wrong. His was a bipolar monochrome world: black and white but no greys. Grey was the casuist's colour. In *Homage to*

Catalonia Orwell had claimed that if ever he saw working men struggling with their 'natural enemies', the police, he knew instinctively which side he was on.[36] The analogy shows precisely the nature of his 'imperialist' model. One was either exploiter or exploited and as he said, in the 'imperialist' power model the exploited were always right and the exploiters always wrong.

Orwell's basic concern, then, was not so much with politics as with human nature. If his human was clearly the part-man and part-beast of traditional dualism, s/he was nevertheless transformed by the nature of the social relationship. Imperialist, and indeed all capitalist social relations, were founded on power and for Orwell it was immaterial whether those who held power believed themselves (erroneously of course) to be motivated by a desire to improve the lot of their fellows or by a naked, cynical desire for gratification; the effect was the same. To attempt to place self-denying ordinances on the powerful, as Confucius and Plato and many later had done, was simple illusion. Power itself had to be defused and 'imperialism' as the base of social relationships replaced by equality. He added to this analysis a transformative insight by which he recognised in the lives of the oppressed a set of values (referred to in shorthand as 'decency') which could form the basis of a democratic, egalitarian society. So much for Orwell's model.

The question is: 'Does the "imperialism" model contribute anything at all to the development of political theories of the ruler-ruled relationship?' There would be general agreement that at first sight the model seems demonstrably simplistic, as consequently, does Orwell's analysis of power relations. The motives which impelled so many to participate in the imperial enterprise could not realistically be written off as invariably exploitative; the intentions of socialist intellectuals and ideologues to improve the lot of the poor (their 'imperial' enterprise) could not plausibly be represented as simply an attempt to exercise power for its own sake. Contrary to the assumptions of the model, the oppressors are *not* always wrong. Nor does the evidence (even Orwell's evidence) lend much substance to the claim that the oppressed are always right. Moreover, do the oppressed actually possess the qualities Orwell perceives? Violence as well as decency has always played a large part in working-class life; so has gross gender inequality and so, for that matter, has paternal authoritarianism (consider, for example, *Sons and Lovers* by D. H. Lawrence, himself the son of a miner). Do the opposition in Burma today believe that their government is less 'imperialist' than were the British former masters? Have not some of the oppressed become oppressors? And if it *were* true that, all in all, the exploited possessed this quality of 'decency', hasn't Orwell himself portrayed this as a consequence of exploitation? Remove the exigencies through greater disposable income, better welfare provision, housing and so on, and decency will surely atrophy.

There is another, perhaps deeper line of criticism of Orwell's alternative power model. When he speaks of the value of working-class life he is in effect retreating from the public to the private realm. Nowhere does he write about power structures within working-class political movements such as the trade unions. Whereas even Machiavelli recognised the value to the polity of private virtue, he thought it had little place in statecraft.

Is it conceivable that as astute and careful an observer as Orwell was unaware of these criticisms? I believe not. I believe that he thought that working-class values, warts and all, offered the only bastion against 'imperialism'. What Orwell passionately cared about was the better treatment by men of their fellows. As Rorty has suggested, Orwell wrote against those who exercised cruelty even through the rhetoric of human equality.[37] The values of the non-ideological, non-imperialistic socialism that he fought for were, in fact, fundamentally the same as those of non-doctrinaire Christianity. That he selected, simplified and exaggerated in attributing these qualities to the working class in greater measure than any other is surely forgivable; after all, fundamentally he agreed with Huxley's Illidge, in *Point Counter Point*, who declares; 'If you live on less than £5 a week you've damned well got to be a Christian'.[38]

Are the values of the exploited of any political significance if they cannot be articulated? After all, O'Brien insists during his interrogation of Winston Smith that the proles would never revolt, not in a thousand years, not in a million. Winston retained a residual faith in the proles only because their values had survived. Their instinctive loyalty was not to any ideology nor to the state but to each other. There was a moral and political force in their gestures of love, compassion and understanding: in their code of decency. So long as decency survived, so did hope.

When Orwell argued for the penetration of power relations by that private value system which he called decency, he was arguing against Machiavelli's widely-held case for a separate moral category for politics. Machiavelli's injunction to the 'good man', in *The Prince*, is that to become a successful ruler he must learn how not to be good. As

Hampshire writes, 'a fastidiousness about the means employed, appropriate in personal relations, is a moral dereliction in a politician'.[39] Following the Vietnam War this injunction became contentiously relevant to the debate upon the American conduct of the war, the so-called 'dirty hands' debate. This phrase had been highlighted earlier by Jean-Paul Sartre's appropriately titled play *Les Mains sales*,[40] in which the communist leader declared that his hands were dirty right up to the elbow, having been plunged in filth and blood. 'Do you think you can govern innocently?', he asks metaphorically. The debate concerns the relationship between politics and morality, more specifically between public and private morality. Machiavelli's (and Sartre's) contention is that politics is a distinctive activity. Walzer[41] sees three justifications for this view: the politician acts on our behalf, speaks in our name, 'lies and intrigues for us'; the politician rules over us, directs our affairs in a comprehensive fashion; and finally, the politician uses or threatens violence both for us and perhaps against us – he may kill in our name. No-one succeeds in politics without getting his hands dirty and traditional Christian theology made allowances for this. St Augustine's melancholy soldier knew that war could be both just and horrific. Basil the Great, as Walzer reminds us, advised that all who killed even in a just war should abstain from communion for three years because their hands were unclean.[42] There is a general acceptance amongst 'dirty-hands' theorists that, as Machiavelli suggests, 'when the act accuses, the result excuses',[43] but their general project is somehow to constrain leaders morally; dirty their hands may be, but not free.

Few of these theorists actually believe that politics forms an entirely separate category of human activity. After all, we can get our hands dirty in private life, says Walzer, and we can keep our hands clear in warfare. (Orwell's famous account in *Homage to Catalonia* of his refusal at the front to shoot a fascist because he had his trousers down is an excellent example of Nagel's dictum: 'our conflict is with the soldier not with his existence as a human being'.[44]) Hampshire, too, agrees that there can be no 'distinct and clear dividing line' between the public and private realm. Would not the bosses of multinational companies, or indeed the leaders of any large organisation (say, a headteacher of a large secondary school) wish to claim much the same immunity? Some feminist writers have argued that even family life is dominated by structures of power which are public rather than private. So Orwell's argument for the penetration of public life by private values should not be dismissed out of hand. The thrust of his argument is that *no* political system could develop beyond 'imperialism' if it was not founded on a sense of right and wrong and that the most likely source of that moral dimension was to be found in the lives of ordinary people.

'Dirty-hands' issues, entwined as they are within important and complex categories of absolute and utilitarian moral reason, nevertheless confront Orwell's thought only tangentially. These theorists are concerned to understand the paradox of a leader who is directed in his private actions by a moral system which prevents him from injuring others but who, as a political leader, feels compelled sometimes to act immorally on behalf of those he represents. Like Koestler's Spartacus he who alone can understand, acts on behalf of those who cannot. For Orwell, though, as we have seen, those who attain political power do so for self-gratification. If that was not their original motive (but it probably was), it soon becomes their motive. Power is an end not a means and they are not tortured moral souls. Whilst Nagel at least is aware of the 'pleasure of power' and regards it as one of the most primitive of human feelings,[45] even he does not pursue this line of thought. For Orwell the central issue is one which the 'dirty-hands' theorists only touch on; the structure of power itself. The leaders whom these theorists discuss are modern versions of Machiavelli's prince. They may indeed allude to the representative character of a modern democracy but the profundity of the difference such structures make upon the exercise of power is by no means made explicit. What Orwell argues for, of course, is the substitution of traditional ('imperialist') structures of power by not merely representative but truly egalitarian ones, with such consequences as we shall now go on to explore.

Orwell was by no means the first to extol the virtues of the oppressed; Dickens and Tolstoy, among others, could have been said to have done so far more comprehensively. More recently, Vaclav Havel, in an influential essay written in 1978 entitled *The Power of the Powerless*,[46] spoke of a force which stood against Czechoslovakia's totalitarian despotism, openness to truth. The power of truth, he argued, is only a potential power and does not participate directly in any struggle for power, making its presence felt in the arena of being itself. Yet if it can oblige a small, obscure boy to call out that the emperor has no clothes then an entire political edifice may crash to the ground as a consequence: so private values may indeed penetrate power relations. Like Orwell,[47] Havel believes in the overriding political importance of a popular moral system, for he believes that a more just political and economical system can only come from a widely held moral code (and not vice versa *à la* Marx). Havel is clearly working from the same tradition as Orwell but he adds a prescriptive dimension to that tradition. 'There can and must be structures that are open, dynamic and small ... Any accumulation of power whatsoever ... should be profoundly alien ... They would be structures not in the sense of organisations or institutions, but like a community.'[48] This is how Havel perceives that 'decency' might transform 'imperialism'.

It is interesting to note that even modern capitalism has found a version of the Orwellian and Havelian model attractive. John Naisbitt, for example, speaks of the 'radical downsizing' of some major companies. 'Big companies ... are deconstructing themselves and creating new structures, many as networks of autonomous units. Deconstruction is now in fashion, because it is the best way to search for survival.'[49] As one manager of GE explained: 'What we are trying to do is to get that small company soul ... inside our big company body'.[50] A power structure resembling a community; an egalitarian not an imperial power model. What Orwell might have made of this partial conversion of the enemy (for all the wrong reasons?) is an interesting topic for speculation.

Orwell recognised that politics frequently involves choosing the lesser of two evils but believed that the more ordinary people were involved in such decisions the less often morally unacceptable decisions would be taken. To accept the challenge of such involvement would require a genuine commitment to making the policy processes open to ordinary people. For a start, it would mean a political discourse less dominated by jargon. As long as politics remains a specialised activity conducted centrally by intellectuals claiming a special expertise, ordinary people will be effectively disempowered. So long as there exists, within structures of power, a ready potential for one group to dominate and exploit another, it will do so, says Orwell. Conversely, the more power is diffused, the more power structures are disaggregated, the more difficult 'imperialism' becomes. If Orwell is right, it is only by dispersing and demystifying power that society can rid itself of the menace of Big Brother and the threat of 'imperialism', be it fascist, socialist or managerial, for it is only by dispersing and demystifying power that politics may be made accessible to the oppressed. This is what follows from Orwell's 'imperialism' model. Its particular intellectual force lies precisely in depicting the relationship between ruler and ruled in so uncompromising a way and with such a clear message.

The quality of Orwell's contribution to political thought is shaped very largely by its quality as literature, and it is to this theme that I shall now turn. Eagleton and others might wish to argue the absurdity of such a proposition. 'Literature,' says Eagleton, 'in the sense of a set of works of assured and unalterable value, distinguished by certain shared inherent properties, does not exist.'[51] If this were true then perhaps we might need to invent literature, rather like Voltaire's God. Kenneth Quinn clearly thinks it is not true. He argues that literary texts can be distinguished from other texts rather as cars can be distinguished from trucks. They occupy different places in our lives and we use them in different ways. 'We expect poets or novelists to be particular about the words they use. The more particular they are the better the novel or poem is likely to be. But there's more to it than that. A bad novel is still a novel of sorts ... all such texts have something in common: *they work in a particular way...*'[52]

In earlier times literature clearly encompassed every serious discipline, its concern being the whole of knowledge. By the nineteenth century, however, knowledge had fractured and intellectual activity quickly became differentiated. There emerged kinds of writing that quite clearly were consciously instrumental and consciously non-literary. But there was also writing that intended to influence 'by characteristically non-objective techniques, our perception of the world and our moral understanding'.[53] Creative or imaginative writing – literature – is first and foremost an artistic enterprise. It has a structure, a field of significance and it adopts a position to which one can react. In short, 'literature is experience reorganised as a structure of words that can be perceived both as artistic creations and as a representation of life that is essentially true'.[54] Although it may very well be argued that literary boundaries are not as easily demarcated – or for that matter, trucks and cars as easily distinguishable as Quinn suggests (indeed truck-like cars these days enjoy a certain chic), he is surely right to want to distinguish between the aims of creative or imaginative writing and those of other forms of writing. Orwell's imaginative writing – his fiction – for example, is not readily separable from his journalism and neither did he wish it to be. *Down and Out, Clergyman's Daughter*, and *Homage* straddle both, and accounts of Orwell's northern experiences in *Wigan Pier* differ from his diary account. It would be unhelpful, then, to try to draw a distinction between his fiction and journalism: Orwell himself drew no such distinction. This difficulty does not detract from Quinn's central point: recognising a text as literature means recognising that reading it offers the prospect of a literary experience. We read it *differently* to, say, an ESRC document on social science research. Quinn goes on to argue that a literary text has no immediate, easily understood purpose, yet it *does* possess a quality that other kinds of text do not. He encapsulates that quality by suggesting that literature is not primarily concerned with the transmission of information but the sharing of experience.

It is precisely in these senses that Orwell's analysis of imperialism should be viewed. The author attempts to share his experiences of 'imperialism' with us. He has, quite literally, reorganised these experiences so as to represent to us a view of life that many will perceive to be essentially 'true'. This idea of sharing an experience is of fundamental importance to Orwell's project; it is probably the only method open to him to expose us to 'the truth' of imperialism. Were he to have employed the more orthodox philosophical, economic or ideological form of analysis which his critics have called for, then, so far as he was concerned, he would have been sucked into an 'imperialistic' relationship; he would himself have become an 'intellectual' and so an exploiter. Orwell usually used the word intellectual synonymously with ideologue. His intellectual was a spokesman for a system of thought the exclusive nature of which could be penetrated only by other intellectuals; only they would have the key. As an imaginative writer sharing his experiences rather than an intellectual guarding the integrity of a system of thought, Orwell was committed not so much to giving anyone who wanted a duplicate key as to leaving the door open. *That* is the nature of imaginative literature and it represents a medium of communication ideally suited to the moralist who wishes us to realise that political issues are moral issues and that to assign a special moral category to politics is the first decisive step in engendering 'imperialism'.

Orwell attempted to provide us with a metaphor depicting how human relationships should *not* be structured. What Rorty writes à propos of *Animal Farm*, suitably modified, provides a fitting testimony to Orwell's metaphorical analysis of imperialism: Orwell, he writes, 'attacks the incredibly complex and sophisticated character of leftist political discussion ... by retelling the political history of this century entirely in terms suitable for children'.[55] Sartre, who argued that Picasso's great anti-fascist, anti-war painting *Guernica* won not a single convert to the Republican cause, would no doubt think Orwell's project was doomed to failure, yet such evidence as exists[56] suggests that if anything the metaphor is as powerful a means as any of giving, in Calvi's words, 'a voice to whoever is without a voice'.[57]

From *Literature and the Political Imagination*, ed. John Horton and Andrea T. Baumeister (London, 1996), pp. 218–37.

NOTES

[Stephen Ingle focuses on the ways in which Orwell's works explicate the power relationship between those who rule and those who are ruled. Ingle exemplifies this relationship via an imperialist model with *Burmese Days* and shorter works like 'Shooting an Elephant' and 'A Hanging', in which Orwell's own dialectical position as imperial policeman and critic of empire informs his enquiry into justice and exploitation. Ingle turns to class and economics as the underlying factors in any apprehension of the nature of power relations in Britain or the fight against fascism in the Spanish Civil War and begins to tease out the moral and political war against totalitarianism that runs through Orwell's writing. Finally, Ingle considers how Orwell's political thought contributes to an ongoing analysis of colonial and class relations and in this the essay is most elucidatory when read alongside Campbell's and Rorty's essays (nos 4 and 8) in this volume. Eds]

1. Terry Eagleton, 'The Rise of English', in Dennis Walder (ed.), *Literature in the Modern World* (Oxford, 1990), p. 25.

2. Kenneth Quinn, *How Literature Works* (London, 1992), p. 18.

3. Ibid., p. 20.

4. See, for example, the debate generated in the pages of *Political Studies*, 41 (1993) and 42 (1994) by David Beetham's *The Legitimation of Power*.

5. Michael Sheldon, *Orwell: The Authorised Biography* (London, 1991), pp. 13, 15.

6. Stephen Wadhams, *Remembering Orwell* (Harmondsworth, 1984), p. 21.

7. George Orwell, *Burmese Days* (Harmondsworth, 1969).

8. Ibid., p. 24.

9. Ibid.

10. Ibid., p. 28.

11. Ibid., p. 29.

12. Ibid., p. 37.

13. Ibid., p. 66.

14. Sonia Orwell and Ian Angus (eds), *The Collected Essays, Journalism, and Letters of George Orwell* (London, 1968), I, pp. 235–42. Hereafter referred to as *CEJL*.

15. *CEJL*, I, p. 239.

16. *CEJL*, I, p. 46.

17. *CEJL*, I, p. 239.

18. *CEJL*, IV, pp. 330–69.

19. George Orwell, *The Road to Wigan Pier* (Harmondsworth, 1963).

20. Ibid., p. 104.

21. Ibid., p. 189.

22. Ibid., p. 195.

23. George Orwell, *Homage to Catalonia* (Harmondsworth, 1962).

24. Ibid., pp. 8–9.

25. Ibid., p. 15.

26. George Orwell, *Animal Farm* (Harmondsworth, 1958).

27. Such as 'The Lion and the Unicorn', *CEJL*, II, pp. 56–109 and 'England Your England', in *Inside the Whale and Other Essays* (Harmondsworth, 1960), pp. 63–90.

28. George Orwell, *Nineteen Eighty-Four* (Harmondsworth, 1960).

29. Gollo Mann, *Frankfurter Rundschau*, 5 November 1449, Jeffrey Meyers (ed.), *George Orwell: The Critical Heritage* (London, 1975), pp. 277–81.

30. Raymond Williams, *Orwell* (London, 1971).

31. George Kateb, 'The Road to *Nineteen Eighty-Four*', *Political Science Quarterly*, 4 (1966), 565–81.

32. See, *CEJL*, III, pp. 1–37.

33. *CEJL*, II, pp. 155–64.

34. *CEJL*, I, pp. 148–50.

35. *CEJL*, III, pp. 234–44.

36. *Homage to Catalonia*, p. 119.

37. Richard Rorty, *Contingency, Irony and Solidarity* (Cambridge, 1989).

38. Aldous Huxley, *Point Counter Point* (Harmondsworth, 1971), p. 59.

39. Stuart Hampshire, *Public and Private Morality* (London, 1978), p. 50.

40. J. P. Sartre, *Les Mains sales* (Paris, 1948).

41. Michael Walzer, 'Political Action: The Problem of Dirty Hands', in Marshal Cohen et al. (eds), *War and Moral Responsibility* (Princeton, NJ, 1974), pp. 64–6.

42. Ibid., p. 69, note 9.

43. Machiavelli, *Discourses*, Bk 1, Chapter IX, p. 139.

44. Thomas Nagel, 'War and Massacre', in Marshall Cohen et al. (eds), *War and Moral Responsibility*, p. 21.

45. Thomas Nagel, 'Ruthlessness in Public Life', in Stuart Hampshire, *Public and Private Morality*, p. 77.

46. Vaclav Havel, 'The Power of the Powerless', in J. Vladislav, *Vaclav Havel or Living from Truth* (London, 1987), pp. 36–122.

47. What distinguishes Havel from Orwell is that the former allows a role in the process of penetration to intellectuals: Havel's intellectuals did not constitute a pampered and feted cosmopolitan group but dissidents whose stand threatened their liberty and even their lives.

48. Vaclav Havel, 'The Power of the Powerless', p. 118.

49. John Naisbitt, *Global Paradox* (London, 1994), p. 13.

50. Ibid., p. 14.

51. Terry Eagleton, 'The Rise of English', in Quinn, *How Literature Works*, p. 22.

52. Quinn, *How Literature Works*, p. 9.

53. Ibid., p. 43.

54. Ibid., p. 55.

55. Rorty, *Contingency, Irony and Solidarity*, p. 174.

56. See, for example, Stephen Ingle, 'Socialism and Literature: The Contribution of Imaginative Writers to the Development of the British Labour Party', *Political Studies*, 2 (June 1975), 158–67.

57. Italo Calvi, *The Uses of Literature* (New York, 1986), p. 101.

Further Reading

BOOKS AND ESSAYS BY GEORGE ORWELL

Down and Out in Paris and London (London: Victor Gollancz, 1933).
Burmese Days (London: Victor Gollancz, 1935).
A Clergyman's Daughter (London: Victor Gollancz, 1935).
Keep the Aspidistra Flying (London: Victor Gollancz, 1936).
The Road to Wigan Pier (London: Victor Gollancz, 1937).
Homage to Catalonia (London: Secker & Warburg, 1938).
Coming Up For Air (London: Victor Gollancz, 1939).
Animal Farm (London: Secker & Warburg, 1945).
Nineteen Eighty-Four (London: Secker & Warburg, 1949).
The Collected Essays, Journalism and Letters of George Orwell, Vol I–IV, ed. S. Orwell and I. Angus (London: Secker & Warburg, 1968).

BOOKS ON GEORGE ORWELL

Harold Bloom (ed.), *George Orwell* (New York: Chelsea, 1986).
Paul Chilton (ed.), *Nineteen Eighty-Four in 1984: Autonomy, Control and Communication* (London: Comedia, 1983).
Audrey Coppard and Bernard Crick (eds), *Orwell Remembered* (London: Ariel Books/BBC, 1984).
Bernard Crick, *George Orwell: A Life* (Harmondsworth: Penguin, 1980).
Averil Gardner, *George Orwell* (Boston: Twayne, 1987).
Erika Gottlieb, *The Orwell Conundrum: A Cry of Despair or Faith in the Spirit of Man* (Ottawa: Carleton University Press, 1992).
S. J. Greenblatt, *Three Modern Satirists: Waugh, Orwell and Huxley* (New Haven, CT, and London: Yale University Press, 1976).
C. Hollis, *A Study of George Orwell: The Man and his Works* (London: Hollis & Carter, 1956).
Irving Howe (ed.), *1984 Revisited: Totalitarianism in Our Century* (New York: Harper & Row, 1983).
Lynette Hunter, *George Orwell: The Search for a Voice* (Milton Keynes: Open University Press, 1984).

J. Ejner Jenson (ed.), *The Future of Nineteen Eighty-Four* (Ann Arbour: University of Michigan, 1984).

Jasbir Jain, *George Orwell: Witness of an Age* (Jaipur: Printwell, 1986).

William Lutz (ed.), *Beyond Nineteen Eighty-Four: Doublespeak in a Post-Orwellian Age* (Urbana, IL: National Council of Teachers of English, 1989).

Robert Mulvihill (ed.), *Reflections on America, 1984: An Orwell Symposium* (Athens: University of Georgia Press, 1986).

Christopher Norris (ed.), *Inside the Myth, Orwell: Views from the Left* (London: Lawrence & Wishart, 1984).

Bernard Oldsey and Joseph Browne (eds), *Critical Essays on George Orwell* (Boston: Prentice-Hall, 1986).

Daphne Patai, *The Orwell Mystique: A Study in Male Ideology* (Amherst: University of Massachusetts Press, 1984).

Alok Rai, *Orwell and the Politics of Despair: A Critical Study of the Works of George Orwell* (Cambridge: Cambridge University Press, 1988).

J. M. Richardson (ed.), *Orwell x 8: A Symposium* (Winnipeg: Frye, 1986).

John Rodden, *The Politics of Literary Reputations: The Making and Claiming of 'St George' Orwell* (New York: Oxford University Press, 1989).

Alan Sandison, *The Last Man in Europe: An Essay on George Orwell* (London: Macmillan, 1974).

Robert L. Savage, James Combs and Dan Nimmo (eds), *The Orwellian Moment: Hindsight and Foresight in the Post-1984 World* (Fayetteville: University of Arkansas Press, 1989).

Michael Skovmand (ed.), *George Orwell and 1984* (Aarhus: University of Aarhus, 1984).

Edgar George Slusser, Colin Greenland and Eric S. Rabkin (eds), *Storm Warnings: Science Fiction Confronts the Future* (Carbondale: Southern Illinois University Press, 1987).

Richard I. Smyer, *Animal Farm: Pastoralism and Politics* (Boston: Twayne, 1988).

Peter Stansky (ed.), *On Nineteen Eighty-Four* (New York: Freeman, 1983).

Peter Stansky and William Abrahams, *Orwell: The Transformation* (London: Constable, 1979).

Benoit Suykerbuyk (ed.), *Essays from Oceania and Eurasia: George Orwell and 1984* (Antwerp: University Instelling Antwerpen, 1984).

R. J. Vorhees, *The Paradox of George Orwell* (Lafayette: Purdue University Press, 1961).

T. Courteny Wemyss (ed.), *George Orwell* (Westport, CT: Greenwood, 1987).

Raymond Williams, *Orwell* (London: Fontana/Collins, 1971).

Raymond Williams (ed.), *George Orwell: A Collection of Critical Essays* (Englewood Cliffs, NJ: Prentice-Hall, 1974).

George Woodcock, *The Crystal Spirit: A Study of George Orwell* (Harmondsworth: Penguin, 1970).

A. Zwerdling, *Orwell and the Left* (New Haven, CT, and London: Yale University Press, 1974).

ARTICLES AND ESSAYS ON GEORGE ORWELL

Samir Elbarbary, 'Language as Theme in *Animal Farm*', *International Fiction Review*, 19:1 (1992), 31–8.

J. B. Ellis, '*Nineteen Eighty-Four* and *1984*', in *Cinema and Fiction: New Modes of Adapting, 1950–90*, ed. John Orr and Colin Nicholson (Edinburgh: Edinburgh University Press, 1992), pp. 66–74.

Carl Freedman, 'Antinomies of *Nineteen Eighty-Four*', *Modern Fiction Studies*, 30:4 (1984), 601–20.

Frank Gloversmith, 'Changing Things: Orwell and Auden', in *Class, Culture and Social Change* (Sussex: Harvester, 1980), pp. 101–39.

Peter Goodall, '"Was the So-Called Melon Actually a Pumpkin?" Orwell and the Problem of Realism', *AUMLA*, 75 (1991), 1–20.

Ian Haywood, 'Facecrime: George Orwell and the Physiognomy of Politics', *Textual Practice*, 2:3 (1988), 345–66.

Shamsul Islam, 'George Orwell and the Raj', *World Literature Written in English*, 21:2 (1982), 341–7.

David Lowenthal, 'Orwell: Ethics and Politics in the Pre-Nineteen Eighty-Four Writings', in *The Artist and Political Vision*, ed. B. R. Barber (New Brunswick: Transaction, 1982), pp. 335–61.

Deanna Madden, 'Women in Dystopia: Misogyny in *Brave New World, 1984*, and *A Clockwork Orange*', in *Misogyny in Literature: An Essay Collection*, ed. Anne Katherine Ackley (New York: Garland, 1992), pp. 289–313.

Peter Marks, 'The Ideological Eye-Witness: An Examination of the Eye-Witness in Two Works by George Orwell', *Subjectivity and Literature from the Romantics to the Present Day*, ed. Philip Shaw and Peter Stockwell (London: Pinter, 1991), 85–92.

R. K. Meiners, 'Dialectics at a Standstill: Orwell, Benjamin, and the Difficulties of Poetry', *Boundary 2*, 20:2 (1993), 116–39.

John Newsinger, '*Nineteen Eighty-Four* Since the Collapse of Communism', *Foundation*, 56 (1992), 75–84.

Ralph S. Pomeroy, '"To Push the World": Orwell and the Rhetoric of Pamphleteering', *Rhetoric Society Quarterly*, 17:4 (1987), 365–412.

Patrick Reilly, '*Nineteen Eighty-Four* and the Failure of Humanism', *Critical Quarterly*, 24:3 (1982), 19–30.

Andre Reszler, 'Man as Nostalgia: The Image of the Last Man in Twentieth-Century Postutopian Fiction', in *Visions of Apocalypse: End of Rebirth?* ed. Saul Friedlander, Gerald Holton, Leo Marx and Eugene Skolnikoff (New York: Holmes, 1985), pp. 196–215.

John Rodden, 'Decency and Democracy: George Orwell, "the Aspiring Plebian"', *Prose Studies*, 12:2 (1989), 174–92.

Jonathan Rose, 'The Invisible Sources of *Nineteen Eighty-Four*', *Journal of Popular Culture*, 26:1 (1992), 93–107.

Howard Wolf, 'George Orwell and the Problematics of Non-Fiction', *Critical Quarterly*, 27:2 (1985), 23–30.

Notes on Contributors

Beatrix Campbell is the author of a number of books, including *Wigan Pier Revisited* (London, 1984); *The Iron Ladies: Why do Women Vote Tory?* (London, 1987); *Unofficial Secrets* (London, 1988) and *Goliath: Britain's Dangerous Places* (London, 1993).

Simon Dentith is a Reader in English at Cheltenham and Gloucester College of Higher Education and is the author of *A Rhetoric of the Real* (Hemel Hempstead, 1990).

Richard Filloy is Assistant Professor of English at the Lane Community College, Oregon and the author of articles that have appeared in periodicals such as *The Quarterly Journal of Speech* and *The Journal of Advanced Composition*.

Lynette Hunter is Reader in Rhetoric at Leeds University and is the author of *Modern Allegory and Fantasy* (London, 1989); *George Orwell: The Search for a Voice* (Milton Keynes, 1984) and editor of *Toward a Definition of Topos* (London, 1991).

Stephen Ingle is Professor of Politics at the University of Sterling. His publications include *Socialist Thought in Imaginative Literature* (London, 1979) and *The British Party System* (Oxford, 1987).

Alan Kennedy is Professor of English and Head of the English Department at the Carnegie-Mellon University. His publications include *The Protean Self: Dramatic Action in Contemporary Fiction* (London, 1974) and *Reading, Resistance, Value* (London, 1990).

V. C. Letemendia teaches at the University of Toronto.

James Phelan is Professor and Chair of English at Ohio State University. He is the author of *Reading People, Reading Plots* (Chicago, 1989) and *Narrative as Rhetoric* (Ohio, 1996).

Patrick Reilly is a Senior Lecturer at the University of Glasgow. His publications include *Jonathan Swift: The Brave Defender* (Manchester, 1982); *George Orwell: The Age's Adversary* (London, 1986) and *The Literature of Guilt* (London, 1988).

John Rodden teaches rhetoric at the University of Texas, Austin, and is the author of *The Politics of Literary Representation: The Making and Claiming of 'St George' Orwell* (Oxford, 1989).

Richard Rorty is Professor of Humanities at the University of Virginia. He is the author of a number of books including *Objectivity, Relativism, and Truth* (Cambridge, 1991); *Philosophy and the Mirror of Nature* (Oxford, 1980) and *Consequences of Pragmatism* (Hemel Hempstead, 1982).

Michael Walzer is Professor of Social Science in the Institute for Advanced Study, Princeton, NJ, and is the author of *Spheres of Justice* (Oxford, 1983) and *Exodus and Revolution* (London, 1985) and *The Company of Critics* (London, 1989).

Index